14 00/
99 BB

JUSTIFYING VIOLENCE:
ATTITUDES OF AMERICAN MEN

MONICA D. BLUMENTHAL

ROBERT L. KAHN

FRANK M. ANDREWS

KENDRA B. HEAD

 INSTITUTE FOR SOCIAL RESEARCH
THE UNIVERSITY OF MICHIGAN
ANN ARBOR, MICHIGAN

ISR Code No. 3296

Library of Congress Catalog Card No. 74-169101

ISBN 87944-114-3

Printed by Braun-Brumfield, Inc.

Ann Arbor, Michigan

Cover Design by Mary Kay Krell

To
People of Good Will
Everywhere

PREFACE

In a sense, this work was begun as a response to the death of Martin Luther King. While we had been shocked and grieved by the assassination of President Kennedy five years earlier, that event struck us as one of those untoward acts of fate, so strangely disconnected from the world in which it occurs that it falls outside the universe of rational understanding. Unlike the assassination of the President, the death of the great black leader seemed connected to contemporary events in painful and obvious ways. The racial aspect of the killing was undeniable, and while all the reasons for the assassination may never become public, it seemed to us that the act itself had to be regarded in the context of the long history of racial strife and assassination in our country. Moreover, it became clear to us that, whatever racial hatreds were involved in this assassination, the violence of America was not confined to matters of race. When this study was conceived, the most publicized forms of violence were riots in the urban ghettos and student disorders on campuses, but violence saturates other aspects of life in the United States. The high rates of homicide and assault, for example, contribute to the ambient climate of violence.

It may well be that there are some biological determinants of violence, but such factors cannot explain why Americans are far more likely to kill each other with guns than citizens of any other civilized nation. The answer to the question of why people in one culture are more likely to resort to violence than members of another must lie at least in part in the social psychological characteristics of that civilization. It seemed to us that any effort to reduce the level of violence in this country must be preceded by an understanding of the social and cultural determinants of violence.

It was also our conviction that if serious efforts were to be made to reduce violence in the United States, some means of measuring their effects must be found. This study has spent considerable effort measuring attitudes towards violence, especially the extent to which violence is condemned or condoned in our society. To the extent that attitudes are determinants of behavior and to the extent that widely held attitudes supply a favorable or unfavorable atmosphere for the performance of particular acts, attitudes toward violence should serve as predictors of the overall levels of violence in the United States.

The truth of this latter assertion remains to be fully demonstrated, although it is supported by some fragmentary data on the relationship between violent behaviors and the attitudes that justify them. Assuming for the moment that such attitudes do indeed influence behaviors, the measurement of attitudes towards violence assumes a special importance: measuring such attitudes provides hope of assessing the state of the nation or a community before catastrophe actually occurs. It is infinitely better to be able to measure a change in attitudes toward violence and so have the opportunity to act constructively before violence occurs than to wait for annual counts of riots or homicides and so be able to act only on the basis of retrospective measures and social costs already incurred. Moreover, programs aimed at reducing the level of violence in this country should be reflected in changes in attitudes. Thus, it was in the hope that the study of attitudes towards violence would serve as a useful social indicator that this study was begun. It seems to us that one measure of the quality of life in a society must be the level of violence that people are prepared to justify.

In addition to the effort to provide a baseline description of attitudes towards violence we have also attempted to describe the rationalizations which enable people to hold positive attitudes towards violence. Their content is not surprising. Among other things, they include the need to defend oneself, the tendency to exact retribution, the predilection to believe one's friends can do no wrong and one's enemies deserve no quarter. However comprehensible such beliefs and rationalizations may be, they enjoin us to think carefully about the nature of life in the United States, and they remind us of the social principles and institutional arrangements that stand in opposition to violence and revenge. The right to a fair trial, the presumption of innocence until guilt is proven, the stricture that there can be no punishment under the law until guilt has been established are major examples, and are basic to our government and our system of justice. Yet these are swept aside by belief systems that encourage the police to shoot during the course of their duties and that see death and property damage as necessary to the process of producing social change. It is the conflict between such beliefs and the institutions of democracy that gives us most pause and cause for concern.

This research on violence was the product of many people who worked with more than ordinary zeal. The initial conceptualization and early development of the model explaining attitudes towards violence was largely due to the efforts of Robert Kahn and myself. The National Science Foundation made it possible to turn a research speculation into reality at a time when violence was not yet a popular priority for research funding. Frank Andrews was the main architect for the analysis, which made it possible to test our formulations and turn them into quantitative data. Much of the actual labor of executing the analysis was done by Kendra Head. But the project would not nearly have been possible on the basis of these labors alone. Early in the development of the project we had the help of Letha Chadiha, Janet Keene, and Georjean Maggio. Carol Tavris contributed to later developments in our conceptualization of violence and assisted us with our research of the literature. Much of the work on developing a model for scaling the responses to the questions measuring attitudes towards violence was done by Dean Runyan, and a large part of the later steps in the analysis was executed by Toby Jayaratne. Marita DiLorenzi also provided assistance. Robert Friis and Ursula Brandt also contributed to the analysis. Much of the work of typing was done by Marcia Ehrlich and Marcia Jacobson. We are particularly grateful for the editorial assistance of Ms. Jayaratne. We are indebted also to Irene Hess, who drew the sample, to John Scott, who supervised the field operation, and to Joan Scheffler, who supervised the coding.

In addition to those who served as project staff, we owe a debt to many others. We are thankful to Dr. Walter Shervington and Dr. Daniel Jacobs, who made it possible to interview prisoners at the U. S. Federal Penitentiary in Milan. We must also express our debt to the many people who participated with us in the preliminary group discussions which served as the basis for the initial research formulations. To give their names here would not be appropriate since the discussions were confidential in nature; nevertheless, the debt we owe them is real. We wish also to thank our colleagues at the Institute for their helpful advice and well-founded criticism. We are particularly indebted to Charles F. Cannell, Angus Campbell, John R. P. French Jr., and Sidney Cobb.

As this book goes to press, work continues on the relationship between violence and violent behavior. We hope also to repeat the nation-wide study, perhaps in 1973. By so doing, we can begin the development of trend data and can provide first indicators of whether the country is growing more or less violence-prone. We have hopes that the availability of such trend data will in itself stimulate efforts to make violence unnecessary and unrewarding.

There is one other related area of work for which we must also look to the future. Some early discussions of our research findings with people concerned with social practice—police administration, government, law—have brought home to us sharply the gap between social research and social practice. Research findings do not provide policy; it must be invented. The facts never speak for themselves; they must be utilized.

We hope that the next national study of violence will show the effects of such utilization.

Monica D. Blumenthal

Ann Arbor, Michigan
October, 1971

TABLE OF CONTENTS

Page

Chapter 1

INTRODUCTION

Trends of the Times

"Violence is as American as apple pie," says Rap Brown, and whether it is or not, there appears to be a very great deal of it nowadays. A committee of Stanford University scholars recently concluded that America was in a "crisis of violence" (Daniels, Gilula and Ochberg 1970, p. 1), a theme reiterated by the President's Commission on Campus Unrest (1970). Within the last years, two successive presidents have established three major commissions to investigate problems of domestic violence— The National Advisory Commission on Civil Disorders, The President's Commission on the Causes and Prevention of Violence, and the President's Commission on Campus Unrest.

All three commissions expressed deep concern for the society in which we live. The Commission on Civil Disorders (1968) found America moving toward division into two unequal societies. The Commission on Violence (1969) found a level of violence "dangerous to our society," and The Commission on Campus Unrest (1970), commenting on the handling of student disturbances, stated that "a nation driven to using the weapons of war upon its youth is a nation on the edge of chaos."

The consensus of the three commissions that violence in America has risen to alarmingly high levels is based on a variety of observations. The last decade has witnessed a decided increase in the rate of violent crime (Graham 1969). Homicide rates, while not as high as in the 1920's and early 1930's, have almost tripled in the middle classes since 1955 (Homicides on the increase 1970) and are among the leading causes of death among the younger nonwhite population. Moreover, among the industrialized nations of the world—including Canada, Australia, England, Germany, Denmark and Japan—the United States has the highest rate of homicides with guns. Indeed, the rate is seven times greater in our country than in the next highest (Gillin and Ochberg 1970, p. 244).

Forcible rape, assault, and robbery involving force or the threat of

1

force have also increased in proportion to the population during the last 20 years (Morris and Hawkins 1969). "Crime in the streets" has become a household concern. Not only does violent crime present a problem in and of itself; it generates an atmosphere of fear and suspicion that exerts a pervasive effect on American life. Many people are afraid to walk the streets at night, and indeed in some areas of our cities it is not safe to be unescorted. Citizens drive through the central cities with their car doors locked, and in some places motorists have been killed or injured when people hurled rocks at cars from freeway overpasses. In some real way, crime diminishes individual freedoms and reduces the quality of life.

Most crimes receive only brief attention or statistical notice. The last few years, however, have witnessed a series of spectacular multiple murders: the murder of eight student nurses in Chicago, the killing of random individuals by an insane gunman in a tower on the University of Texas campus, the murder of an actress and her house guests by members of the cultish Manson "family" and the killing of a California ophthalmologist with his entire family and secretary.

Not long before, the nation had witnessed in quick succession the assassination of President Kennedy, Martin Luther King and Senator Robert Kennedy. Moreover, assassination is far from rare in the United States. The staff of the President's Commission on Violence (Kirkhan, Levy and Crotty 1969, p. 119) reported that the United States ranked 13th among 83 nations studied in respect to the number of top-ranking officials assassinated between 1918 and 1968.

Urban Disturbances

The past decade has also been marked by a variety of urban disturbances. Such disturbances are not new, and episodes of political violence have occurred with great frequency and on a large scale at other times in American history. Nevertheless, there has been a rapid increase in the rate of such events since the 1950's, which were generally placid except for serious riots in Detroit and Harlem (Kirkhan, Levy and Crotty 1969). The number of politically violent events occurring at the present time is larger than at any previous time in American history.

Urban disturbances range from episodes involving small crowds throwing rocks and bottles at police cars to such riots as those in Detroit, Watts, and Newark, resulting in the loss of many lives and millions of dollars.

Urban disturbances, which many consider violence initiated for the purpose of social change, brought with them the violence of social control as well. The report of the Commission on Civil Disorders (1968, p. 107) leaves little doubt that agents of the law, attempting to restore order, often responded to their mission of regaining social control in excessive or inappropriate ways. Analysis of the deaths incurred during the riots studied by the Commission provided overwhelming evidence that most of the lethal force exerted during riots was used by the police and National Guard on riot participants and bystanders, some of whom were killed in their own homes.[1]

The Commission found both the police and the National Guard poorly trained in riot control and inadequately equipped to deal with civil disturbances. The Commission report points out that rifles, bayonets, and machine guns are weapons appropriate for war but not for controlling civil disorders (1968, p. 502), and yet these have been the weapons supplied to the National Guard on riot missions. The police were rarely found to have an adequate supply of protective equipment (1968, p. 491), and neither they nor the Guard agents were adequately supplied with nonlethal weapons for crowd-control (1968, p. 492).

A new pattern of violence seemed to emerge in the urban experience toward the end of the decade. Although the Commission on Civil Disorders dismissed as baseless reports of conspiracy behind the sniping in the 1967 riots (1968, p. 9), the threat of a black conspiracy was widely discussed. The press began to emphasize organized sniping in many disorders, with attendant implications of widespread conspiracy on the part of militant blacks. Some social scientists reviewing the data interpreted the reported incidents as harbingers of a conspiratorial, organized violence of a revolutionary character.[2] Detailed investigation from Brandeis University's Lemberg Center for the Study of Violence, on the other hand (Knopf 1970, p. 13ff), indicated that elements of conspiracy in the incidents of alleged sniping have been rare. Irrespective of the accuracy of the press reports and interpretations, the reporting itself probably added to the climate of apprehension and fear.

The intricate spiral of relationships among fear, violence for social change, and violence for social control is neatly illustrated by the over-reported and dramatic conflict between the police and the Black Panthers, a conflict which was much in the public eye in the late 1960's and early 1970's. The Black Panther Party was founded in Oakland in 1966 by Bobby Seale and Huey Newton. Part of their stated intention in forming the party was to defend the black community against suppression by the police, who were regarded as agents of "repression" and of the "white

---

[1] For a compelling and vivid account of the chaos, the reader should consult the sections of the Commission on Civil Disorders report which chronicle the Detroit and Newark riots.

[2] For example, see Janowitz 1969, pp. 317-339.

power structure" (Cleaver 1969, p. 165ff). Arming party members, if not all blacks, was described as a necessary part of self-defense.

In the interest of such self-defense or defense of the community, the Panthers initiated a program of action in which armed black patrols maintained a kind of surveillance over police activities in Oakland, California (Cleaver 1969, p. 200). This activity was viewed as threatening by the police, who responded with various retaliatory actions, especially the frequent stopping and questioning of Panthers on minor issues. These acts in turn were perceived by the Black Panthers as harassment and repression. There were armed confrontations, and the Panthers began stockpiling arms, many of them apparently illegal (New York Times, December 28, 1969, p. 42). This stockpiling was reported by informers to the police, providing the latter with legal opportunities for raids on Panther headquarters. Some of these raids were conducted with minimal injuries on both sides, but many resulted in the wounding and death of both police and Panthers (New York Times, November 13, 1970, p. 38).

In one instance, the Chicago killing of Fred Hampton and Mark Clark, there was considerable evidence of reckless and uncontrolled police action (Epstein 1971, p. 77) with the raiding police at the front and back doors of the apartment shooting dozens of rounds as they mistook each other's fire for continuing Panther resistance. Throughout the lengthy Black Panther dispute, the conflict-supporting effect of the rhetoric of violence was particularly apparent, with police and Panther supporters alike all too ready to believe wildly exaggerated tales of violence—for example, the allegation that 28 Panthers had been murdered by the police within two years (Epstein 1971, p. 77) or that within a six-month period over 100 attacks on police had been made by "black extremists fomenting racial turmoil" (New York Times, January 3, 1970, p. 6).

It seems reasonable to suppose that this series of interchanges, extensively reported by all media, fanned white fears of armed black revolution and black fears of white repression, and contributed to a hardening of attitudes among both blacks and whites. In any event, what started as a local conflict became a nationwide series of confrontations marked by escalating violence from all participants.

Student Disturbances

The ebb and flow of different forms of violence is not yet well understood. For whatever reasons, some reduction in urban disturbances coincided in recent years with an increasing amount of student unrest, disruption, and violence on college campuses. "Trash" became a verb as students expressed their anger and dissatisfaction through property damage. Moreover, the disturbances appeared to spread not only from one campus to another, but to students in high schools and even junior high schools. In addition, the disturbances assumed a virulence that had been previously lacking. In the fall of 1968, San Francisco State College kept its doors open only with the daily presence of 200 to 600 policemen (Orrick 1969, p. 1). Even so, the college was obliged to close entirely on several occasions. For the first time the question was seriously raised as to whether institutions of higher learning, with their special frailties and limited sanctions, could withstand onslaughts of this kind.

Student disruptions became increasingly turbulent, as bombings and arson began to appear in conjunction with college disturbances. At the same time, radical student groups splintered, and the white radical non-student terrorists, the Weathermen, attained national prominence. Terrorist tactics, off-campus and on, escalated the level of fear and violence.

As student protest appeared to increase, so did violent control of student demonstrations and other youth-led disturbances. Expert, judicial, and public opinion was divided. Many people in the nation were shocked at the televised actions of the Chicago police against the demonstrators during the 1968 Democratic Convention, but a large majority seemed to find the police actions justified (Robinson 1970). The Violence Commission staff thought otherwise, describing the action as a "police riot" (Walker 1968, p. xxii).

The President's Commission on Campus Unrest (1970) suggested that the measures used by the police in controlling the 1968 disturbances at Columbia University were more forceful than those used to control the earlier Berkeley campus disturbance. Students and faculty were beaten, and the level of force employed was described as "counter-violence" and "excessive force and violence" by the Commission (1970, p. 37). The Commission points out that "both before and after Columbia, every police bust gave rise to charges of police brutality. Far too often, they were true." The behavior of law enforcement officers acting in other campus disturbances was condemned by the Commission on Campus Unrest following the tragic deaths of students at Kent State University and Jackson State College. In both cases local authorities absolved the law officers of blame.

Violence and counter-violence, blame and blame returned; these themes echo relentlessly through the decade of the sixties.

Unsolved Social Problems

Notable in the reports of the three Presidential Commissions appointed to study civil unrest and violence since 1967 is the idea that violence springs from unsolved social problems. The Commission on Civil Disorders report (1968, p. 10) describes pervasive racial discrimination and segregation, in employment, education and housing. It describes black urban immigration and a white exodus, resulting in massive concentrations of impoverished blacks in the central parts of major cities. It depicts these urban centers as ghettos where segregation and poverty converge to destroy the opportunity of the young. The Commission report cites the frustrated hopes and unfulfilled expectations of black Americans, their political powerlessness, and an ambient climate of approval and encouragement of violence as the bases of the ghetto disturbances.

The President's Commission on Campus Unrest (1970, p. 62), on the other hand, emphasizes the passionate attachment of the new youth culture to principles celebrating the romance of human life and the unique humanity of the individual. These involve opposition to materialism, competition, conformity, and technology. More important, the Commission finds in the youth culture a profound ideological commitment to human equality and peace. These commitments are not based on personally endured privations, since most student protesters come from affluent families (Horn and Knott 1971), but instead derive from the innermost conscience of the young. That America has not fully lived up to its national ideals nor yet fulfilled its promises of human dignity and equal opportunity feeds both urban and campus disturbances.

Moreover, as the Commission on Violence points out, the failure to meet our social obligations contributes to the etiology of crime, as well as civil disturbance. The Commission states:

> To be a young, poor male; to be under-educated and without means of escape from an oppressive urban environment; to want what society claims is available (but mostly to others); to see around oneself illegitimate and often violent methods being used to achieve material gain; and to observe others using these means with impunity—all this is to be burdened with an enormous set of influences that pull many towards crime and delinquency (To Establish Justice 1969, p. xxi).

This point is underscored by former Attorney General Ramsey Clark in his book *Crime in America* (1970, p. 66) in which he describes in compelling terms the association between crime and the social facts of poverty, stopped-up toilets, crowded city ghettos, under-education, premature adult death, and high infant mortality rates. If anything like consensus can be found among experts, it is on the proposition that the three major types of contemporary civil violence—urban riots, campus disturbances and crime—all flow from the wellsprings of unsolved social problems.

Defining Violence

Before proceeding further, it would be well for us to define what we mean by violence. Of late, the word has been used in a variety of ways. Garver (1969) speaks of psychological violence and as we shall show later, there are wide differences of opinion among Americans about what behaviors constitute violence, in spite of the fact that most Americans agree violence is "bad." The Commission on Campus Unrest recognized this confusion in the spoken language as to the meaning of violence and took great care to differentiate between dissent, disruptive protest and violent protest. Dissent, the Commission finds a valuable part of American life which may be manifested by vigils, meetings and demonstrations. Disruptive protest is manifested by activities which interfere with the normal functioning of organizations, and is typified by some sit-ins and some forms of picketing. Violent protest is defined by the Campus Unrest Commission as protest which involves bodily injury.

According to Webster's International Dictionary, violence is a force which injures or abuses. Such a meaning of "violence" includes both personal injury and property damage. It is in this sense that we will use the word, albeit we recognize that not all Americans use the word in the same fashion.

Violence and the State

Violence in some degree has always been considered a legitimate instrument of the state, and it is widely held that knowledge of the state's right to use violence is an important restraint on criminal behavior. Certainly the delegation to the state of the right to use violence is a device by which men seek to maintain order among themselves and to insure the survival of the social arrangements in which they live. Moreover, in states which are not totalitarian in nature, violence is threatened or used to maintain order with the implied consent of the governed, and is to this extent legitimate.

Violence is only one of many resources available to the state for maintaining social control. Rewards, persuasion, influence and nonviolent sanctions can all be used to maintain order, and are so used. Violence is a method of last resort, often used for its symbolic value rather than for its immediate effect (Gamson 1968). Capital punishment is a case in point. The death of a particular individual is not only the execution of a man, punishment for some past crime and prevention of any other by him, it is also the "proper" disposition of the abstract murderer and a symbol of the power of the state. Even now, after a moratorium of several years on capital punishment in the United States, the majority of American men believe that execution is a proper punishment for the state to use in cases of murder.

The legitimacy of violence by the state depends upon acceptance of the authority of the state by the citizens, and ultimately on the agreement of the governed that the social values which violence is used to maintain are desirable and just. When the state uses force to serve goals which are not regarded as socially desirable by a substantial portion of the polity, such violence tends to be regarded as illegitimate, at least by the opposition. To some degree the use of force by opposition groups has been explained and justified in similar terms.

For example, the riots of the 1960's have been described as a direct result of the blacks' sense of discrimination and inequality (Grimshaw 1968). The high prevalence of looting has been described as a symbolic response to their economic deprivation and as a form of protest against current conceptions and definitions of property rights (Dynes and Quarantelli 1968). Similarly, arson has been described as a method of protest and redress against consumer exploitation (Fogelson 1970).

In such interpretations of the ghetto riots, the sense of relative deprivation has been assigned a major role. This sense of deprivation is not based primarily on the absolute circumstances in which the individual may be living, nor on his present circumstances in comparison to the past. By these standards, living conditions for black Americans have been improving (Pettigrew 1967). Relative to the living standards of other Americans, however, blacks are deprived, and for many of them this frame of reference has become dominant. Moreover, black Americans have been coming more and more to feel that the discrepancy between what they expect and what they are likely to achieve is not so much a function of their own inadequacies and deficits as it is a result of a social situation imposed upon them.

It is with this background in mind that the use of force by the state to control civil disturbances must be considered. The order which law-enforcement agencies seek to maintain is by definition the existing order. What is written in the law, rather than what is to be written, serves as the basis for enforcement actions. The issue of legitimacy arises especially in those situations where the order which the state seeks to maintain involves the very principles against which some groups seek to protest. The use of the police to disperse groups protesting segregation laws provides a classic example of such a situation.

In such cases the legality of a violent action by the police or other agencies of the state must be differentiated from the legitimacy of that act in the eyes of the population at large and in particular subgroups. An action may be legal and at the same time be illegitimate in the view of many concerned with it. For an action to be legitimate as well as legal, it must evoke or at least not contradict a generalized attitude of identification with the state (Gurr 1970, p. 185). To the extent that there is disagreement about the social goals at which actions of the police are directed, for example in controlling student protests or ghetto disturbances, there are likely to be elements in the population which regard the police actions as illegitimate.

The legitimacy of the state itself in the eyes of its citizens is in part dependent on their agreement with its major apparent goals, their perception that the government is in general attempting appropriate implementation of those goals and that, to the extent that this is not the case, there are available means of altering governmental policy and practice. If there are groups within the society which perceive the status quo as harmful, the means for producing orderly change unavailable or hopelessly ineffective, they are likely to see the use of violence by the state as illegitimate. To them the use of force becomes a political issue, and its use by the state may generate counter-violence on their part as they bid for an increased share of power and resources. This hypothetical sequence seems especially likely when violence is used to control actions of protest.

Organizations do not change easily, and societies are still more resistant to planned change. To some extent resistance to change must be included in any social system; if every impulse or attempt to create change were instantly successful, there would never develop any patterns of sufficient stability to deserve the name of system or society. In the American experience, the notions of change and resistance to change, constitutional amendment and checks and balances are taught to every child in school and experienced in one connection or another by most adults. As Gardner (1970, p. 65) puts it, "The competition of interests inherent in our pluralism acts as a brake on concerted action. The system grinds to a halt between crisis. . . .It simply won't move without vigorous leadership."

Unfortunately, it sometimes happens that those groups that see the necessity for producing social change rapidly are those with least access to or sophistication about the legitimate means of producing such changes. Such groups are unlikely to be able to use persuasion, which is based on mutual trust and easy access, or influence, which is based on a *quid-pro-quo* exchange of resources (Gamson 1968, p. 169). Hence they are driven to search for other means, and may be reduced to violence.

Escalation

These are interpretations and assumptions but they fit the pattern of escalating violence to which we have been witness. The sequence of protest, force, and counter-force has been apparent in the cities and on the campus. It is visible also in respect to crime, where increasing rates of violent crime appear to be coupled with strong demands on the part of the public for more punitive laws and more stringent law enforcement.

To the extent that violence is the tool of those already suffering from feelings of disfranchisement, the state, in an effort to control violence, employs it against the already disfranchised. Such groups, with little to lose and much to gain, are likely to respond with escalated counter-violence, and thus the cycles continue until some new element intervenes to redefine the situation, or until there is an overwhelming and repressive force.

The danger of repression as a response to civil disorder has been emphasized by both the Campus Unrest Commission and the Commission on Violence. Indeed, the basis for dealing with disorder has already become a major political issue. The preventive detention provision of the District of Columbia Omnibus Crime Bill, for example, has been cited as a model for the nation by the federal administration, but has been criticized widely because it permits the imprisonment of a suspect without bail and before trial, if in the judgment of a magistrate the suspect is "likely to commit further crimes if . . . free" (Schrag 1970). Moreover, the "no knock" provision of the same law is regarded by many lawyers as a violation of Constitutional prohibitions against illegal search and seizure. The Organized Crime Control Act of 1970 allows a judge to impose a 30-year sentence on a person convicted of a felony if the judge decides that the person is a "dangerous special offender." Such laws are defended as necessary to control violence, and attacked as eroding the safeguards to civil liberties provided by the Constitution. They illustrate the process of escalation and they emphasize increased punishment rather than decreased alienation.

Pragmatic Effects

The idea that people low in power and high in alienation are most likely to resort to the instrumental use of violence has been often expressed (Tilly 1970, p. 26; Gamson 1968, p. 169). That likelihood increases when the alienated individuals perceive themselves as members of a group with less access to valued resources than other groups around them. Add to this a substantial increase in expectations, and it becomes still more likely that violence will be appealing.

In a statement which acknowledges the complaints and injustices under which minority groups labor, the Commission on the Causes and Prevention of Violence states that the twin objectives of social order must be to make violence both *unnecessary* and *unrewarding*. It can be argued that we have failed thus far to do the first and are behaving irrationally with respect to the second. The country was slow to change its racial policies and practices when urged to do so through conventional channels of dissent and litigation, but some conspicuous efforts have been made by both government and the private sectors to bring about changes in the wake of violence.

The 1967 riots resulted in the establishment of the Commission on Civil Disorders, which focused national attention on racial problems, and at the same time that the federal government moved into action, numerous local governments sought to redress the grievances of the black community. Of twenty cities selected for intensive study by the Commission on Civil Disorders, all but three responded to riots with action programs designed to ameliorate such grievances (Hahn 1970). These programs were undertaken seriously, although they have been variously successful. The violence of the urban riots apparently evoked a response, albeit not always an effective one.

We believe, however, that violence has evoked other responses as well, that many people who decry disruptions and disturbances produced by minority groups also call for the use of stringent and forceful police methods. Not only is the use of violence by the state seen as proper to control disruptions; the state may be regarded as entirely blameless in its use of violence and the responsibility for its use may be placed on those against whom the official violence was addressed. The local grand jury investigating the slaying of four Kent State students during a campus disturbance found the National Guard free of responsibility in the slayings, and blamed the college administration for its "attitude of laxity and permissiveness" (New York Times, October 17, 1970). In addition the grand jury accused some faculty members of an over-emphasis on the right to dissent. No guardsmen were cited in the indictments against persons involved in the Kent State disaster, but the University president, faculty and students were held responsible. Moreover it was the acts of students, not guardsmen, which the grand jury found "irresponsible" and "violent." The Commission on Campus Unrest, on the other hand, found the shootings unjustified and inexcusable.

In these respects, Kent State represented a drama that was acted out again in the killing of two students at Jackson State College. In that situation also, a federal court found the shootings unjustified while local officials found the state police entirely without blame.

Clearly, events seen as violent evoke unintended violent responses as well as efforts at remedial action. Moreover, the views of violence are partisan, and the assignment of responsibility seems more a political issue than a matter of law.

A Nation Divided

In 1968 the Commission on Civil Disorders concluded (1968, p. 1) that the United States was moving toward "two societies, one black, one white—separate and unequal." The Commission viewed the riots of the 1960's as a response to the conditions of ghetto life, and pointed out that the black ghettos were created and maintained by the institutions of white society. The polarization between black and white was seen as an increasing but not irreversible phenomenon which could destroy the nation if unchecked.

At that time student protest was relatively inconspicuous. Since then, however, it has become increasingly prominent. Student activist groups have often seen themselves on the same side as the blacks, and much of their protest has been concerned with "white racism." But blacks do not necessarily see white students as their allies, and some black activist groups have restricted their membership to blacks. To some extent, student activists may be seen as an articulate fragment of society, alienated from their elders and set apart also from those they wish to help.

Still other subgroups in the nation have made themselves heard in terms that suggest divisiveness rather than pluralism. In 1968 the development of a substantial third party in the South was based on an appeal to the racial fears of the white lower middle classes, groups which feel they are most likely to bear a disproportionate share of the costs of social change (Rossi 1970). The so-called "hard hats" have also emerged as a conservative bloc, specifically opposed to blacks and student activists. In Pittsburgh in 1969, 4,500 white construction workers' union members marched into town to protest the forced integration of unions (New York Times, August 30, 1969, p. 1). In New York's Times Square, union members demonstrated in an expression of direct opposition to the peace movement and the students active in it. Meanwhile, within the "youth movement," hippies gave way to yippies and the Students for Democratic Society spun off the terrorist, non-student Weathermen. Certainly there are deep cleavages between black and white, but there are gaps between other groups as well.

The emergence of such contesting subgroups adds to the problems of violence. Such groups hold different values and conflicting goals. For example, the student protesters in the antiwar movement regard the war in Vietnam as essentially immoral, to be abandoned at the earliest opportunity (Skolnick 1969, p. 34). The "hard hats" believe that ending the war without a clear military victory would be an affront to patriotism and an insult to national honor. Moreover, many of the other values expressed by student protesters are directly destructive of the beliefs by which the hard hats maintain their self-esteem in the face of limiting economic and social realities (Lane and Lerner 1970).

Differences between these groups in respect to the legitimate use of violence are serious, and these differences in themselves can become the subject of violent contest.

Types of Violence

Given the complex nature and serious consequences of violent behavior, it becomes important to understand it more fully. For example, what are the attitudinal concomitants of such behaviors? What perceptions and beliefs evoke or prevent them? How are violent behaviors rationalized and justified?

Such questions cannot be answered by studying violence as if it were all of one piece. Clearly, one must distinguish between violence that is instrumental and violence that is expressive. The differences between the two types of violence lie not so much in the affect involved as in the qualities of planning and intent. It may be part of human nature to feel some violent impulse toward the object of one's anger—and, for that matter, to become angry at the object of one's violence. But expressive violence arises primarily in response to feelings of hate or rage, while in the case of instrumental violence such feelings are secondary, although they may arise during the course of committing violent acts. Instrumental violence is violence used to some end. Sometimes it is a show of strength, which it is hoped will lead to a change in the distribution of power. Often it is seen by its proponents as a last resort, an effort to gain some desired goal in situations where persuasion and political influence cannot be used to accomplish the same end (Gamson 1968).

Within the category of instrumental violence it is necessary to distinguish between that which is institutionalized and that which is not. Police action which results in personal injury is a form of violence which has an institutional basis, and which may be legal and legitimate, depending on the circumstances. The use of violence by a robber to gain possession of money is neither institutionalized nor legitimated, and even the thief would not defend his acts on this basis. On the other hand, instrumental violence which is used in an effort to produce social change, though neither legal nor institutionalized, may be regarded as legitimate and justifiable by some groups albeit not by the society at large.

We believe that violence can be usefully thought of in terms of two dichotomies: first, violence that is primarily expressive, and violence that is primarily instrumental. Second, instrumental violence can be divided into violence that is instrumental for maintaining social control and existing institutions, and violence used instrumentally to change the existing institutions and power structure.

It seems reasonable to expect that individuals might have quite different attitudes toward these different kinds of violence. For example, one would not expect revolutionaries and officers of an existing regime to hold similar attitudes toward capital punishment for insurrection. Similarly, some radical college students might endorse violence as a tool for producing social change while condemning violence as a means of social control. Others might commend the use of violence for social control while condemning it as a tool for social change. In short, one could expect people to differ on such issues, and expect also that a given person could hold a variety of attitudes toward violence depending on the type of violence in question.

In addition, each type of violence can be regarded either from a position of moral absolutism or relativism; that is, each can be regarded as absolutely wrong or right, or as justifiable under some circumstances and not under others (Spiegel 1968). If a person takes a relativistic position toward violence, it becomes necessary to ask under what circumstances he believes violence is justified.

The Field of Force

For any particular set of circumstances and for any particular person, the level of violence considered justifiable may be regarded as the resultant of opposing forces, some of which tend to drive the level down until no violent act is perceived as justifiable, and others of which tend to drive the level up so that acts of extreme violence become justifiable. A number of these forces can be specified, and may be considered the major substance of the research described in this book. They include the following:

1. *Basic cultural values against violence:* The Judaeo-Christian ethic, widely espoused in this country, states that "Thou shalt not kill." In addition, a prominent theme in the New Testament is the concept of the Golden Rule, that one ought to treat one's neighbors as one would like to be treated oneself. Both injuctions seem directly relevant to the problem of violence, and both should act to mitigate the justification of violent behaviors.

2. *Basic cultural values in favor of violence:* The Bible, in less gentle passages, also provides the basis for values more sanguineous than loving. "Eye for eye, tooth for tooth, hand for hand, foot for foot" provides considerable grounds for violence of one kind or another. Moreover, in the United States we have glorified the hard riding, straight shooting frontiersman who settled arguments with the action end of his gun in calm disregard of whatever legal assistance might be available. This aspect of our heritage has been widely disseminated and popularized by the mass media.

In addition, some concepts of masculinity, for example machismo, imply positive values toward violence, as does the long established tradition of the right of every man to commit violence in self-defense. To the extent that an individual cleaves to such values, he should be likely to justify higher levels of violence.

3. *Identification with the person or group committing the aggression:* The extent to which the individual perceives himself to be allied with the membership, motives, and goals of an aggressor can be regarded as a force tending to make the particular act of violence seem more justified than if the same act were committed by a neutral party. For example, if an individual regards the police as his agents, a body designed for his protection, he would be more apt to see beatings and shootings committed by the police in the course of their duties as justified, than if he regards the police as not committed to his welfare.

The intentions of persons or groups involved in violence may be important in determining the extent to which an individual identifies with such persons. To the extent that the aggressor in a situation is perceived as having meant well, a specific act of violence may be forgiven him. On the other hand, the perception that the aggressor has "evil intentions" or "immoral motives" or is deliberately destructive will weaken the justification of his violent action and lead to a reduction in the amount of force seen as permissible.

Similarly, the extent to which the individual perceives the aggressor in negative terms and is negatively identified with the aggressor will act as a force to make the violent act appear less justified.

4. *Identification with the victim of the aggression:* The same range of relationships, from very positive to quite negative identifications, is possible between an individual and the person or group which is the victim of an act of violence. The perception of the target group as a peer group or reference group to which empathic considerations are usually extended will tend to make an individual view as less justified an act of violence directed at that particular group. The strength of the force acting to make the violent act seem less justified will be determined by the degree to which the individual identifies with the target group.

Negative identification with a target group is no less important in explaining attitudes toward violence in particular circumstances. It seems clear that categorizing a target group as alien or out of the range of identification has often been used as a justification for violence. There is ample evidence, for example, that some Southerners have regarded blacks as a lower form of life, and it is likely that similar attitudes may characterize the perceptions of other ethnic or social groups by other subpopulations (Smelser 1968, p. 101ff). If a group is perceived in such a fashion as to be excluded from the kind of consideration which is extended to persons with whom there is positive identification, different standards of behavior may be perceived as applicable. (We don't treat our aging relatives, for example, in the same fashion that we treat our aging pets.) Propaganda efforts in wartime systematically attempt to characterize the enemy as subhuman or as the personification of evil, so that the violence committed against them appears justified. It is interesting, for example, to recall that as a nation we were horrified during World War II when Hitler killed several thousand people in the bombing of Rotterdam, but expressed little concern when 100,000 were killed in the American firebombing of Dresden (Zinn 1970, p. 79). In short, it seems reasonable to suggest that negative identification with the victims of a violent action serves as a force tending to increase the level of justification for a particular act of violence.

5. *Definition of violent behavior:* The above factors are likely to influence the degree of violence justified, to the extent that the behavior under consideration is seen as violence. To the extent that the behavior, however forceful and destructive, is not regarded as violence, it will be less necessary for the individual to justify the action in the terms listed above.

Research Design

In the summer of 1969, we conducted a survey of attitudes and values regarding violence. The universe sampled consisted of men aged 16 through 64 living in the conterminous United States. The sample, although selected so that the data would be representative of American men as a whole, was chosen to include a larger number of black respondents than would have been produced had a single sampling rate been used. In all, 1,374 respondents were interviewed with a structured interview schedule yielding an overall response rate of 80 percent. (Details of the sample are included as Appendix A.)

To test our hypotheses regarding the role of values, identification with the aggressors and victims of violence, and definitions of violence in determining the level of violence justified, the interview was designed to measure attitudes pertaining to student disturbances, ghetto riots and violence in general. So, the study assessed the respondent's attitudes toward how much violence would be required to produce the social changes desired by students; how much would be required to bring about changes desired by blacks; and how much violence would be necessary to bring about change in general. Secondly, the survey inquired how much violence the respondent judged necessary to control the student disturbances on campus, black disturbances in the ghettos, and, in respect to a less political case, how much violence was necessary to control the activities of "hoodlum gangs."

In line with the notion that an important component in the attitudes justifying violence is the extent to which the respondent identifies with the actors in a particular episode of violence, the respondent was asked questions measuring the extent to which he identified with student demonstrators, black protesters, and the police. The extent to which such feelings modify attitudes toward violence is examined in detail in this study.

Respondents were also asked to define various acts such as "student protest," "police frisking people" and so on in an effort to determine whether or not the respondent defined particular acts as violence.

Whether or not the respondent holds certain acts to be violent, adheres to certain values, and identifies with certain groups can be thought of as being the product of events and circumstances in the respondent's past and present life. Such things as the year in which the respondent was born (i.e., his age), his race, and his parent's socio-economic background are among the earliest relevant facts. In later childhood are education and religious training as well as the multitudinous inputs that come from family, neighborhood and the social environment of the child. Among the adult influences which must be considered are socio-economic class, income, occupation, region of residence, whether the respondent lives in a city or on a farm, and whether or not he has served in the military. These variables are shown in Figure 1.

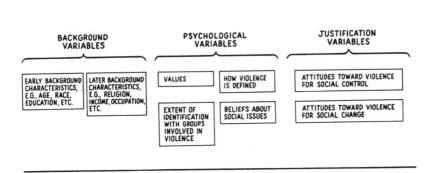

Figure 1. Analytic Model

Summary

Violence is becoming an increasingly ubiquitous phenomenon in the United States. Individual violence, as reflected in the statistics on homicide and assault, appears to be on the increase, as do acts of collective violence. Urban disturbances, which many regard as a form of violent protest, increased during the 1960's. Inevitably these were accompanied by the violence of social control as the police attempted to restore order.

While urban disturbances appeared to reach a peak during the late 1960's, protests on campus assumed a more virulent character. Buildings on campus were trashed, and in later years burned and bombed. Police were called to campus more frequently, and some of the police behaviors assumed aspects which the President's Commission on Campus Unrest called "counter-violence."

Three Presidential Commissions addressed themselves to the problems of domestic violence and found that crime, ghetto riots and campus disturbances all stemmed at least in part from the social problems of our time. Racial discrimination, poverty, and inequalities in opportunity and justice, all were cited as well springs for the violent protest of city and campus.

To many who regarded the urban and campus disturbances as a form of social protest, the violence used by the police to restore order acquired a political meaning. That is, the actions of the police were seen less as legitimate means of restoring order than as repressive measures employed by the state to suppress protest against legitimate social grievances. Such a view lends itself to the proposition that further violence in the interests of change is required to overcome the suppressive forces.

Such background considerations lead to the view that in order to study attitudes toward violence several different types of violence need to be differentiated. Particularly, distinctions need to be made between instrumental violence that is used to maintain social order and instrumental violence which aims to produce social change. Moreover, one might think that attitudes toward such types of violence would be influenced by a person's principal values and by the extent to which he sympathizes with the goals of those who are contenders in violent scenarios. This monograph reports the results of a survey of attitudes toward violence of a representative, random sample of American men.

Chapter 2

ATTITUDES, CAUSES, AND CURES

American Concern with Violence

To understand American attitudes toward violence, we must understand what acts Americans consider violence, how concerned they are about it, what they see as its causes, and how they propose to cure it.

We begin with the matter of concern. The initial question in the interview raised that issue rather than the issue of violence:

> *In this study we are interested in people's views about many different things. What things going on in the United States these days worry and concern you?*

Table 1 shows the percentage of respondents who gave answers directly relating to violence, such as riots, war and crime, and the percentage of respondents giving answers that might be construed as relating to violence by some, but not by others. Included among these are respondents who mentioned protests, such as sit-ins, and those who mentioned persons sometimes seen as causing violence—communists, anarchists, militant groups, and the like. In all, 65 percent of American men responded with one or more of these items.[1]

As a second question, the respondent was asked:

> *Could you mention some (other) things you've heard about in the last few years that involve violence?*

Table 2 shows the more frequent responses to this question.

---

[1] Subsequent text, charts and figures will refer to "American men," "all men," "all respondents," and similar phrases. The relevant age range—16-64—will usually not be stated. However, the statements and statistics are based on data for men in this age range only. These data were collected in the summer of 1969. Strictly speaking, we can only say what was true among American men at that time and we have used the past tense for that reason, when direct references to the data are made.

Table 1

Percentage of Respondents Reporting Violence-Related Items
As Matters of Concern
(all respondents; N=1,374)

War	36%
Riots	22
Protest	14
Violent people	9
Crime	7
Other violence	2
"Nonviolent" concerns	35

Note: The respondent was allowed four different answers if he wished, so that the total percent on this table exceeds 100. Sixty-five percent of the respondents mentioned at least one violence-related concern; some mentioned more than one.

War was mentioned most often by American men as a matter of concern in the summer of 1969. When they were asked to mention "violent things," however, many more American men spoke of racial problems than of war—39 percent compared to 10. Within the category of race-related issues, ghetto riots were mentioned most often, but many respondents simply said, "racial problems," and a small number mentioned nonviolent protests such as sit-ins. Civil disturbances, riots, uprisings and protest in which the respondent did not specify the involvement of either students or blacks were mentioned next most often, followed by student protest. Taken altogether, 68 percent of the respondents mentioned protests and civil disturbances, both racial and nonracial, as being related to violence, a substantially larger number than the 27 percent who mentioned crime, and the 7 percent who spoke of young people, juvenile delinquents, communists and anarchists. Within this latter combined category, more respondents mentioned young people in connection with violence than mentioned communists. Almost nobody talked about police brutality, although the violent events of the 1968 Democratic Convention were mentioned a number of times.

These data indicate that American men were overwhelmingly oriented toward the domestic scene when they thought about violence, and particularly to that aspect of the domestic picture which involved some element of dissent. Concern with violence is extensive, and the concern is greater with respect to collective violence and civil disorder than with respect to crime.

Table 2

Percentage of Respondents Reporting "Things" Involving Violence
(all respondents; N=1,374)

Racial problems, riots and protests	39%
Civil disturbances and protest (not including student and black protest)	28
Student protest and rebellion	26
Crime	27
War	10
Juvenile delinquents, young people, Communists and others	7
Police violence	2

Note: The respondent was allowed up to three different answers to this question, so the total for this table exceeds 100 percent.

Beliefs about the Causes of Violence

The sequence of questions inquiring what the respondent saw as causes of violence began as follows:

> *People nowadays have many ideas about what causes violence. Thinking about the problem generally, what do* **you** *think causes violence?*

Table 3 shows the responses given most frequently.

Table 3

Percentage of Respondents Reporting Designated Causes of Violence
(all respondents; N=1,374)

Lack of understanding, communication, trust, and respect between people; interpersonal differences, lack of love; hate	20%
Frustration and general dissatisfaction, feeling discriminated against, changes not happening fast enough, people not getting what they want	15
Anarchists, radicals and communists	12
Racial concerns, protests, etc.	10
Concern with law, order, courts, police matters	9
Economic concerns	8

The largest single category revolves around the issue of lack of understanding and communication, mistrust and hatred. One-fifth of American men gave such reasons as the causes of violence, some stating their opinions simply, others eloquently:

> I think the inability for groups of people . . . to discuss disagreements of any kind leads to rebellion and rebellious acts.

> I'll say they are not human toward one another, the people of both races.

Next to the lack of communication and understanding, American men mentioned frustration as a cause of violence, people wanting things they can't have, the feeling that changes in the society will not be made fast enough and general feelings of dissatisfaction. It seems that Americans consider very seriously the proposition that the roots of violence lie in the social and human conditions of our time.

Along a rather different line, the response that was made at the third highest frequency blamed violence on specific groups of individuals. Eight percent of the population mentioned anarchists or agitators as a cause of violence, and an additional 4 percent attributed the problem to communists.

Eight percent of American men mentioned economic concerns as causing violence. The lack of jobs, inflation, taxes, low wages, and discriminatory employment practices—all were cited in this category.

Ten percent of American men mentioned racial problems as causal in violence. Discrimination, prejudice, segregation, and the resulting dissatisfaction and frustration on the part of blacks were mentioned most often. Blacks were twice as likely to mention such concerns as whites. In addition, 6 percent of the respondents who did not specifically mention race mentioned infringement of the rights of others and "people not being given their rights" as causes of violence. It seems likely that many who answered in this fashion were thinking of racial problems, although they did not say so directly.

Table 3 also shows that 9 percent of American men felt that the state of the law, the police, and the courts were causal factors in the production of violence. Disrespect for the law and a general lack of law and order were the predominant themes of answers falling in this category.

The emphasis on social factors as the major causes of violence is even more apparent in the answers given to more specific questions. Respondents were asked to say yes or no with respect to seven possible causes of violence. Even allowing for some possible bias toward agreement, the magnitude and rank order of the data in Table 4 are impressive. When asked directly, the overwhelming majority of Americans said that social conditions contribute substantially to violence. Almost 90 percent believed that discrimination causes violence, and about three-quarters felt that poverty and inadequate employment cause violence. Over 70 percent believed that the lack of good education causes violence.

Table 4

Percentage of Respondent Agreement and Disagreement
About What Causes Violence
(all respondents; N=1,374)

	Yes	No	Total
Discrimination	89%	11%	100%
Poverty	76	24	100
Lack of good jobs	72	28	100
Poor education	71	29	100
Not being able to keep up with changes	66	34	100
Not feeling important	46	54	100
Can't live up to what's expected	36	64	100

In these opinions, Americans share the perceptions of social scientists (Fogelson 1970), at least in respect to the issues involved in racial violence. Discrimination, racism, economic exploitation, and substandard education have been repeatedly cited as causes of the urban riots that characterized the late 1960's. In view of the fact that the vast majority of the respondents also cited racial protest or other protest issues as the types of violence that most concerned them, it seems reasonable to assume that many respondents were seriously addressing themselves to the issues involved in domestic violence.

Causes and Cures

Remedies are not merely the mirror images of causes; life is far too complicated for that. Nevertheless, effective remedies must be logically related to causes, and it is appropriate to search for such relationships. Our inquiry about the remedies people proposed for violence began, like the sequence about perceived causes, with an open question:

What do you think should be done to prevent big city riots?

The answers to this question are presented in Table 5. The single most frequent proposal is to prevent big city riots by force. Only 9 percent of all men had mentioned concerns connected with the police or the law as causal in producing violence, but 18 percent mentioned bolstering the police (either through more and different weaponry or through the use of additional forces) as a method of preventing violence. In addition, 15 percent mentioned stricter or more punitive laws as ways of preventing violence. In all, more than 30 percent of American men mentioned stricter laws and increased force as means of preventing violence.

Table 5

Percentage of Respondents Reporting What Can Be Done To Prevent Big City Riots
(all respondents; N=1,374)

More police, national guard, force, gas, guns	18%
Economic changes	16
Stricter, more punitive laws and stricter law enforcement	15
Improved communication and understanding	14
Better education	13
Social change in general	8
Better housing	7

On the other hand, the majority of responses have to do with social and economic improvements of various kinds. Economic and social problems, and the frustration they generate, had been mentioned as prominent causes of violence, and the proposed cures are consistent with this emphasis. Improvement of economic conditions, welfare programs, self-help programs, improved education, an end to discrimination, better housing and improved judicial procedures all were mentioned.

On balance, we take the response pattern of causes and cures as a hopeful sign. As a nation, we appear to be willing to concede that the seeds of disorder may lie within the social problems of our time. We can hope that the nation will increasingly direct itself to correcting those conditions which laymen and social scientists agree are the wellsprings of violence.

Measuring Attitudes Toward Violence

Americans take violence seriously. As we have seen, in the summer of 1969 substantial numbers of American men spontaneously mentioned violence and its cognates as sources of concern. Moreover, judging from the nature of the responses given to questions about the causes of violence and the means of preventing it, many Americans appear to have done some serious thinking on the problem. But how much do Americans actually condone or condemn violence? To what extent are they prepared to justify violence? And when they do justify it, what kind of violence do they have in mind?

In measuring attitudes toward violence, it becomes necessary to differentiate between types of violence, and to specify the kind of violence one is talking about. For operational purposes, we had defined violence as behaviors which lead to bodily injury or substantial property damage. On the basis of this definition, arson, homicide, war and automobile accidents would all be considered violence. It seems reasonable to suppose that attitudes toward such different types of violence might vary considerably. Moreover, in considering how violence might be conceptualized, it is apparent that naming a particular behavior or act is not in itself sufficient to evoke definite attitudes toward it. If one is to venture an opinion about a homicide, one wants to know not only that a man was killed, but also the circumstances surrounding the act and the motivation of the actors. To kill an enemy soldier in battle, to shoot your wife's lover, or to kill an unarmed burglar are very different matters. There are profound differences also between sniping at police in a ghetto, sniping at a passerby from a university tower, and sniping at the tower sniper. Still different is killing a darkly dressed pedestrian crossing the freeway in the middle of the night. Nevertheless, all these events involve the death of one person at the hands of another.

Two threads can be sorted out of this tangle: one is the presence or absence of intent, the other the motivation underlying the action. When intent is lacking, as is generally thought to be true in the case of accidents, the violent events are generally regarded as acts of God or matters of chance. The perpetrators of such acts are viewed as unfortunate, or at worst careless. Rarely do we conceive of such people as intrinsically bad or evil, although such attitudes are common in respect to persons who commit other types of violence. In any case, attitudes toward "accidental" violence are different from attitudes toward violence committed by an intending human being.

If intent is present, for example, if a homicide is committed purposefully, the question of motivation arises. To begin with, a gross distinction can be made between those motivations that are comprehensible to the average observer and those that are not. In the latter case, the violence is viewed as being "senseless" or sick, for example, the killing of eight nurses by Speck. Here the attitudes toward the perpetrator of the act are generally that he ought to be removed from society, cured if possible, institutionalized at least. For the victims, such acts tend to be viewed as unfortunate accidents.

On the other hand, if the motivation of the perpetrator of a violent act seems sane and comprehensible, the motives underlying the act might become important determinants of attitudes toward the act. One set of attitudes might prevail if the act is regarded as a response to severe frustration, another if it is a response to threat or a matter of self-defense. Still other attitudes might predominate if the act of violence is instrumental, for example, if violence is used as a tool to produce social change or as an instrument of the state to maintain social control.

A prominent theme in the domestic violence which has occurred in the United States is the conflict between those who believe that law and order must be maintained with force and those who feel that violence is necessary in producing social change. Because of the importance of this conflict, and because the task of measuring attitudes toward many different types of violence was not practicable for one study, a considerable portion of the interview was devoted to examining attitudes toward violence when it is used for producing social change and attitudes toward violence as a means of maintaining social control.

Attitudes Toward Violence for Social Control

In order to measure attitudes toward the use of violence for social control, the respondent was asked how the police should handle a variety of disturbances. In each case the respondent was read a brief scenario describing a disturbance and then handed a card on which he was asked to indicate how the police should handle the situation described. The exact format of these questions was:

	Almost Always	Sometimes	Hardly Ever	Never
A. The police should let it go, not do anything.	☐	☐	☐	☐
B. Police should make arrests without using clubs or guns.	☐	☐	☐	☐
C. Police should use clubs, but not guns.	☐	☐	☐	☐
D. The police should shoot, but not to kill.	☐	☐	☐	☐
E. The police should shoot to kill.	☐	☐	☐	☐

The set of questions on how the police should handle disturbances was repeated three times; once in relation to student disturbances, once in relation to ghetto disturbances, and once in respect to a situation that did not involve protest. The last of these was included in order to measure attitudes toward violence in circumstances not complicated by political issues or partisan support. In a sense, we wanted the respondent's general attitude toward violence for social control, but preliminary work made it seem wise to specify a particular situation rather than leave it to the respondent's imagination. For this reason, we chose for the third scenario a situation involving hoodlum gangs. It represented collective violence of a type which is not uncommon in the United States, but which does not involve attitudes toward civil rights, discrimination, blacks, students or social change, all of which are intricately involved in attitudes toward the student and ghetto disturbances which we wished to study.[2]

Police Force and Hoodlum Gangs. The question asking the respondent his opinion about how the police should handle situations involving hoodlum gangs was as follows:

> *There have been times when gangs of hoodlums have gone into a town, terrified people, and caused a lot of property damage. How do you think the police should handle this situation?*

The respondent was then handed a card on which items A, B, C, D, and E were printed as shown above and he was allowed to fill it out without further interference from the interviewer. The percentage distribution to this question is given in Table 6.

Table 6 tells us a variety of things. To begin with, there was a great deal of agreement that some action must be taken. Eighty-one percent of American men answered "never" to the statement that "the police should let it go, not do anything." This indicates a strongly action-oriented motif; the possibility that the situation might just blow over and go away if ignored occurred to very few. Something must be done and, in the context of the question, that something must involve the police.

Second, 80 percent of all men believed that the police should make

---

[2] Preliminary testing of this set of questions demonstrated that there was no appreciable difference in the frequency of responses when the format to which the respondent answered was "almost always," "sometimes," "hardly ever," and "never," and when he was asked to respond with "agree a great deal," "agree somewhat," "disagree somewhat," and "disagree a great deal." The former wording was adopted since it seemed to fit the questions better.

Table 6

Percentage of Respondents Reporting How the Police Should Handle Hoodlum Gangs

(all respondents; N=1,374)

	Almost Always	Sometimes	Hardly Ever	Never	Total
A. The police should let it go, not do anything.	7%	6%	6%	81%	100%
B. Police should make arrests without using clubs or guns.	28	52	9	11	100
C. Police should use clubs, but not guns.	18	62	11	9	100
D. The police should shoot, but not to kill.	20	44	23	13	100
E. The police should shoot to kill.	5	27	24	44	100

arrests without using either clubs or guns, "almost always" or "sometimes," and an equal number believed that the police should make arrests in such a situation using clubs but not guns. There is less agreement about the appropriateness of the use of guns in controlling hoodlum disturbances. Sixty-four percent felt that the police should shoot, but not to kill, "almost always" or "sometimes" in such situations. Half that number, 32 percent, felt that the police should shoot to kill.

There are interesting patterns in these statistics. Their "center of gravity" is toward minimal rather than maximal force—arrest or the use of clubs without guns. But a substantial majority support the use of guns (shoot, but not to kill) at least sometimes. The most substantial break is between the percentage of respondents who felt that shooting but not killing is appropriate (64 percent), and the percentage who felt that the police should shoot to kill "almost always" or "sometimes" (32 percent). It is known that the use of firearms in any kind of an assault increases the probability of death by a very large amount. For example, criminal assaults with guns are five times more likely to end in the death of a victim than assaults with knives (Gillen and Ochberg 1970, p. 249). There is a large element of chance in the amount of damage a bullet does; the difference between life and death is often a matter of millimeters, and aim is difficult in respect to a moving target. One might speculate that respondents who felt that the police should shoot but not kill anyone in the process might have had a somewhat optimistic notion about the accuracy with which guns can be used.

In this context, the difference between the number of American men who said that it was never appropriate to shoot to kill and the number who felt it was never appropriate to shoot at all is interesting. Both these responses seem life-conserving in intent. Yet while 44 percent felt that killing in hoodlum disturbances was never justified, only 13 percent felt that shooting was never justified. One wonders whether there would be a revision in the public's attitudes toward the use of firearms by the police if the connection between the use of firearms and accidental homicide were made more concrete in the public mind, or whether deadly accidents are easily accepted.

Whether the average American man views human life in a somewhat casual fashion or of supreme value is not easily asked or answered. We approached the issue in relative rather than absolute terms:

> *Some people say that stealing or damaging property is as bad as hurting people. Others say that damaging property is not as bad as hurting people. What do you think?*

Forty-six percent replied that damaging property is as bad as hurting people, while 54 percent said that hurting people is worse. It is possible that some respondents construed this question to include hurting people in minor ways; nevertheless, the responses to the question suggest a value on property almost commensurate with that on persons. However, American men seemed to take a more serious view of personal injury when the question was phrased differently, so that the respondent might be more likely to apply it to himself (Table 7):

> *Do you think it would be worse to become a permanent cripple, or to lose an uninsured home through fire, or are they equally bad? . . . Would you say it was a lot worse or just somewhat worse?*

Table 7

Percentage Responses to Whether It Is Worse
to Become Crippled or to Lose Your Home
(all respondents; N=1,374)

Becoming a cripple is a lot worse	69
Becoming a cripple is somewhat worse	7
Losing a home is as bad as becoming a cripple	20
Losing a home is worse	4
Total	100%

Ghetto Riots and Student Disturbances. When American men were queried about the control of ghetto disturbances, their attitudes toward police action were virtually identical with those held in respect to the control of "hoodlum gangs" (Table 8).

Table 8

Percentage Responses to How the Police
Should Handle Ghetto Riots
(all respondents; N=1,374)

	Almost Always	Sometimes	Hardly Ever	Never	Total
A. The police should let it go, not do anything.	3%	9%	11%	77%	100%
B. Police should make arrests without using clubs or guns.	30	51	10	9	100
C. Police should use clubs, but not guns.	15	65	12	8	100
D. The police should shoot, but not to kill.	14	47	22	17	100
E. The police should shoot to kill.	4	26	19	51	100

However, when questioned about the control of campus disturbances, American men saw less need for police force than in the other two situations (Table 9). Almost nine out of ten responded that campus situations should generally be controlled without clubs or guns. In other words, there is overwhelming support for the use of moderate police methods. Sixty-two percent of the respondents felt that the police should "never" shoot to kill in campus disturbances, while an additional 19 percent felt that such tactics should "hardly ever" be used. These figures show more support for the use of peaceful methods than in the case of hoodlum disturbances, where only 44 percent of the respondents felt that the police should never shoot to kill, with an additional 24 percent stating such methods should hardly ever be used.

Nevertheless, it is sobering to think that 19 to 32 percent of the respondents felt that the police should shoot to kill "almost always" or "sometimes" depending on the particular situation. These figures represent a significant minority of American men, interviewed in the summer of 1969, before the deaths in campus disturbances at Kent State University

Table 9

Percentage Responses to How the Police
Should Handle Student Disturbances
(all respondents; N=1,374)

	Almost Always	Sometimes	Hardly Ever	Never	Total
A. The police should let it go, not do anything.	4%	12%	14%	70%	100%
B. Police should make arrests without using clubs or guns.	38	49	6	7	100
C. Police should use clubs, but not guns.	16	60	15	9	100
D. The police should shoot, but not to kill.	16	32	25	27	100
E. The police should shoot to kill.	3	16	19	62	100

and Jackson State College had occurred. Nineteen percent of them agreed that the police should shoot to kill in student disturbances. One cannot help but ask to what extent such attitudes contributed to the tragic deaths which have occurred on college campuses since that time. Indeed, one must also ask to what extent American attitudes toward the use of firearms by the police contributed to the deaths incurred in the ghetto disturbances of the 1960's. Most of such deaths were attributed to the police and to the National Guard, and the Commission on Civil Disorders (1968, pp. 327, 489ff.) asserted that neither group of enforcement agents had had sufficient training in riot control, and that there were problems in communication and command. The President's Commission on Campus Unrest (1970, pp. 2-55) came to similar conclusions in respect to campus disturbances. Under these circumstances, one might expect that personal attitudes could have played a large role in determining individual behaviors.

One might interpret the action-oriented, stop-them-by-shooting-if-necessary motif, which is prominent in the responses to these questions, as implying that some American men see the problem of maintaining social control less as a problem in civil administration than as a "war against crime." Surely this phrase has been sounded often enough that one might suspect that it is ringing in the ear of the man on the street (Schira 1968,

p. 414; Blum 1968, p. 418). Laws and due process are suspended in wars, and the aim is to dispatch the enemy as promptly as possible. We will show later that persons who recommended high levels of police force were more likely to see those against whom police force is used as having the kinds of undesirable characteristics often attributed to a national enemy.

War involves summary justice. One dispenses with juries and there is no appeal. These data suggest that some Americans are prepared to admit such procedures in civil disturbances, dispense with the usual courtroom procedures, and delegate to the policeman not only the power to arrest and subdue but the power to execute on the spot.

Attitudes Toward Violence for Social Change

The converse of the use of violence to maintain social control is the use of violence to produce social change. While the former implies an interest in maintaining the status quo, the latter seeks to disrupt that equilibrium for the sake of actualizing a different set of priorities.

Attitudes concerning the use of violence as a means of producing social change were measured with the following set of questions:

	Agree a Great Deal	Agree Somewhat	Disagree Somewhat	Disagree a Great Deal
A. Changes can be made fast enough without action involving property damage or injury.	☐	☐	☐	☐
B. Protest in which some people are hurt is necessary for changes to come fast enough.	☐	☐	☐	☐
C. Protest in which there is *some* property damage is necessary for changes to be brought about fast enough.	☐	☐	☐	☐
D. Protest in which there is *much* property damage is necessary before changes can be brought about fast enough.	☐	☐	☐	☐
E. Protest in which some people are killed is necessary before changes will take place fast enough.	☐	☐	☐	☐

Again, the respondent was given a card and asked to check the appropriate responses in respect to three situations intended to parallel those described in the questions relating to violence for social control. The first situation related to student demonstrations, the second to black protests, and the third set asked about the general necessity for violence in bringing about change. (The references to hoodlums were omitted as irrelevant to efforts at social change.)

The exact wording of the questions describing the student situation was as follows:

> *As you know, many white students feel changes are needed in society. Do you agree with the students that some changes* **might** *be needed?*

> *In trying to bring about change, students sometimes demonstrate in such a way that property is damaged and the police have to be called. We would like to know how much you agree with each of these opinions about how much violence is necessary for the students to bring about changes?*

Table 10 gives the responses of all those men who had agreed some change might be needed in response to the preceding question (93 percent). These results will be discussed jointly with those shown in Tables 11 and 12.

The questions inquiring about the use of violence to bring about changes for blacks were as follows:

> *Many Negroes (black people/colored people) feel changes are needed in our society. Do you agree that some changes* **might** *be needed in the United States to make life better for Negroes (black people/colored people)?*

> *In trying to bring about changes, some Negroes (black people/colored people) have protested sometimes in such a way that the police had to be called. We would like to know how much you agree with each of these opinions about how much violence is necessary for the Negro (black people/colored people) to bring about changes.*

Table 11 gives the percent distribution of responses for those respondents who had agreed some changes might be needed to make life better for blacks (91 percent).

Table 10

Percentage Responses to What Level of Violence Is Necessary
to Bring About Change for Students

(all respondents who felt change was needed; N=1,241)

	Agree a Great Deal	Agree Somewhat	Disagree Somewhat	Disagree a Great Deal	Total
A. Changes can be made fast enough without action involving property damage or injury.	62%	25%	8%	5%	100%
B. Protest in which some people are hurt is necessary for changes to come fast enough.	6	15	18	61	100
C. Protest in which there is *some* property damage is necessary for changes to be brought about fast enough.	5	14	25	56	100
D. Protest in which there is *much* property damage is necessary before changes can be brought about fast enough.	4	5	13	78	100
E. Protest in which some people are killed is necessary before changes will take place fast enough.	4	5	6	85	100

The exact wording for the general situation was as follows:

Some people feel that important changes can only be brought about through violence; others say violence is not necessary. What do you think?

Every respondent was asked this question, since there was no preceding question which gave the option of saying no change was needed.

In some respects, the most significant finding in these tables is the least obvious; it is the fact that 91 percent of all American men agreed that "some changes might be needed to make life better for blacks," and 93 percent agreed with the students that "some changes might be needed" in

Table 11

Percentage Responses to What Level of Violence Is Necessary
to Bring About Change for Blacks

(all respondents who felt change was needed; N=1,212)

	Agree a Great Deal	Agree Somewhat	Disagree Somewhat	Disagree a Great Deal	Total
A. Changes can be made fast enough without action involving property damage or injury.	58%	24%	12%	6%	100%
B. Protest in which some people are hurt is necessary for changes to come fast enough.	6	17	22	55	100
C. Protest in which there is *some* property damage is necessary for changes to be brought about fast enough.	6	19	22	53	100
D. Protest in which there is *much* property damage is necessary before changes can be brought about fast enough.	4	6	16	74	100
E. Protest in which some people are killed is necessary before changes will take place fast enough.	4	5	7	84	100

society. The questions, of course, were put with considerable qualification
—*some* changes, *might* be needed. Nevertheless, there is an expressed readiness for change, in the abstract and in unspecified kinds and amounts.

When one turns to the questions that specify the pace and cost of change, the proportion of change-endorsers drops precipitously as the hypothetical costs in life and property increase. The distribution of responses for each item (A-E) is virtually identical across the three situations. In all cases the vast majority of Americans agreed with the first item (A) that changes *can* be brought about fast enough without action involving property damage or injury. This item may be interpreted either as a statement by the respondent as to what is possible, or as a statement about

Table 12

Percentage Responses to What Level of Violence Is Necessary
to Bring About Change

(all respondents; N=1,374)

	Agree a Great Deal	Agree Somewhat	Disagree Somewhat	Disagree a Great Deal	Total
A. Changes can be made fast enough without action involving property damage or injury.	62%	25%	8%	5%	100%
B. Protest in which some people are hurt is necessary for changes to come fast enough.	4	15	25	56	100
C. Protest in which there is *some* property damage is necessary for changes to be brought about fast enough.	4	17	23	56	100
D. Protest in which there is *much* property damage is necessary before changes can be brought about fast enough.	3	7	15	75	100
E. Protest in which some people are killed is necessary before changes will take place fast enough.	3	6	6	85	100

what is likely. However, 18 percent of American men disagreed with the item when the questions were asked in relationship to changes needed by blacks (Table 11). It is as though almost one-fifth of our male population had given up the hope that such changes can be made peacefully.

The next four items (B,C,D,E) are phrased not so much in terms of what is possible, as in terms of what is *necessary;* that is, what will actually be required to produce change. Necessity seems to be the language with which we excuse ourselves and rationalize unpleasantness; it is necessary to spank children and fire incompetent employees, even if it pains the parent or employer and, apparently in the eyes of some Americans, it is necessary to use violence to bring about social change. Like the first item, these four can be interpreted as an indication of despair that change will ever come about in a nonviolent way or they can be seen as an endorsement of violence.

Inspection of Tables 10 to 12 shows that, on the whole, American men did not agree that violence is necessary to produce social change. Nevertheless, in all three situations 9 percent of the male population thought that "protest in which some people are killed" would be necessary to bring about needed change, while between 19 and 23 percent felt that protest involving some personal injury would be needed. Similarly, 9 to 10 percent of American men felt that protest involving extensive property damage would be required to bring about change, while 19 to 25 percent agreed that protest involving some property damage would be required.

There are at least two ways of looking at these figures. On the one hand, we can congratulate ourselves that the great majority of men are so committed to the idea that change can be produced without violence. On the other hand, we can ask ourselves whether it is really desirable or safe to have one-quarter of our male population believing that some degree of violence is required to produce change in our society. The eruption of violence does not require participation by the majority, but only by a small group who adopt such methods and who receive social support from a larger number of their fellows.

Indices of Violence

For many purposes it is convenient to combine responses to these many items, and speak in terms of two indices or dimensions—violence for social control and violence for social change. The regularity of responses across the three basic situations encouraged such combination. Accordingly, the three sets of questions dealing with the amount of force the police should use to handle a disturbance were combined into a single scale. This scale is called Violence for Social Control; the higher the score on this scale, the more violent the level of police force recommended. (A more detailed presentation of the scaling is presented in Appendix D.)

A variety of patterns can be formed in response to the questions asking how the police should handle different situations. Moreover, the meaning of a particular response is quite different if answers to other items in the set differ. For example, suppose a respondent answers "hardly ever" to the question which inquires if the police should use clubs. His answer to that question takes on a very different meaning if he also says they should make arrests without using clubs or guns "almost always" and shoot (either to kill or not to kill) "never," than if he says they should shoot "almost always" or "sometimes." In the first case, the pattern is essentially nonviolent in nature; in the second case the pattern implies a maximal use of force. The nature of the pattern is taken into account in the scaling.

Figure 1 gives some typical responses for high, moderate, and low scores on the scales of Violence for Social Control:

Violence for Social Control Score		Make arrests without clubs or guns	Use clubs	Shoot but not to kill	Shoot to kill
Lowest	0	sometimes	never	never	never
		almost always	sometimes	never	never
	4	sometimes	sometimes	hardly ever	hardly ever
		almost always	sometimes	sometimes	hardly ever
		almost always	sometimes	hardly ever	hardly ever
Highest	9	sometimes	sometimes	almost always	sometimes
		hardly ever	sometimes	sometimes	sometimes
		never	never	sometimes	sometimes

Figure 1. Violence for Social Control: typical response patterns on how the police should handle big city riots.

Violence for Social Change Score		Some people hurt	Some property damage	Much property damage	Some people killed
Lowest	1	disagree a great deal	disagree a great deal	disagree a great deal	disagree a great deal
		agree a great deal	agree a great deal	disagree a great deal	disagree a great deal
	4	disagree somewhat	disagree somewhat	disagree somewhat	disagree somewhat
		agree somewhat	agree somewhat	agree a great deal	agree a great deal
Highest	7	agree a great deal	agree a great deal	agree somewhat	agree somewhat
		agree a great deal	agree a great deal	agree a great deal	agree a great deal

Figure 2. Violence for Social Change: typical response patterns on what level of violence is necessary to bring about change.

Similarly, the three sets of questions relating to how much violence was seen as necessary for social change to occur fast enough were combined into a single scale. This scale is called Violence for Social Change. Again, the higher the score on the scale, the more the respondent agreed that property damage and personal injury were necessary to produce social change. (Details of the scaling are given in Appendix D.) Figure 2 gives some typical sets of responses for high, moderate and low scores on the scale of Violence for Social Change.

Summary

American men in 1969 were greatly concerned with violence, over 65 percent spontaneously mentioning some form of violence when asked what things going on in the United States "nowadays" concerned them. The greatest degree of concern was with violence as it relates to protest and dissent, 65 percent of American men mentioning such issues. Almost half felt that violence is due to lack of communication between people (particularly blacks and whites), frustration at the problems of modern living, and other contemporary social problems. When asked whether specific social problems such as unemployment, discrimination and lack of education contribute to causing violence, from 70 to 89 percent agreed that such conditions contribute to violence. However, when asked how violence could best be prevented, a large number of respondents (30 percent) mentioned more police force and stricter, more punitive legislation. Apparently, in the thinking of many American men the cure for violence is not related to its cause.

There was widespread consensus among American men that disturbances such as those caused by hoodlums, student demonstrations, and inner-city upheavals should be handled by minimal amounts of police force whenever possible. From 80 to 87 percent of Americans agreed that police ought to make arrests in such disturbances without using clubs or guns "almost always" or "sometimes." Seventy-six to eighty percent thought that such arrests should be made using clubs but not guns "almost always" or "sometimes." There was considerably less agreement about the appropriateness of the use of guns in such disturbances. From 48 to 64 percent of American men, depending on the specific situation, felt that the police should shoot (but not to kill) "sometimes" or "almost always" in controlling such situations, while from 19 to 32 percent felt that the police should shoot to kill.

Over 90 percent of American men felt that some change of the type advocated by students and blacks might be needed, and about 90 percent agreed that such changes could be made without action involving property damage or personal injury. However, about 20 percent believed that protest involving some property damage or personal injury is necessary to bring about change at a sufficiently rapid rate. About 10 percent believed that protest involving extensive property damage and some deaths is necessary to bring about change fast enough. The 10 percent figure is a relatively small one, but it represents an estimated 5 million men in the United States, a substantial number. That this number of American men felt that changes will not come about at a sufficiently rapid pace unless major violence occurs and that almost a quarter believed that some violence is necessary to bring about change at a reasonable rate may reflect the extent to which American men believe that our social system is not willing or able to deal with the social problems of our times.

Chapter 3

BACKGROUND, BELIEF, AND BEHAVIOR

When one asks who is violent, the answer is often phrased in terms of background characteristics—usually characteristics that describe persons other than the speaker. Thus, the violent are said to be the young, the uneducated, or the irreligious. How much truth is there in such generalizations? To what extent are such characteristics associated with different attitudes toward violence and with violent behavior?

We have already seen that Americans have varying beliefs about the extent to which the causes of violence are found in social problems. It seems reasonable to think that such beliefs might be reflected in people's attitudes toward violence for social change, and toward the use of force to maintain social control. In other words, we can ask to what extent general attitudes and beliefs about social problems appear to determine specific attitudes toward violence.

Lastly, we can ask to what extent such attitudes toward violence are expressed in violent behavior. Knowing what a man thinks is one thing; finding out what he does is something else. People often have opinions they do not act upon and do things they don't believe in, so it is important to determine the extent to which the atitudes investigated in this study are reflected in behaviors. The last part of this chapter will deal with these issues.

Background Characteristics and Attitudes Toward Violence

Table 1 shows the association between some demographic characteristics of American men and their attitudes toward Violence for Social Control and Violence for Social Change.

Table 1

Violence for Social Control and Violence for Social Change
in Relation to Some Demographic Characteristics
(all respondents; N=1,374)
(gammas)[a]

Demographic Characteristics	Violence for Social Control	Violence for Social Change
Age	.09	-.14
Education	-.15	-.11
Family income	-.04	-.17
Experience in South	-.11	-.11
Town size	-.12	.13
Race	-.23	.64

[a] Gammas are a measure of association designed to measure relationships between ordinal categories (Freeman 1965, p. 79).

In general, the relationships between these variables and attitudes toward violence are small, with race the sole exception. One cannot predict attitudes toward violence from background factors alone. Nevertheless, the patterns of relationship are meaningful and interesting.

Age

Perhaps the most striking fact in these data, given the much-discussed gap between old and young, is the stability of attitudes toward violence across age groups. Nevertheless, the age of a man does seem to be associated with his attitudes toward violence and the association varies with the type of violence. Figure 1 shows the relationship between age and Violence for Social Control. On the whole, teenagers in the sample were most likely to recommend peaceful patterns of handling disturbances and least likely to recommend the most forceful methods. In this, they differed from all other age groups in the population.

On the other hand, teenagers scored higher than any other age group on the index of Violence for Social Change (Figure 2). Only 26 percent of those under 20 fell into the lowest categories on Violence for Social Change, compared to 41 percent of those in their twenties and 44 percent among American men as a whole. Moreover, with increasing age, the percentage advocating high levels[1] of Violence for Social Change decreases steadily.

---

[1] Low, moderate and high levels of Violence for Social Change refer to scores of 1, 2-3, 4-7 on the measure of Violence for Social Change. In the population as a whole, 44, 37 and 19 percent fell in these categories respectively.

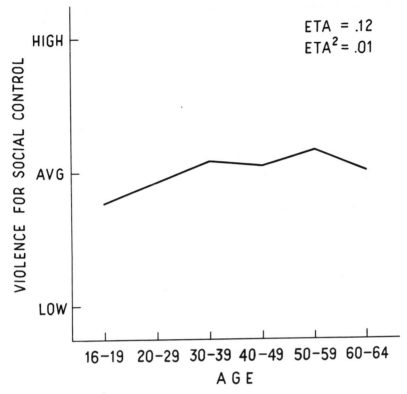

Figure 1. Mean Violence for Social Control in relation to age (all respondents; N=1,374).

Note: The "average" score is based on our sample of 1,374 American men aged 16-64. About two-thirds of these men had scores falling between the points marked "high" and "low."

Whether the association between attitudes toward violence and age, particularly in adolescence, is a function of the life cycle or a particular characteristic of the younger generation of today remains to be seen. Nevertheless, the association between age and attitudes toward violence is consistent with the fact that some violent behaviors are known to be more frequent among the young. This is true, for example, of rioting (Singer 1968, p. 12; Luby, Mendelsohn, Fishhoff and Wehmer 1968, p. 32) and homicide (Wolfgang 1958, p. 65ff).

Education

Figures 3 and 4 show the relationship between education and attitudes toward Violence for Social Control and Social Change. Lack of education is associated with the justification of higher levels of violence

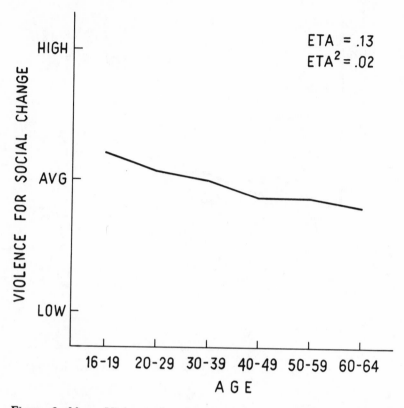

Figure 2. Mean Violence for Social Change in relation to age (all respondents; N=1,374).

for both purposes but there are some interesting differences. With respect to Violence for Social Control, men with the least education were most likely to recommend the most forceful patterns of police response.[2] As education continues through high school, the advocacy of Violence for Social Control declines steadily. Among college graduates, a markedly larger percentage recommend the least forceful police methods. Thirty-seven percent of those who had completed college recommended such patterns of police behavior, compared to 22 percent of those graduated only from high school, and 15 percent of those with less than a seventh grade education.

---

[2] In discussing the Violence for Social Control measure the term "low," "moderate" and "high" (or "least," "moderate" and "highest") refer to those who scored 0-2, 3-6, 7-9 on that measure. For the population as a whole, 24, 52 and 24 percent fell into these three categories.

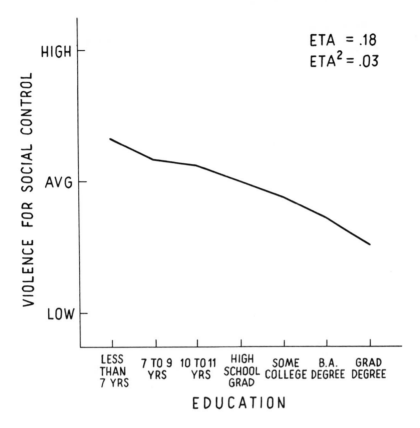

Figure 3. Mean Violence for Social Change in relation to education (all respondents; N=1,374).

Less well-educated respondents recommended higher levels of police force. Thirty-four percent of those with less than seven years of school recommended such measures, compared with 22 percent of those with some college education. Men who had completed some graduate education were even less willing to see forceful methods used. Only 8 percent of men with graduate degrees recommended the highest levels of Violence for Social Control. The most educated men in our nation appear to be least convinced that such force is required.

The relationship between education and Violence for Social Change is not as marked as the relationship between education and Violence for Social Control. In general, however, the less educated the respondent, the more likely he is to score high on Violence for Social Change (Figure 4).

The index of Violence for Social Change can be interpreted as a

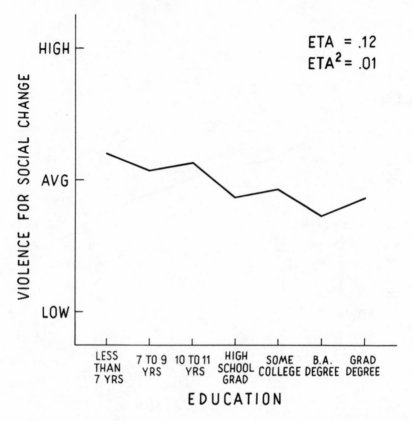

Figure 4. Mean Violence for Social Change in relation to education (all respondents; N=1,374).

measure of the cynicism with which American men view the ability or the willingness of our social system to bring about social change without violence, since the questions are phrased in terms of how much violence is necessary to bring about change "fast enough." It can also be interpreted as an indirect measure of the range of nonviolent alternatives that men can envision. In either light, it makes sense that those with less than a high school education, and presumably with more pressing economic problems, would be both less sophisticated about means of producing change and more inclined to despair that needed change can be brought about fast enough without violence.

Income, Region and Religion

The amount of family income is also related to attitudes toward violence, though not so consistently as education. There is no relationship between income and attitudes toward Violence for Social Control (Figure 5). However, as Figure 6 shows, there is a definite relationship between income and attitudes toward Violence for Social Change. Men with a family income below the median ($8,690) were above average on Violence for Social Change, while those with above-median incomes were lower on this index of violence.

Figures 7 and 8 show that all in all not much of the difference among people in attitudes toward violence can be explained on the basis of the region in which they live. Regional prejudices run strong in some places, but they get little support from our data. True, persons living in the

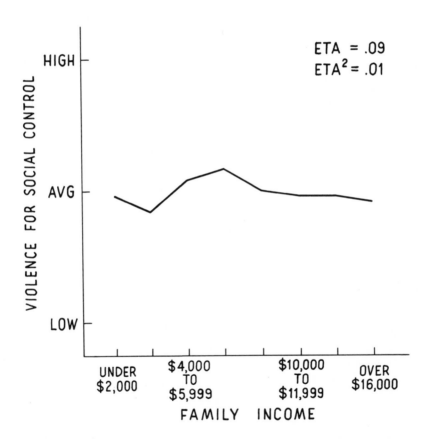

Figure 5. Mean Violence for Social Control in relation to family income (all respondents; N=1,374).

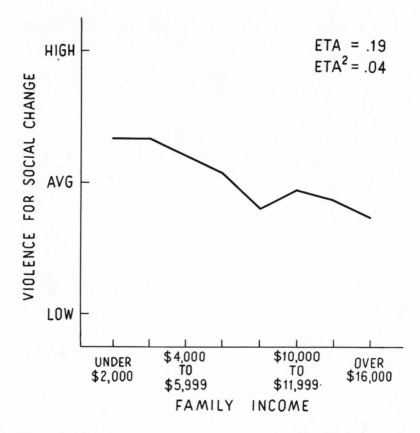

Figure 6. Mean Violence for Social Change in relation to family income (all respondents; N=1,374).

New England States were least likely to recommend the highest levels of Violence for Social Control and most likely to recommend the lowest levels. Men living in the South and the Border states[3] were more likely to recommend high levels of Violence for Social Control, but these differences are not striking. There is almost no variation by region in respect to attitudes toward Violence for Social Change except for the Mountain States, which contained relatively few respondents.

---

[3] The South as defined in this study includes Alabama, Arkansas, Florida, Georgia, Louisiana, Mississippi, North Carolina, South Carolina, Texas, and Virginia. The Border states include Kentucky, Maryland, Oklahoma, Tennessee, and Washington, D. C.

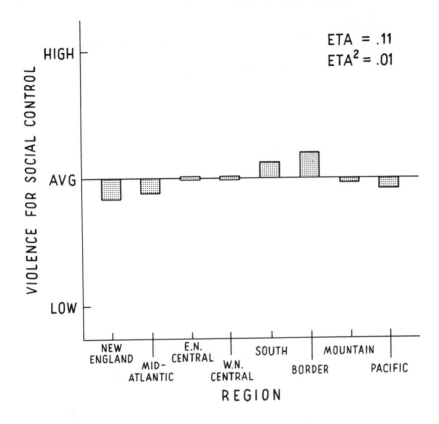

Figure 7. Mean Violence for Social Control in relation to region (all respondents; N=1,374).

Note: This figure and many subsequent figures are drawn so that each bar represents how much the average for a category is above or below the national average. Roughly two-thirds of the men in our national sample had scores falling between "high" and "low" on the vertical axis.

Figures 9 and 10 show that few differences in attitudes toward violence stem from a man's religion. Jews were more likely to recommend low levels of Violence for Social Control than any other religious group. Catholics were also more likely to recommend low levels of Violence for Social Control. Whether these attitudes are partly a reflection of the minority experience is a matter for speculation.

In respect to attitudes toward Violence for Social Change, only men professing no religion were noticeably different from the average (Figure

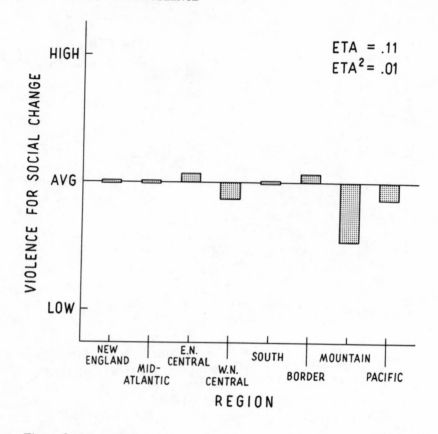

Figure 8. Mean Violence for Social Change in relation to region (all respondents; N=1,374).

10). Such persons were almost twice as likely to fall into the highest categories of Violence for Social Change as were members of the population at large.

There is a small relationship between place of residence (town size) and attitudes toward violence. Men living in cities were less likely to advocate high levels of police force than those who lived in small town or rural areas, in spite of the higher rates of crime and civil disturbances in large cities (Figure 11). On the other hand, men living in large cities scored relatively high on Violence for Social Change (Figure 12). More than others, they tended to believe that change will not come about fast enough in the absence of protest involving property damage and personal injury.

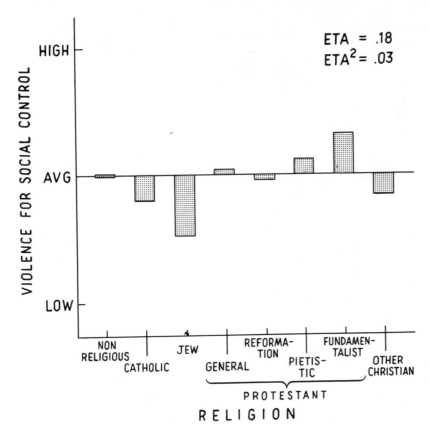

Figure 9. Mean Violence for Social Control in relation to religion (all respondents; N=1,374).

Group Membership and Attitudes Toward Violence

Table 2 shows attitudes toward violence among several special groups within the general population—blacks and whites, college students and white union members. These subpopulations were chosen for study because they are not merely demographic categories, but groups of social and political significance. As one might have suspected, blacks and whites differed considerably; blacks were less likely than whites to recommend high levels of police force as a means of social control. In this they resembled college graduates, whose attitudes we have already discussed (Figure 3). College students, however, were not different from the white population at large in respect to Violence for Social Control. This is

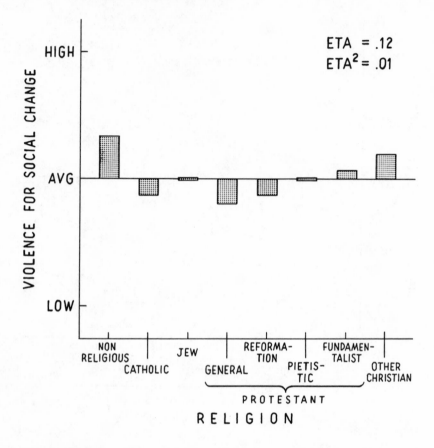

Figure 10. Mean Violence for Social Change in relation to religion (all respondents; N=1,374).

intriguing since, as we have seen earlier, the endorsement of violence for social control was less prevalent among men who had completed college. It remains to be seen whether this tendency will hold for the present generation of students.

Differences between whites and blacks are large in respect to attitudes toward Violence for Social Change. Only 11 percent of blacks disagreed strongly with all statements that property damage or personal injury would be necessary to bring about change fast enough, and over half of them fell in the four highest code categories on the measure of Violence for Social Change. The corresponding figures for whites were almost an inversion—48 and 14 percent.

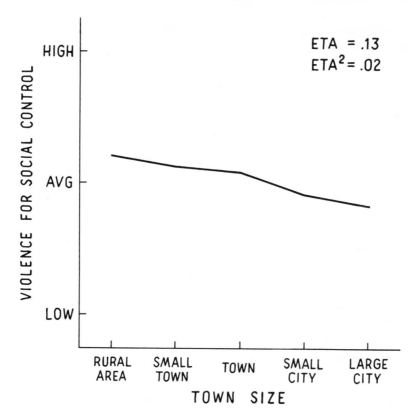

Figure 11. Mean Violence for Social Control in relation to town size (all respondents; N=1,374).

As we suggested earlier, persistent agreement with the statements comprising the scale of Violence for Social Change may be interpreted as reflecting a profound pessimism that social changes will come about at a reasonable speed without violence. It is not surprising that in our society blacks would be more likely than whites to fall victim to such hopelessness. There can be very little doubt that as a group blacks feel a greater need for social change than whites, and are more despairing of its progress. In any case, blacks were much more likely than whites to agree that violence was necessary to bring about change at what they perceived as a reasonable rate.

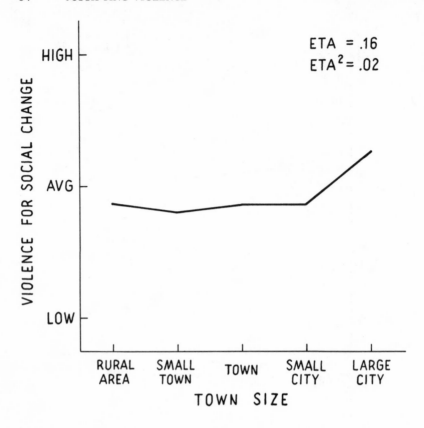

Figure 12. Mean Violence for Social Change in relation to town size (all respondents; N=1,374).

Tables 3 and 4 present some of the data for blacks that are summarized in the indices of Violence for Social Control and for Social Change. As Table 3 indicates, the dominant black response pattern favors police action rather than inaction in case of ghetto riots, and a substantial majority of blacks supported the making of arrests with clubs under such circumstances. Indeed, half of all black respondents said that the police should sometimes shoot in order to control ghetto riots—but not to kill. The white response pattern, as we have said, was still more supportive of the use of force by police.

Twenty-seven percent of black respondents indicated disagreement with the proposition that "changes can be made fast enough without

Table 2

Percentage Responses to Violence for Social Control
and Violence for Social Change for Whites,
Blacks, College Students and White Union Members

		All Respon- dents	Whites	Blacks	College Students	White Union Members
		(N=1,374)	(N=1,046)	(N=303)	(N=63)	(N=279)
Violence for Social Control						
Low	0-2	24	23	37	25	16
	3-6	52	51	46	54	54
High	7-9	24	26	17	21	30
		100%	100%	100%	100%	100%
Violence for Social Change						
Low	1	44	48	11	35	47
	2-3	37	38	37	38	39
High	4-7	19	14	52	27	14
		100%	100%	100%	100%	100%

Table 3

Percentage Responses to How the Police
Should Handle Ghetto Riots
(black respondents; N=303)

	Almost Always	Sometimes	Hardly Ever	Never	Total
A. The police should let it go, not do anything.	6%	26%	24%	44%	100%
B. The police should make arrests without using clubs or guns.	28	56	9	7	100
C. The police should use clubs, but not guns.	14	56	19	11	100
D. The police should shoot, but not to kill.	15	35	17	33	100
E. The police should shoot to kill.	3	15	12	70	100

action involving property damage or injury" (Table 4). This is a minority of blacks, but it is almost twice as large a proportion as that of whites giving similar responses. Moreover, about half of all black respondents thought that changes could not be brought about without some property damage or some personal injury; only one-fifth of white respondents shared this view.

As the statements became more extreme, the differences in response patterns between black and white increased. A significant minority of black respondents—27 percent—agreed with the statement that "protest in which some people are killed" would be "necessary for black people to bring about changes." The corresponding percentage for whites was only 5. These responses by blacks are not specific to the question about racial protest. Almost identical scores were obtained in answer to the questions about student protest and about social change in general. It is the black experience with attempted social change and the resistance to change that seems reflected in these responses.

College students differed more from whites in general in their attitudes toward Violence for Social Change than toward Violence for Social Control. Moreover, they were slightly more inclined to assert the necessity for violence in producing change at a reasonable rate than were persons in the general population. These differences are modest, however, and can be explained in terms of age. College students were not different from other men in their twenties.

White union members were picked as a contrasting group of particular interest. Some union groups have expressed themselves strongly in the political arena over the last few years, generally against student protest and sometimes against racial integration, particularly in respect to integration of the unions themselves. On this basis one might have expected union members to be more in favor of Violence for Social Control, and less apt to see any necessity for using violence to produce social change. On the other hand, there has been some violence in relation to labor disputes in recent years and there is a long history of violence in the labor movement. While these facts might not lead union members to favor the use of violence for bringing about changes desired by students and blacks, they might make plausible the use of violence to bring about other types of changes.

In any case, Table 2 shows that white union members in the United States are not particularly different from other whites in their attitudes about violence.[4]

---

[4] There is a slight trend, however, for white union members to score somewhat higher on both violence measures than men of similar occupational status who are not union members.

Table 4

Percentage Responses to What Level of Violence Is Necessary
to Bring About Change for Blacks

(black respondents who felt change was needed; N=303)

	Agree a Great Deal	Agree Somewhat	Disagree Somewhat	Disagree a Great Deal	Total
A. Changes can be made fast enough without action involving property damage or injury.	38%	35%	17%	10%	100%
B. Protest in which some people are hurt is necessary for changes to come fast enough.	15	34	26	25	100
C. Protest in which there is *some* property damage is necessary for changes to be brought about fast enough.	15	34	25	26	100
D. Protest in which there is *much* property damage is necessary before changes can be brought about fast enough.	12	17	27	44	100
E. Protest in which some people are killed is necessary before changes will take place fast enough.	9	18	12	61	100

Beliefs About Social Issues and Attitudes Toward Violence

In Chapter 2 we observed that many American men agreed that the roots of violence lie in social problems. It might be argued that such attitudes would modify attitudes toward violence, perhaps in respect to the extent that the respondent believes violence necessary to bring about social change, but even more in respect to the amount of police force he feels appropriate to maintain social control. On the other hand, considerations of legitimacy intervene between perceived social ills and the justification of violent remedies. For the vast majority of people, one can assume that the use of force by the state (and therefore by the police) is seen as legitimate under many circumstances, but that the use of force by citizens to bring about change is seen as illegitimate—even if the changes themselves are perceived to be needed. Prediction was not attempted, but these issues were investigated empirically.

A composite measure was constructed to show the extent to which the respondent believed that lack of good jobs, poverty, poor education and discrimination caused violence. The more the respondent agreed that violence was caused by such factors, the higher his score on this measure, the Social Causes Index. (For details of index construction see Appendix C.) Table 5 shows the relationship between beliefs about whether social conditions cause violence and Violence for Social Control. If the individual believes that social problems do not contribute to violence at all, he is apt to recommend very stringent police measures; 65 percent of such people fell into the highest category of Violence for Social Control, in contrast to only 18 percent of those who believe that poverty, lack of good jobs, discrimination and a poor education all contribute to producing violence. Moreover, among those who do not believe that social problems contribute to violence only 8 percent recommended low levels of police force compared to a national average of 24 percent.

This finding suggests that if the general population were more educated in respect to the social problems of contemporary America, the attitudes of those who are for the use of very high levels of force to maintain social control might change to more moderate levels.

Table 5

Percentage Responses to Belief in Social Causes of Violence
in Relation to Violence for Social Control
(all respondents; N=1,374)

		Belief in Social Causes					
Violence for Social Control		Low 1	2	3	4	High 5	All Respondents
Low	0-2	8	19	18	25	28	24
	3-6	27	52	54	50	54	52
High	7-9	65	29	28	25	18	24
	Total	100%	100%	100%	100%	100%	100%
	N	(61)	(111)	(190)	(313)	(678)	

Men who believed that social problems contribute to the development of violence were more likely to score high on Violence for Social Change (Table 6). Even among those most convinced of the social-problem origins of violence, however, the large majority oppose the idea that violence is necessary for social change.

Table 6

Percentage Responses to Belief in Social Causes of Violence
in Relation to Violence for Social Change
(all respondents; N=1,374)

Violence for Social Change		Belief in Social Causes					All Respondents
		Low 1	2	3	4	High 5	
Low	1	76	53	51	44	38	44
	2-3	15	32	35	37	41	37
High	4-7	9	15	14	19	21	19
	Total	100%	100%	100%	100%	100%	100%
	N	(52)	(105)	(182)	(303)	(677)	

Attitudes Toward the Courts and Violence for Social Change

One of the specific social issues investigated in this study was the extent to which American men believed the courts were fair. Each respondent was asked the following questions:

> *Some people have told us the courts nowadays treat some people better or worse than others. Do you think that* **rich** *people and* **poor** *people are likely to be* **treated the same** *by the courts or* **not***?*

> *Do you think that white people and Negroes (black people/colored people) are likely to be treated the same by the courts or not? . . . Who is treated better?*

> *Do you think the courts treat people like yourself* **better** *or* **worse** *than others, or* **about the same***?*

The responses to these questions are shown in Table 7.

It is a striking and sad commentary on the state of our society that only one-fifth of American men believed that the courts were likely to treat the rich and poor alike (Table 7). Less spectacular, but still distressing, is the finding that less than half believed that blacks and whites were treated equally by the courts, a belief that is widely shared among both blacks and whites. The courts are intended as the keystone of justice and equality. It is to them that the citizen turns for redress of grievances. If equality cannot be found in court, where in the government is it to be found? That so many American men believed it is not available in the judicial process suggests either that the perception of unequal treatment by the law is a longstanding condition of life or that there has been a serious erosion of faith in government.

Table 7

Percentage Responses to Questions Concerning the Fairness
of the Courts for Whites, Blacks and All Respondents

DO THE COURTS TREAT RICH AND POOR ALIKE?

	All Respondents (N=1,374)	Whites (N=1,046)	Blacks (N=303)
Poor treated better	1	1	0
Poor and rich treated same	20	20	14
Rich treated better	79	79	86
Total	100%	100%	100%

DO THE COURTS TREAT BLACKS AND WHITES ALIKE?

	All Respondents (N=1,374)	Whites (N=1,046)	Blacks (N=303)
Whites treated better	40	38	66
Same treatment, whites, blacks	43	44	29
Blacks treated better	12	13	2
Sometimes yes, sometimes no	5	5	3
Total	100%	100%	100%

WOULD YOU BE LIKELY TO BE TREATED THE SAME
AS OTHERS BY THE COURTS OR NOT?

	All Respondents (N=1,374)	Whites (N=1,046)	Blacks (N=303)
Treated worse	10	6	34
Treated same	80	82	63
Treated better	10	12	3
Total	100%	100%	100%

It is interesting that 80 percent of American men thought that rich people are better treated by the courts than poor people, but only 40 percent thought that whites are treated better than blacks. This finding is not easy to interpret, in view of the fact that blacks are much more likely to be poor than are whites.[5] It may mean that people are more willing to acknowledge economic than racial discrimination.

An interesting discrepancy in the data is that while 66 percent of blacks felt that whites were treated better in court than blacks, only 34 percent of blacks believed that they themselves would be likely to receive worse treatment. Nevertheless, this is a substantially higher percentage of blacks than whites, only 6 percent of whom believed that they themselves would be apt to receive worse than average treatment in court. One might guess that the difference between the number of blacks who believed that they themselves were likely to receive worse treatment and those who believed that blacks in general were unequally treated by the courts reflects the natural human tendency to deny unpleasant prospects and believe that bad things are more likely to happen to the other fellow than oneself.

It is plausible that attitudes toward the essential fairness of the courts should be related to attitudes toward the use of violence to produce social change. If violence for social change is inversely proportional to the perceived legitimacy of government and to the perceived adequacy of existing social machinery, then those who think the courts unfair might be more likely to lean toward violence as a means of producing social change. To test this notion, the responses to the three items about the courts were combined into the Court Fairness Index; the more the individual thought the courts were apt to be fair, the higher was his score on this index. (For details of index construction see Appendix C.)

Figure 13 shows the expected inverse relationship between perception of court fairness and scores on Violence for Social Change. The relationship is shown separately for all men and for blacks, and is more marked for blacks than for American men in general. However, men of both races who thought the courts were unfair were more likely to feel that violence was necessary for social change than were others.

Attitudes Toward Violence and Violent Behavior

We have dealt thus far with attitudes toward violence, but what a man thinks is not necessarily what he does, and it is therefore necessary to inquire whether the attitudes we have explored are in any way related to

---

[5] In our sample 51 percent of blacks had incomes under $6,000 a year compared to 19 percent of whites.

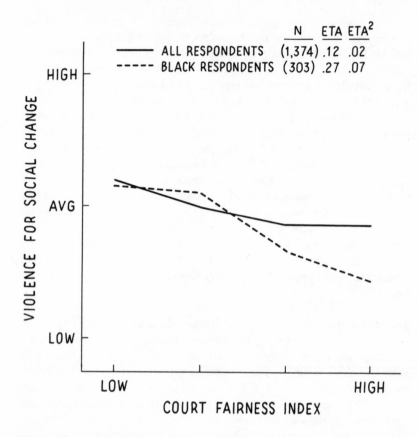

Figure 13. Mean Violence for Social Change in relation to Court Fairness Index for all respondents and black respondents.

violent behaviors. It seems reasonable to expect attitudes to be reflected in behaviors; indeed, most psychologists include the tendency to act as part of the definition of an attitude. While it is unlikely that all people holding a certain attitude would directly express their attitudes by means of similar behaviors, and while it is equally unlikely that all people who behaved in certain violent ways would have uniform attitudes toward violence, we nevertheless expected that individuals who had exhibited violent behaviors would be more likely to hold attitudes favoring violence than persons in the general population.

Student Disturbances. In conjunction with the present research, two adjunct studies were undertaken to investigate the relationship between attitudes toward violence and behavior. The first involved 29 students who were arrested or identified as participating in disturbances on several consecutive nights near The University of Michigan campus. The students interviewed had been part of a large crowd attracted to the attempt, mostly by "street people" and high school youths, to "liberate" a street of several blocks adjacent to the campus. The area is heavily populated with student rooming houses and apartments, stores and restaurants, and the effort to take over attracted a predictably larger secondary crowd of interested onlookers and fringe participants. There were attempts at dispersal and control of the crowd by University representatives and city officials; there was also a considerable introduction of force by police from the office of the county sheriff.

This particular disturbance occurred at the same time that we were in the process of collecting data from the national sample. Consequently, we decided to interview some of the male college students who were involved in the disturbance. Our respondents consisted mainly of those college students who had been arrested (about one-quarter of the arrestees), plus a few others who were nominated by the student arrestees as having been involved in the disturbance.

Whether or not the police acted well in that disturbance is an important but partisan matter which is not relevant to the present analysis. What is relevant is that a number of young people were arrested and charged with a variety of offenses, including property damage and physical assault. It is not possible to say with certainty whether individual arrestees had committed acts of violence. At least one arrestee complained tearfully that he had merely been on his way to the Undergraduate Library when the arrest was made, and others may have been mere bystanders. Nevertheless, acts of violence, including rock-throwing and fighting, did occur during the disturbance and it seems possible that some of the arrestees might have been involved in such acts. Moreover, the arrestees might be regarded as having acted in the interest of social change; after all, "liberating" a street is a social change of sorts. If there is an association between attitudes toward violence and violent behaviors, we would expect the arrestees to hold attitudes toward Violence for Social Change more favorable than those of college students at large. Table 8 shows that this is indeed the case.

It can readily be seen that the participants in the street disturbance were considerably more inclined to express opinions which resulted in high scores on Violence for Social Change than were college students in general. Moreover, college students on the whole were more apt to agree with the necessity of violence to bring about change fast enough than were men of similar education who were not in school at the time. The majority of such men were in the lowest category of Violence for Social Change; only 4 percent of the student arrestees were in this category. The arrestees

Table 8

Percentage Responses to Violence for Social Change for
Student Arrestees, College Students, and Nonstudents with
Some College or More

Violence for Social Change		Student Arrestees (Participants in U of M Street Disturbance)	College Students (National Sample)	Nonstudents with Some College or More (National Sample)
		(N=29)	(N=63)	(N=304)
Low	1	4	35	52
	2-3	37	38	34
High	4-7	59	27	14
	Total	100%	100%	100%

expressed opinions in line with what we expected. However, their opinions were measured after their participation and arrest, and it is not possible to say whether their participation in the disturbance was a result of such attitudes or whether such attitudes were developed later, to rationalize the behaviors. We can say from these results that those who have shown a tendency to act violently in behalf of social change will have relatively high scores on the measure of Violence for Social Change. We cannot make the reverse inference with confidence, that is, that those who score high on the Violence for Social Change measure are more apt to behave violently. But it seems likely that among those who score high on this measure, there may be a group, of unknown size, more apt to use violence instrumentally to produce social change than are those making low scores.

Study of Prisoners. The second study carried out in conjunction with the national survey examined the relationship between attitudes toward violence and violent behaviors among prisoners at the federal penitentiary in Milan, Michigan. The Milan Penitentiary is a minimum security prison housing approximately 550 prisoners. Because of the nature of the prison, most of the offenders sent there were convicted of relatively minor crimes (car theft was the most frequent offense) and were serving short-term sentences. Moreover, the average age of the prisoners was quite young (modal age of 21), and there was a high proportion of blacks (about 40 percent) in comparison with the general population.

A random sample of the prison population was selected, every tenth prisoner being included in the sample. Fifty-two of the prisoners in the sample were interviewed with the same schedule of questions used in the national sample. In addition, the record of the prisoner was systematically coded for mentions of violent behavior. The violent behaviors cited included those in the history of the prisoner (for example, whether he had been in fights at home or at school, whether he had been accused of wife-beating or assaults and so on). Also included were behaviors for which the prisoner was booked or convicted in the past, and the nature of the offense for which he was presently serving a prison sentence. Finally, the prisoner's record was examined for mentions of violent behavior recorded during his prison stay. The various types of violent behavior were then summarized on a scale, the Violent Behaviors Index. (For details of index construction see Appendix C.)

It is not entirely clear how the violent behaviors of the prisoners should be expected to relate to the attitudes we measured. Certainly, the acts of these prisoners hardly fall in the category of either Violence for Social Control or Violence for Social Change. The violence used in commission of a crime is often instrumental, but its purpose is personal rather than political. Moreover, the violence committed in the prison and recorded in the earlier history of the prisoners seems often to have derived from passion rather than politics. On the whole, however, one might suspect that these young men, having been the objects of attention from the police, would be inclined to favor less forceful means of social control than American men at large. Indeed, Table 9 shows that this is the case.

Table 9

Percentage Responses to Violence for Social Control
for Prisoners and Matched Sample[a]

Violence for Social Control		Prisoners (N=52)	Matched Sample (N=i42)
Low	0-2	42	27
	3-6	54	54
High	7-9	4	19
	Total	100%	100%

[a] Because of the age and racial composition of the prisoners, a group having comparable characteristics was selected out of the national sample for this analysis.

How the prisoners should have been expected to score on Violence for Social Change was even less clear. One might suppose that since many of these young men came from impoverished and deprived social circumstances, and since they themselves had been called to task by the police and the courts, they might be inclined to favor higher levels of Violence for Social Change than individuals in a group of similar age and racial composition selected from the general population. Table 10 shows that this is the case.

Table 10

Percentage Responses to Violence for Social Change
for Prisoners and Matched Sample

Violence for Social Change		Prisoners (N=52)	Matched Sample (N=142)
Low	1	12	32
	2-3	35	36
High	4-7	53	32
	Total	100%	100%

Nevertheless, the prisoners' data do not answer the question about what different relationships might be expected between types of violent behaviors and attitudes toward the two kinds of violence measured here. We had no reason to assume that the behaviors should relate more toward Violence for Social Control or Violence for Social Change, but expected that the violent behaviors would be associated in some degree with both measures. This proved to be correct (Figures 14 and 15); the Violent Behaviors Index correlates with Violence for Social Control and Violence for Social Change equally, with a gamma of .3. This finding supports the notion that people's behaviors are related to their attitudes, and provides some support for the validity of the two violence measures. Those who behave more violently are inclined to express attitudes favoring violence.

Summary

Attitudes toward violence are related to some extent to background characteristics, although the relationships are not very strong. In respect to age, teenagers were least likely to recommend high levels of Violence for Social Control, and there is a tendency for the level of police force

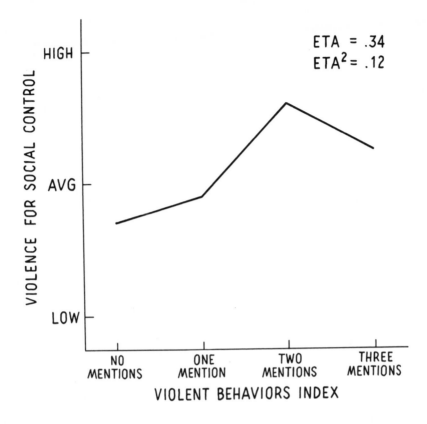

Figure 14. Mean Violence for Social Control in relation to Violent Behaviors Index (Milan prisoners; N=52).

recommended to increase with increasing age. On the other hand, young people were more likely to agree that protest involving property damage and injury is necessary for change to come about fast enough. People with lower incomes were more likely to score high on Violence for Social Change than were those who are better off financially. Differences in attitudes toward violence associated with region and religion are quite small. Jews and Catholics were less apt to recommend high levels of Violence for Social Control.

Among various special groups in the population, black men were apt to score low on Violence for Social Control, while white union members and college students were not particularly different from other whites in regard to this measure. However, college students were apt to score somewhat higher on Violence for Social Change than were whites in

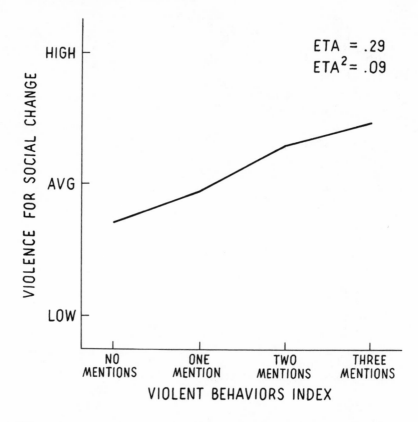

Figure 15. Mean Violence for Social Change in relation to Violent Behaviors Index (Milan prisoners; N=52).

general, although they do not appear to differ in this from their age mates. Black men were apt to score higher than college students on Violence for Social Change, over half falling into the four highest categories on this measure compared to 19 percent of American men in general. White union members do not differ from the rest of the population in respect to their attitudes toward Violence for Social Change, in spite of the fact that they were not generally favorably inclined toward black protesters and student demonstrators.

Among American men in general, those who do not believe that poverty, lack of jobs, inadequate education and discrimination contribute to causing violence were likely to recommend very high levels of Violence for Social Control. On the other hand, such individuals were apt to score low on the Violence for Social Change measure. In respect to a specific issue, the fairness of the courts, 79 percent of American men believed that the rich are treated better than the poor, and only 43 percent believed that blacks and whites are treated equally. Less than 30 percent of blacks believed the two races receive equal treatment in court. The extent to which the individual believes the courts are fair is associated with attitudes toward Violence for Social Change; the less the individual believed the courts are fair, the more likely he was to score high on Violence for Social Change.

Two small studies were carried out to test the proposition that attitudes toward violence are to some extent related to violent behaviors. In the first study, a number of college students who were participants in a street disturbance were interviewed with the same questions used to measure attitudes in the national sample. These college students were shown to have much higher scores on the Violence for Social Change measure than were college students in the national sample. In the second study, a group of prisoners in a minimum security federal prison were interviewed. The prison records of these individuals were coded for mentions of violent behavior and the results correlated with the scales measuring attitudes toward violence. There was a low correlation in the expected direction between attitudes toward both Violence for Social Control and Violence for Social Change and the index of violent behaviors. These two studies support the notion that there is an association between attitudes toward violence and violent behaviors.

Chapter 4

THE MEANING OF VIOLENCE

What Men Call Violence

Americans are concerned about violence and use the word often, but what do they really mean by it?[1] When people speak of protest as "violence," are they thinking only about protest that involves property destruction and personal injury? When people talk about "police violence," are they referring to actions which involve personal injury, or are they using a derogatory term for police behavior in general? And is there agreement among Americans on the answers to these questions, or do our disagreements about violence extend to the meaning of the word itself?

These are matters of semantics, but they go beyond the meaning of words. The question must also be asked whether the language we use has the power to influence the course of events. Does the very fact that a behavior is labeled "violence" bring into play a set of attitudes and opinions about how such behaviors should be dealt with, or is the choice of rhetoric without influence on subsequent actions?

To find out something about the context in which American men think of violence, respondents were asked:

What violent events in the United States are of the most concern to you?

Table 1 shows that in 1969 American men were concerned about racial problems, student protest, crime, and protest generally. Only a small

---

[1] Some explanation of our own use of the word violence is in order. We have reserved the term for *activities inflicting damage on persons or property*. In questioning respondents about violence for social control and social change, we were careful not to use the word violence. Instead, we worded the questionnaire items in terms of specific behaviors that constituted violence in terms of *our* definition—damaging property, hurting people, beating students, and the like. When the word is used as respondents defined it (whatever that may have been) it will appear in quotation marks.

71

Table 1

Percentage Responses Regarding Violent Events In the U.S. of Most Concern[a]

(all respondents; N=1,374)

Racial problems	30%
Student protest	23
Crime	20
Protest	19
Violent people	5
War	4
Police brutality	1

[a] Each respondent was allowed two answers to this question, and not all answers fell in the categories shown in Table 1; hence responses do not sum to 100 percent.

percentage mentioned concern about war. Almost none mentioned violence on the part of the police.

These answers are interesting but not in themselves easy to interpret. For example, consider the large percentage of American men who mentioned protest and student protest as the violent events which most concerned them. Does this mean that American men regard all dissent as protest, and protest as violence in itself? Or are those who mention protest as the type of violence which concerns them thinking of episodes of protest that led to property damage and personal injury?

To concentrate the attention of respondents on the semantic issue of what kinds of behaviors are regarded as violence *per se,* the following questions were asked:

> *Here is a list of nine things that have been in the news. Tell me if you think about these as violence. I don't mean if they lead to violence, but if you think about them* as **violence in themselves.**
>
> *Do you think of* **student protest** *as violence?*

The respondent was then asked about police beating students, police shooting looters, burglary, sit-ins, draft card burning, looting, not letting people have their civil rights, and police stopping to frisk people. In each case the question was phrased:

> *Do you think of _____ as violence?*

Table 2 gives the percentage of respondents classifying each of these acts as violence in itself or as not violence.

Table 2

Percentage of Respondents Defining Certain Acts as Violence

(all respondents; N=1,374)

	Yes	Both	No	Total
Do you think of looting as violence?	85%	3%	12%	100%
Do you think of burglary as violence?	65	5	30	100
Do you think of draft card burning as violence?	58	4	38	100
Do you think of police beating students as violence?	56	14	30	100
Do you think of not letting people have their civil rights as violence?	49	8	43	100
Do you think of student protest as violence?	38	15	47	100
Do you think of police shooting looters as violence?	35	8	57	100
Do you think of sit-ins as violence?	22	9	69	100
Do you think of police stopping to frisk people as violence?	16	10	74	100

The table is arranged according to the frequency with which the respondents labelled these acts as violence. Looting was considered violence by the largest percentage of American men, and by a substantial margin; burglary was next highest, closely followed by draft card burning and police beating students. These were the majority responses on the list.

Fifty-eight percent of American men thought that burning a draft card was violence, in and of itself; 38 percent thought student protest was violence, and 22 percent felt sit-ins were violence. Clearly, many Americans find acts of dissent violence *per se*. This finding is not inconsistent with the results of other research. While the question of whether or not Americans thought dissent as such was violent had not been asked before, a number of previous surveys have inquired about the right to free speech and protest. Respondents in such studies have usually agreed that free speech is desirable in principle, but they have often objected to the exercise of that right in specific cases. For example, in 1953 only 19 percent of a national sample felt that members of the Communist party should be allowed to speak on the radio. In 1965, 59 percent felt that "people have the right to conduct peaceful demonstrations against the war in Vietnam," a small proportion in light of the specific limitation to "peaceful demonstrations." And, in 1969, the year in which this study was conducted, only 38 percent of Americans felt that "students have a right to make their protest" (Erskine 1970).

The Carnegie Commission on Higher Education spoke as if in anticipation of these findings:

> Most campus protest has taken the form of dissent, not disruption. However, there has been some tendency in the public reaction to [condemn] protest activity as well as disruption. The American public seems to show limited tolerance for mass protest activities, even when these are within the bounds of law.
>
> This substantial disapproval suggests that many Americans may not distinguish sufficiently between organized dissent and disruption (Ann Arbor News, March 14, 1971, p. 1).

Definition and Disagreement

According to Webster (1969) violence is the exertion of physical force so as to injure or abuse. If one has something like this definition in mind, one must surely say that acts such as the "police beating students" or "shooting looters" are violent. After all, even if you do not consider a beaten student or a shot looter abused, both are likely to be injured. In view of the dictionary meaning of the word, it is curious that only 35 percent of American men defined "police shooting looters" as violence, and only 56 percent defined "police beating students" in this manner. Of the behaviors about which we inquired, these two involve the most force and are the most likely to lead to injury, and yet they are not the acts most likely to be called violence.

Why did more people define draft card burning as violence than defined beating students as violence? Is the reasoning that "violence" is bad, the actions of the police good, and that consequently their acts are not violence? What essential meaning leads American men to define an act as violence? And for that matter, do they all mean the same thing?

The last question can be answered more readily than the first. When one considers the question of probable agreement and disagreement among American men on the meaning of violence, certain groups of people who might be expected to differ in their opinions come readily to mind. For example, in the early 1960's sit-ins were widely used to desegregate various facilities. Our data show that a sizable number of American men regarded such tactics as violence. One might guess that black people and their sympathizers would be less inclined to this view than those people in the population who are opposed to desegregation. Similarly, one might expect that college students would be less likely to regard student protest as violence than groups who have taken public stands against such issues. In Table 3, which addresses itself to the issue of whether or not American men are agreed about what they call "violence," opinions are presented for five identifiable subgroups in the population. These include blacks, white people who at some point in our interview expressed fears of being discriminated against by blacks[2] (the reverse discrimination whites), college students, college graduates, and white union members. Some union groups have on occasion aligned themselves against both blacks and students. For example, the "antipeace" rally that occurred in Times Square in May, 1970, and the march in protest against the integration of construction unions in Pittsburgh can be thought of as demonstrations of anti-student, antiblack feeling.

Table 3 shows large differences of opinion among such groups of American men as to what acts are "violence." For example, only 4 percent of college students and 15 percent of blacks defined sit-ins as "violence," but 40 percent of whites who spontaneously mentioned fears of being discriminated against by blacks called sit-ins "violence." Similarly, 59 percent of blacks defined the "police shooting looters" as violence, but only 23 percent of white union members did so.

Table 3 shows that, of the groups examined, blacks were most likely to see police actions leading to personal injury as "violence." College students and college-educated men were more likely than the general population to define such acts as violence, but they were not as likely to do so as were blacks.

Activities such as draft card burning, sit-ins, and student protest, which do not intrinsically involve the use of destructive force, but which do entail dissent and have sometimes led to damage and injury, were called "violence" by many American men. College students and those with

---

2 Replies implying or expressing a fear of "reverse discrimination," a fear of the government giving preferential treatment to blacks at white expense, emerged in response to several questions. A respondent was selected for inclusion in this analysis group if his reply to one or more of the following items was coded as implying or expressing a fear of reverse discrimination: first, items asking what things in general, and what violent things concerned the respondent; second, a question asking his opinion on causes of riots; and third, a question asking *in what way* the respondent felt his life would change if black protesters achieved their goals.

Table 3

Percentage of Respondents in Selected Subgroups
Defining Certain Acts as Violence

	College Students	College Degree & Over	White Union Member	Reverse Discrim. Whites	Blacks
	(N=63)	(N=172)	(N=279)	(N=187)	(N=303)
Police beating students is violence	79%	66%	45%	47%	82%
Police shooting looters is violence	43	50	23	26	59
Police frisking is violence	16	16	10	13	34
Looting is violence	76	79	91	89	74
Burglary is violence	47	54	67	73	70
Student protest is violence	18	22	43	54	23
Sit-ins are violence	4	13	24	40	15
Draft card burning is violence	26	35	63	74	51
Denial of civil rights is violence	54	45	40	42	70

college degrees were least likely to label such action "violence." Blacks, although somewhat more likely to consider such acts "violence" than the college-educated, were less likely to do so than American men in general, and far less likely to do so than white union members or whites who feared reverse discrimination. The tendency to call property damage such as looting and burglary "violence" was very general, although college students and those with college degrees were somewhat less apt to do so than were others.

What is Meant by Violence

These data imply that American men differ greatly in what acts they call "violence," and that many people do not use the word as a description of forceful action which leads to injury or abuse. How then is the word used, and what does it mean when an action is labeled "violence?" This question is difficult to answer, because the explanation of meaning is always difficult. It is least so, perhaps, when one can point directly to the physical object or event that exemplifies and gives reality to the word in question. Thus we teach children, pronouncing the word apple, for example, and at the same time presenting the object for sight and touch and taste.

As we attempt to explain more abstract and difficult concepts, and to do so in circumstances less convenient for direct experience, we must explain the meaning of one word in terms of other words—it is "the same as," or "something like," or "opposite from" other known concepts. In this fashion we locate a new or undefined term in an existing semantic space. That space is always in some degree idiosyncratic, because it is formed from individual experience, which is ultimately unique. But there are commonalities enough to permit communication, although we may sometimes deceive ourselves and others that we are "talking the same language" when we are doing so only in linguistic and not in semantic terms.

To understand better the meaning of violence to American men we tried to determine which words in our list of nine acts (looting, burglary, draft card burning, etc.) respondents defined similarly and which they saw as far apart in meaning. From such an analysis, we learned what things respondents would give a common label; for example, if a respondent called sit-ins violence, what other things was he likely to consider violence and what things not violence?

Figures 1, 2 and 3 present the results of this analysis for American men as a whole, for blacks, and for those with some college education. The latter two groups were sufficiently different with respect to these semantic issues to require separate analysis. In each figure the closeness of one item to another indicates the degree of association; items shown close together are likely to be defined similarly.

All three figures show that if the respondent called one police action violence, he was likely to call all police actions violent, and conversely if he labelled one police action as not violence, he was likely to say no police actions are violence. The figures also show that, regardless of how the respondent defined police actions, he was likely to define actions involving dissent (protest, sit-ins, and draft card burning) and acts involving property damage (looting and burglary) as opposite to police actions. Thus, if he said that police actions were not violence, he was likely to say that protest and burglary were; if protest and burglary were not violence in his lexicon, then police beating students or shooting looters were violence to him.

American men in general did not differentiate among burglary, draft card burning, looting and sit-ins in applying the label of violence or nonviolence. These items tend to be defined alike by an individual, although his definition may differ from his neighbor's. Because these items are defined similarly and opposite to the way police acts are defined, it

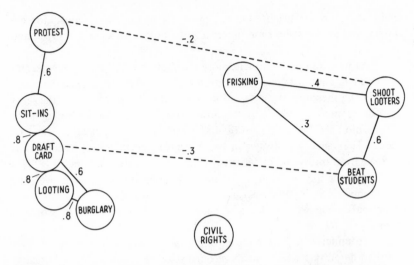

Figure 1. Relationships among definitional items (all respondents; N=1,374).

Note: Numbers on Figures 1-3 showing associations between definition items are gammas. Solid lines indicate positive relationships; broken lines indicate negative relationships.

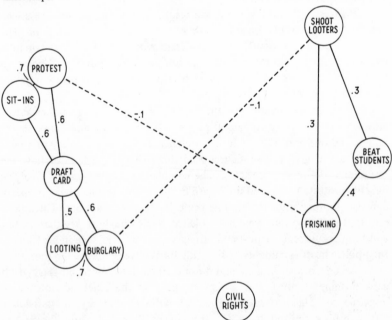

Figure 2. Relationships among definitional items (black respondents; N=303) (gammas).

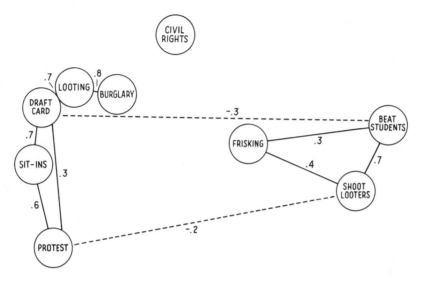

Figure 3. Relationships among definitional items (high education respondents; N=374) (gammas).

seems possible that people use the word "violence" as a term meaning illegitimacy. The logic underlying such usage might be something as follows: The state alone can exercise major force within the law. This is "legitimate violence," and legitimate violence is not really violence. The police are agents of the state; therefore their acts are legitimate and therefore not violent. Protest, dissent, burglary and the like are forceful actions against the state, illegitimate and hence violent.

This line of reasoning may be equally convenient for those who question the legitimacy of the state. For them it might run something as follows: The state (for whatever reasons) is not legitimate to me; the police are agents of an illegitimate state, therefore their acts are violent. Moreover, dissent is an attempt to change the state in such a way that it becomes more responsive to disfranchised elements in the population. Thus dissent is legitimate, and it is therefore not violent.

Such a line of reasoning would explain why a substantial number of black people called police procedures such as frisking, which in itself involves little force, "violence;" it would also explain why many American men called actions of dissent such as sit-ins, which in themselves involve almost no force, "violence."

Figures 2 and 3 show that not all respondents handle the language similarly. While American men as a whole tended to lump acts of protest with burglary and theft, blacks and those with some college education differentiated acts of protest from looting and burglary.

Thus, the three figures show some generalities and some differences in the ways American men used the word "violence." Certain classes of action tend to be defined similarly (either as violence or not violence). However, different subgroups in the population vary greatly in whether or not a specific act is likely to be called "violence" (Table 3). For example, while the majority of blacks regarded police actions as "violence," only a small percentage of white union members did so. Certain behaviors tend to be given a common label, but the label may be "violence" or "not violence," depending on the person doing the labelling.

These facts raise a new question: what is the semantic explanation of this pattern of agreement and disagreement? More specifically, does the disagreement arise because people have different ideas about the underlying meaning of the concept "violence," or because they have different ideas about the specific phenomena to which we asked them to make the response of "violence" or "not violence?"

Table 4 sheds some light on this question, and suggests that the underlying meaning of the word "violence" (that is, how "violence" is defined) is similar for most men, even if the specific acts to which the word is applied are not. The table is based upon a widely-used analytic technique—the semantic differential. Work by Osgood, Suci and Tannenbaum (1957) has demonstrated that the meaning of words can be defined by means of three dimensions: the evaluative dimension, the activity dimension, and the potency dimension. In order to assess how the respondent thought of the word violence, the interviewer handed him a card on which six scales were identified, and made the following statement:

> *Here are some words that have been used to describe violence. The first words are strong and weak. Do you think violence belongs at the* **strong end** *or at the* **weak end** *or* **in between**? *Please point to where you think it belongs.*

In addition to the strong-weak scale (representing the potency dimension), the respondent was asked to locate the word "violence" on a semantic differential scale ranging from good to bad, valuable to worthless (the evaluative dimension), and fierce to peaceful (representing the activity dimension). Because it seemed relevant to the current rhetoric of violence, two additional scales were used—necessary-unnecessary and avoidable-unavoidable.

Table 4 shows that on the whole American men tended to view "violence" as bad rather than good, worthless rather than valuable, fierce

Table 4

Percentage Responses to the Semantic Meaning of Violence
(all respondents; N=1,374)

	1	2	3	4	5	6	7	
Good	1%	1%	2%	11%	9%	17%	59%	Bad
Valuable	4	3	5	16	9	16	47	Worthless
Fierce	55	16	10	10	2	3	4	Peaceful
Strong	30	14	13	18	6	7	12	Weak
Necessary	2	2	4	16	10	16	50	Unnecessary
Avoidable	24	13	9	22	10	9	13	Unavoidable

rather than peaceful, and as unnecessary rather than necessary. They also are more inclined to call it strong than weak, and a little more likely to think it avoidable than unavoidable, but opinion on these matters is more scattered. Agreement on the semantic meaning of the word is not universal but it is substantial.

If there is not universal agreement about the meaning of the word violence, are differences of opinion about what the word means distributed in a special way in the population? For example, do young and old, black and white men mean the same thing when they talk about "violence?" Table 5 shows that there is virtually no association between whether a respondent believes that violence is strong or weak, fierce or peaceful, or bad or good, and such demographic characteristics as age, education, income, town size, or region. The only semantic difference in what "violence" means appears to be between blacks and whites.

Table 5

The Semantic Meaning in Relation to Some Demographic Characteristics
(all respondents; N=1,374)
(gammas)

	Semantic Meaning of Violence		
Demographic Characteristics	Strong-Weak	Fierce-Peaceful	Good-Bad
Education	-.08	.09	-.10
Age	.02	-.09	.24
Experience in South	-.03	.12	-.09
Town size	-.04	.04	-.10
Family income	-.04	.01	-.03
Race	.26	.15	-.33

Table 6 shows that blacks tended to describe "violence" as weaker, less bad, and less fierce than do other groups. If this semantic difference accounted for the difference in what acts blacks call "violence," one would suppose that blacks might be more apt to call the less fierce, weaker actions (such as sit-ins and protest) violence, and that they would be less apt to call forceful actions (such as police beating students or shooting) violence. But the data show that exactly the opposite is the case. It is blacks who were most apt to call police acts "violence," and it is blacks rather than the other groups who were more apt to say protest activities are not violence. Consequently, it is unlikely that the difference between blacks and other groups in respect to how the word "violence" is semantically described will explain the large differences in what acts are defined as violence. This point can be illustrated by comparing the large differences between blacks and white union members in respect to their definition of police actions as violent or nonviolent (Table 3) with the relatively small difference in how these two groups described "violence" semantically (Table 6). They show much larger differences in whether or not they define protest and police actions as "violence" (Table 3) than in how they describe the meaning of the word.

Table 6

Percentage Responses to the Semantic Meaning of Violence
for Whites, Blacks, College Students and White Union Members

		Whites (N=1,046)	Blacks (N=303)	College Students (N=63)	White Union Members (N=279)
Strong	1-2	46	30	54	43
In between	3-5	37	40	36	35
Weak	6-7	17	30	10	22
	Total	100%	100%	100%	100%
Fierce	1-2	73	65	80	74
In between	3-5	21	27	19	18
Peaceful	6-7	6	8	1	8
	Total	100%	100%	100%	100%
Good	1-2	2	6	4	1
In between	3-5	20	34	27	16
Bad	6-7	78	60	69	83
	Total	100%	100%	100%	100%

The Rhetoric of Violence

Another way of considering how semantic notions of the word "violence" relate to whether or not particular behaviors are called "violence" is to bring the two sets of responses into a single table. To facilitate this, the items in which the respondent defined behaviors as violence or not violence were combined into three indices. *Are Police Acts Violence?* is an index based on the three items involving police behaviors (shooting looters, beating students, and frisking people). *Is Protest Violence?* is an index of the three items referring to protest activities (sit-ins, student protest, and draft card burning). *Is Burglary-Looting Violence?* is an index that combines definitional responses about burglary and looting. In each case, the higher the score on the index, the more of those acts the respondent defined as "violence."

Table 7 shows the relationship between the semantic characterization of "violence" and whether protest, police actions and property damage are defined as violence or not violence. Whether the respondent regarded violence as strong or weak bears no relationship to how likely he was to define either protest, police actions or property damage as violence. Whether the respondent regarded violence as fierce or peaceful bears very little relation to how he defined protest and property damage, and still less relationship to his perception of police activities. It appears that the extent to which an individual sees violence as being forceful, that is, strong and fierce, is only minimally related to whether or not he describes a particular set of behaviors as violence.

Table 7

The Semantic Definition of Violence in Relation to What Acts Are Defined as Violence

(all respondents; N=1,374)

(gammas)

Semantic Definition of Violence	Acts Defined as Violence		
	Is Protest Violence?	Are Police Acts Violence?	Is Burglary-Looting Violence?
Strong-Weak	-.01	.06	.04
Fierce-Peaceful	-.14	.10	-.13
Good-Bad	.20	-.17	.23
Necessary-Unnecessary	.28	-.21	.20

Table 7 also shows how the respondent's notion of whether violence is good or bad and necessary or unnecessary relates to how he defined protest, police behavior and property damage. Here the relationships are a little larger. The more the respondent saw violence as bad and unnecessary, the more likely he was to define protest activities and property damage as violence, and the less likely to define police activities as violence. One might guess that the rationale underlying this association is: violence is unnecessary, police activities are necessary, therefore, police activities must not be violence. A similar rationale can be used to explain the relationship between the good-bad dimension and the respondent's definition of protest and police activities.

Returning now to the question of what American men mean when they define a particular act as violence, we can draw the following conclusions. On the whole, Americans view violence as fierce, strong, unnecessary, avoidable and bad. One could infer that when behavior is seen as not having such qualities, it is not defined as violence. For example, when the police shooting looters is defined as not being violence by the majority of Americans, one can imagine that Americans might think of such police actions as fierce and strong, but neither avoidable nor bad, and certainly necessary. In addition, the tendency of American men to define police behaviors such as shooting looters as not "violence," while defining much less forceful actions executed by those who are not police as "violence," might be interpreted as implying that the word violence is associated with illegitimacy in the mind of the public. If violence is committed by a legitimate power, it is not seen as violence.

Definitions and Attitudes Toward Dissenting Groups

If the respondent who labels a particular act as violence does indeed mean thereby that the act is unnecessary, illegitimate, and bad, one might guess that he would also be inclined to regard the individuals committing such acts as bad, worthless and outside the law. It is commonly assumed that evil is done by evil men, and there is evidence that the respondents tend to think this way. Of those who called student protest violence, 54 percent believed that student demonstrators were "looking for trouble," in contrast to only 30 percent of those who felt student protest was not violence (Table 8). Similarly, of those who believed that student protest was violence, 67 percent also believed that student demonstrators were untrustworthy, in contrast to 42 percent of those who did not believe student protest was violence (Table 9).

Table 10 shows a definite relationship between whether or not the respondent defined acts of protest as violence (high index score on Is Protest Violence?) and how he perceived white student demonstrators. If

Table 8

Percentage Responses to the Perception of Student
Demonstrators as Helpful, in Relation to Whether
Student Protest Is Defined as Violence

(all respondents; N=1,374)

	Is Student Protest Violence?	
	Yes	No
Are white student demonstrators helpful?		
Looking for trouble	54	30
Not one way or the other	27	30
Trying to be helpful	19	40
Total	100%	100%

Table 9

Percentage Responses to the Perception of Student
Demonstrators as Trustworthy, in Relation to
Whether Student Protest Is Defined as Violence

(all respondents; N=1,374)

	Is Student Protest Violence?	
	Yes	No
Can white student demonstrators be trusted?		
Can't be too careful with them	67	42
Don't know	11	13
Can be trusted	22	45
Total	100%	100%

they were seen as helpful, trustworthy, and having goals whose attainment
would change the respondent's life for the better, the respondent was less
likely to call protest actions "violence" than if student demonstrators were
seen as looking for trouble, untrustworthy, and having goals whose attainment would change the respondent's life for the worse.

Table 10 also shows a relationship between how white student
demonstrators and black protesters were perceived, and whether or not
police actions were called violence. The more positively these two groups

Table 10

Definitions of Protest and Police Actions in Relation to Attitudes
Toward White Student Demonstrators, Black Protesters, and Police

(all respondents; N=1,374)

(gammas)

Identification Items	Is Protest Violence? Index	Are Police Acts Violence? Index
White Student Demonstrators[a]		
Are helpful vs. looking for trouble	-.38	.30
Do not dislike people like the respondent vs. dislike people like the respondent	-.17	.11
Are trustworthy vs. untrustworthy	-.38	.23
Will make life better vs. worse	-.30	.37
Black Protesters		
Are helpful vs. looking for trouble	-.40	.31
Do not dislike people like the respondent vs. dislike people like the respondent	-.09	.09
Are trustworthy vs. untrustworthy	-.42	.34
Will make life better vs. worse	-.28	.36
Police		
Are helpful vs. looking for trouble	.14	-.46
Do not dislike people like the respondent vs. dislike people like the respondent	.16	-.35
Are trustworthy vs. untrustworthy	.06	-.41
Will make life better vs. worse	.12	-.23

[a] The more positively the respondent views the group of people asked about, the higher the score on the item.

were viewed, the more likely the respondent was to label many police acts as violence. At the same time, police actions were more likely to be called violence if the respondent believed the police to be untrustworthy, looking for trouble, apt to dislike people like himself and having goals whose attainment would change his life for the worse.

In short, American men tend to define acts of dissent as "violence" when they perceived the dissenters as undesirable people. It is not possible to say that protest is defined as violence because protesters are seen as evil, or that protesters are seen as evil because of the way protest is defined. Probably each perception reinforces the other. Our semantic interpretation and prediction is that defining a set of behaviors as violence is not only associated with a whole set of attitudes about the actors, but sharpens and simplifies those attitudes, and gives sanctions to punishment.

In any case, the phenomenon of labeling and definition deserves to be taken seriously. Something is known about the effects of labeling people, and more is being learned. People tend to become what you call them, presumably in response to differential treatment as well as language. As Eliza says so nicely to Professor Higgins, the difference between a lady and a washerwoman is not how she talks or what she does but how you treat her. In a series of experiments, Rosenthal and Jacobson (1968) showed that it is possible to improve the IQ of a group of students simply by telling the teacher that these students (randomly selected) are promising. The child rises to meet the expectation of the world around him, presumably because the treatment he receives is in some way different from the treatment received by his fellows.

In keeping with the same principle, students of juvenile delinquency have come to the conclusion that an important part of the process of "criminalization" is labeling the prospective criminal delinquent. If this labeling occurs, the individual is more likely to become a criminal than another person who has committed the same delinquent act but is not labeled delinquent (Spitzer 1969). Again, presumably the mechanism by which the "labeled" delinquent is propelled to crime includes differences in the treatment given to him and his unlabeled counterpart. One might expect that labeling behaviors could have effects no less than labeling people, and that defining a set of behaviors as violence could have social consequences in and of itself.

Rhetoric and Attitudes Toward Violence

To some extent the consequences of labeling certain actions violence can be explored with the present data. We can ask, for example, whether people who define protest as violence not only tend to view dissenters rather negatively but also recommend more forceful ways of handling protest. Figure 4 shows that the more the respondent is inclined to call acts of protest violence, the higher the levels of police force he recommends to control campus disturbances.

The same principle applies when ghetto disturbances are considered (Figure 5). The more inclined the respondent was to call protest violence, the more stringent were the measures that he recommended for the control of such disturbances. Labeling an act violence is related to the actions one recommends for handling such behavior.

The pattern of definition, attitude, and advocated behavior can be investigated with respect to police actions as well as actions of protest and dissent. To do so is important not only because it constitutes a kind of replication of the protest analysis just described, but also because the police and the protesters are contending groups, and one might expect

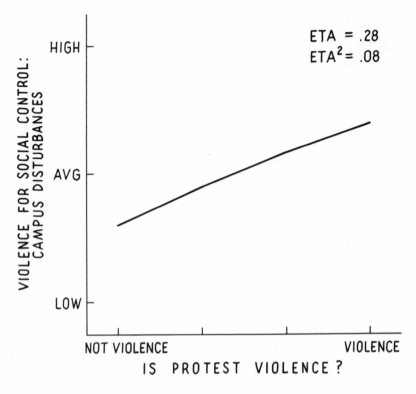

Figure 4. Mean level of force the police should use to control campus disturbances[a] in relation to whether or not the protest is labeled violence (all respondents, N=1,374).

[a]This variable, *Violence for Social Control: Campus Disturbances,* is a scale derived from the set of questions about how the police should handle campus disturbances, described in Chapter 2. This variable is also called Violence for Social Control: Students (cf. Chapter 6). In general, the higher the score, the more forceful the patterns of police behavior recommended. Details of the scaling are presented in Appendix D.

additivity or interaction between the semantics of protest and police action. Figures 6 and 7 show that indeed there are relationships between calling police actions violence and advocating police force to control disturbances in the ghetto or on the campus. However, the direction of the semantic effect (if we may be permitted the causal inference) is directly opposite to the effect of calling a protest action violence. The more the

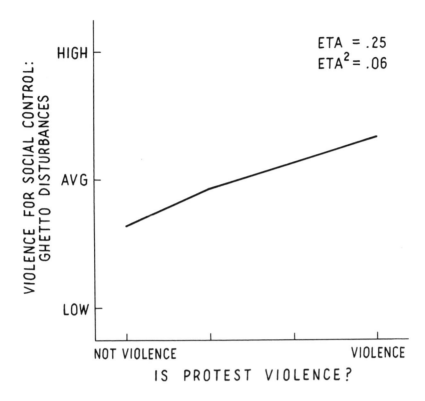

Figure 5. Mean level of force the police should use to control ghetto disturbances[a] in relation to whether or not protest is labeled violence (all respondents; N=1,374).

[a]This variable, *Violence for Social Control: Ghetto Disturbances,* is a scale derived from the set of questions about how the police should handle ghetto disturbances described in Chapter 2. This variable is also called Violence for Social Control: Blacks (cf. Chapter 6). In general, the higher the score, the more forceful the patterns of police behavior recommended. Details of the scaling are presented in Appendix D.

respondent tended to say that police actions are not violence, the higher the levels of Violence for Social Control he recommended in both the ghetto and student situations. It is as if the act of saying that such police actions as "shooting looters" are not violence allows the individual to justify actions which could be less easily rationalized if they were labeled violence. Violence, after all, is generally regarded as bad (Table 4), and if

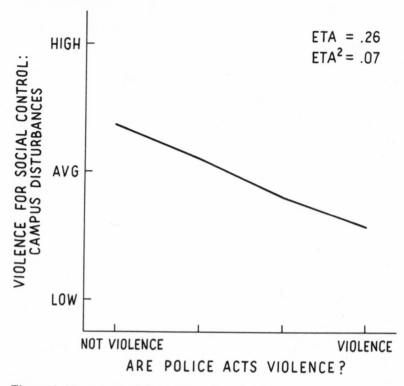

Figure 6. Mean level of force the police should use to control campus disturbances in relation to whether or not police acts are labeled violence (all respondents; N=1,374).

something is bad, one ought not to do it. Consequently, if one defines police actions as violent, one is less likely to advocate such measures in the control of disturbances. Defining injurious or even deadly actions in other terms makes them easier to recommend and justify, a phenomenon of language and social action that has been especially observable in the politics of war and persecution.

Table 11 shows the previously described effects in combination. Using a Multiple Classification Analysis,[3] we find that the effects of

---

[3] The Multiple Classification Analysis (MCA) is an analytic technique designed (Andrews, Morgan and Sonquist 1967) to examine interrelationships between several predictor variables and a dependent variable within the framework of an additive model. The statistics show how each independent variable relates to the dependent variable (by means of the eta), and how much of the variation can be explained by each independent variable (by means of the eta squared). The analysis also shows

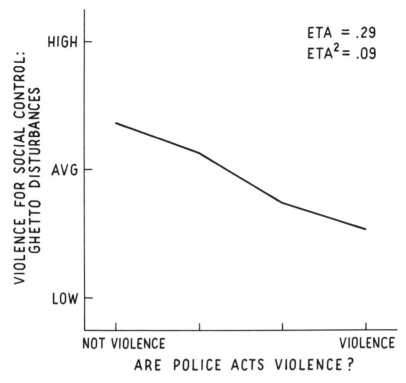

Figure 7. Mean level of force the police should use to control ghetto disturbances in relation to whether or not police acts are labeled violence (all respondents; N=1,374).

defining protest as violence and police actions as not violence are additive; that is, individuals who felt that protest is violence and also that police actions are not violence recommended higher levels of Violence for Social Control than persons who only defined protest acts as violence or who only defined police actions as not violence. Most of the variation is

how strongly the independent variables taken altogether relate to the dependent variable (by means of the Multiple R (the square of the multiple R expresses the relationship as the percentage of variance explained). In addition, the technique provides an estimate of what the multiple R might be expected to be in the population as a whole if the analysis were repeated (the population estimate of the multiple R).

The analysis also supplies an estimate of what the *independent* contribution of the predictor variables is in respect to the multiple R squared, the beta squared. This statistic is not generally included in our tables, but is sometimes referred to in the text.

Table 11

Definitional Indices in Relation to Violence for Social Control
(all respondents; N=1,374)

Predictor Item	eta	eta^2
Is Burglary-Looting Violence? Index	.15	.02
Are Police Acts Violence? Index	.32	.10
Is Protest Violence? Index	.29	.08

Multiple R $= .40$	(population estimate $= .40$)
Variation Explained (R^2) $= 16\%$	(population estimate $= 16\%$)

explained by the Protest and Police Acts Indices. The Burglary-Looting Index makes no independent contribution to the overall correlation. Together these indices explain 16 percent of the variation in attitudes toward Violence for Social Control.

Tables 12 and 13 show that the association between definitions of violence and the advocacy of Violence for Social Control holds for both whites and blacks when these data are analyzed separately. The results cannot be attributed to differences in opinion between whites and blacks about what constitutes violence nor what levels of Violence for Social Control are appropriate. They speak to very general processes in individuals and societies.

It has been said that the rhetoric sometimes used in reference to confrontations is inflammatory and leads to the escalation of violence (President's Commission on Campus Unrest 1970, p. 10). Our data demonstrate that there is indeed a relationship between rhetoric and the level of

Table 12

Definitional Indices in Relation to Violence for Social Control
(white respondents; N=1,046)

Predictor Item	eta	eta^2
Is Burglary-Looting Violence? Index	.16	.02
Are Police Acts Violence? Index	.31	.09
Is Protest Violence? Index	.28	.08

Multiple R $= .39$	(population estimate $= .38$)
Variation Explained (R^2) $= 15\%$	(population estimate $= 15\%$)

Table 13

Definitional Indices in Relation to Violence for Social Control

(black respondents; N=303)

Predictor Item	eta	eta^2
Is Burglary-Looting Violence? Index	.10	.01
Are Police Acts Violence? Index	.25	.06
Is Protest Violence? Index	.32	.10
Multiple R $\quad = .39$	(population estimate = .36)	
Variation Explained (R^2) $= 15\%$	(population estimate = 13%)	

Violence for Social Control that people find justifiable. That, of course, is not the end; one might expect that the levels of violence used for social control would be one of the determinants of the level of violence for social change, and that the escalation might continue to some new crisis. Indeed, the Commission on Campus Unrest (1970, p. 2) has underscored one aspect of this point, stating that: "The use of force by police is sometimes necessary and even legal, but every unnecessary resort to violence is wrong, criminal, and feeds the hostility of the disaffected."

Implications and Speculations. Three facts must now be considered in combination. We have just seen that defining particular acts as violence or nonviolence has definite implications about the level of force deemed appropriate to deal with them. We saw earlier (Table 3) that American men are by no means of one opinion on what acts constitute violence. And we have seen from the moment of our first encounter with the indices of Violence for Social Change and Violence for Social Control (Chapter 2) that American men hold widely differing opinions about such matters.

Using Table 3 as a point of departure, one might draw the following sketch. Let us imagine a draft-card-burning demonstration near a college campus, and the response to it by a group of white union members. Table 3 tells us that 26 percent of college students regard burning a draft card as violence. Thus, not only the participants, but most of the student population of which they are a part, consider the action nonviolent. Within this population one would not expect the sanctions that are employed against violent acts to be operative in the case of draft card burning.

However, 63 percent of white union members regard burning a draft card as violence. Moreover, only 45 percent of union members feel that the police beating students is violence. One can see where a union group might decide that police beating a few students in the course of breaking up a demonstration at which draft cards were being burned was an appropriate, morally justifiable means of social control. Some members might even urge such action by the local police.

On the other hand, 79 percent of college students in the United States regard the beating of students by police as violence. Thus the average college student has a point of view which is substantially opposed to that of many white union members: he would regard the act of burning a draft card as nonviolent and the act of the police clubbing the student in response to this act as violence. If the scenario were played out, both groups would regard themselves as morally outraged and put upon, simultaneously and for opposite reasons.

Nor is the plot line limited to the burning of draft cards. It could be initiated with a number of the definitions in Table 3, and it is not difficult to think of real events in contemporary history that follow this pattern all too closely.

One might speculate further that a violent police response to a demonstration involving draft card burning might radicalize even the nonparticipant students, bringing them closer to acts involving substantial property damage and personal injury. According to our data, approximately one-fifth of American males believe that some property damage or personal injury is necessary for desirable social changes to be brought about fast enough. It seems likely that, when an act of dissent regarded as nonviolent by the dissenters is responded to by actions which the dissenters regard as inappropriate and violent, they will lose some of their motivation to refrain from more forceful acts of protest. If the response to protest actions intended as nonviolent is of the same order as the response to intentionally destructive actions, it seems reasonable to expect that while some people may be driven off, others may be driven toward violent protest—particularly if such actions appear to have been more effective on occasion.

If peaceful protests and destructive acts are all put under the umbrella of "violence," those protesters who already consider property damage and personal injury as necessary in social reform will move toward the radical end of their repertoire.

If the society at large draws no line between sit-ins and arson, protesters are unlikely to do so.

Summary

American men on the whole are generally agreed that acts against property such as looting and burglary are violence. However, many Americans also regard acts of protest such as sit-ins and draft card burning as "violence" in and of themselves, although others do not regard such acts as violent. There are approximately as many men who regard police actions such as "beating students" and "shooting looters" violent, as look on dissent as "violence." However, how particular acts of violence are defined varies widely in different subgroups in the population such as college students, blacks and white union members.

The difference between groups in respect to whether or not particular acts are defined as violence cannot be explained by differences in their explanation of the semantic meaning of the word. Rather, it appears that labeling an act "violence" is a statement that the act in question is not legitimate, good or necessary.

Whether or not a particular act is called violence can be explained in part by attitudes toward the group performing such acts. Those who tend to sympathize with student demonstrators and black protesters are less likely to call acts of protest violence than are those who do not. In addition, those sympathetic to such dissident groups are more likely to label police actions such as "shooting looters" and "beating students" violence than are those who are unsympathetic. On the other hand, it is those unsympathetic to the police who are most likely to label the police actions studied "violence."

Whether or not a specific behavior is defined as violence is not a trivial matter. The extent to which protest is seen as violence appears to be a significant factor in determining the level of violence which will be justified in the service of social control. And the extent to which police behaviors involving personal injury are seen as not violent in nature appears to escalate the level of violence for social control considered reasonable.

The choice of words we use does make a difference in attitudes about how disturbances should be handled. Things which are seen as violence are provocative of a retaliatory response. Since, as a nation, we are not agreed on what actions are violent, the opportunity for escalation of our domestic war through injudicious use of language seems endless.

Chapter 5

VALUES AND VIOLENCE

Introduction. The concept of values is important but problematical in philosophy and the social sciences, and there is little agreement on definitions, determinants, or outcomes. For present purposes, however, we can begin with definitions very close to colloquial usage. When we say that a person "has values," we mean that he has enduring beliefs that certain ways of behaving or certain states of existence are preferable to others, for himself and for other people as well. When we accuse a person of "having no values," we mean that he lacks such enduring beliefs about what actions and states ought to be preferred, and that his behavior is therefore determined wholly by other factors—for example, his immediately-felt needs. (What is more likely, of course, is that the person so accused has values, but values different from those of his accusers.)

Values are best defined, we believe, as motives; indeed, values and needs are the two major categories of motives. Both values and needs motivate goal-directed behavior by a person, and their doing so can be understood as a process of making desirable or preferable certain objects, actions, or states of affairs.

With respect to such objects, actions, or states, the various needs and values of an individual may be congruent or in opposition to each other. For example, an individual who has a strong need to achieve may also hold the value that diligent and persistent work is a virtue; both the need and the value motivate him to a high level of job performance. On the other hand, in certain circumstances his need to achieve may urge him to act in ruthless ways toward others, while some other of his values (kindness, for example) opposes such actions. Such opposition of needs and values is common. It seems that the major functions of values, in any group or society, are to control need-induced behavior and to evoke behavior that is not need-induced.

For the individual, values are developed through a process of socialization. The child is born with certain needs or innate predispositions to behavior; he is not born with values. These he learns through social reinforcement by significant persons in his life. His parents praise and reward certain of his attitudes and behaviors, and disapprove or punish others. At first the child may conform to his parents' values only because of anticipated rewards or punishments, but as time passes values are internalized, and their control over his behavior becomes independent of external sanctions. The child's behavior becomes a complex function of his needs and values, and we say that he has acquired a "conscience."

From the individual's introspective view, the distinction between needs and values is easily expressed. The motivating forces of values are experienced as feelings of "oughtness." "Ought" and "ought not" are the language of values; "want" and "don't want" are the language of needs. When the two are in opposition, the conflict can be painful, and the action that satisfies needs at the expense of strongly held values typically induces persistent feelings of guilt. Mark Twain allowed Huckleberry Finn an eloquent and resentful speech on the subject. Huck had decided to flout the racial values of his society by befriending a runaway slave, and found himself feeling "kind of ornery, and humble, and to blame, somehow." And he resented the values that would not be silenced. "A person's conscience ain't got no sense, and just goes for him anyway. If I had a yaller dog that didn't know no more than a person's conscience does, I would poison him. It takes up more room than all the rest of a person's insides, and yet ain't no good, nohow" (Clemens 1958, p. 194).

In studying the tendencies of American men to justify violence, we wanted to understand the effects of values, both those that condone and those that condemn violent acts. More specifically, we inquired about five values: retributive justice, kindness, self-defense, how people are valued relative to property, and how humanistic values are regarded in comparison to more materialistic ones. Treating these concepts as values implies a number of things, some testable in the present research, some merely assumed. For example, we assumed that a person's beliefs about preferred human actions or states of being in these areas of value are relatively stable and enduring, and that these values serve as standards against which the individual judges his own behavior and that of others. We expected that a person's values would influence directly the amount of violence he considered justifiable for social change or social control, and this expectation was confirmed to some extent. We expected that personal values would themselves be predictable to some extent from the background characteristics of the individual and his family, and this expectation also is given some confirmation. Finally, we assumed a tendency toward consistency or balance within individuals, a tendency for their more specific attitudes to be consistent with their values. This assumption is explored in the present analysis, particularly in terms of the relationships between values and attitudes toward violence, the individual's identification with various social groups, and his definition of certain activities as violent or nonviolent. These issues are the subject matter of the present chapter.

That portion of the analysis which explored the relationship between values and attitudes toward Violence for Social Control is conducted on a special subset of the data. In answering the questions that measure this type of violence, it was possible for respondents to give answers which were logically inconsistent, and some people did so. Inconsistent answers are more difficult to interpret than consistent ones, and they have been excluded from this analysis.[1] However, the associations based on the consistent data alone are not necessarily descriptive of the relationships for all American men. Except for the analysis of values in relation to Violence for Social Control, which is conducted on data from consistent respondents only, the chapter is based upon the full sample.

Retributive Justice

"People who commit murder deserve capital punishment." "Violence deserves violence." "An eye for an eye and a tooth for a tooth is a good rule for living." "When someone does wrong, he should be paid back for it." "It is often necessary to use violence to prevent violence."

These statements reflect the value orientation that we have called retributive justice, an ancient and important concept in the justification and rationalization of violence. Every student of the Old Testament learns it—eye for eye and tooth for tooth. Every diplomat invokes it to explain and justify the wars in which his country engages. Many parents teach it, and every parent hears at some time from the lips of his child: He started it! He hit me first!

It is interesting to speculate on the effects of these precepts in human affairs, and to test their logical limits. If violence occurred *only* as retribution for violence, of course, there would be no violence at all; it would never be provoked. But if violence *always* brought retribution, what then? Two dramatically different possibilities present themselves, depending on where one locates the starting point in a violent sequence and how one appraises the relative force of the initial and retaliative acts. If the protagonists agree on these matters, the violent episode may be brief and self-limiting. A strikes B; B returns the blow. Hands are shaken and all is well.

But such an episode has the quality of cinema rather than reality. Life is not so neatly episodic, and in an endless sequence of events starting points become arbitrary. Which blow was unprovoked and which retribu-

---

[1] For a detailed description of the consistency measure, see Appendix D.

tive becomes correspondingly confused, as bewildered parents, labor arbitrators, and historians discover. The objective observer sees only a series of violent acts by A and B, a process without an identifiable beginning or imminent end. But A insists that the initial act of violence was done by B, and that the episodes of violent provocation and justifiable retaliation form a sequence properly described as B-A, A-B; B-A, A-B; etc. His antagonist agrees to the description of the process but not to its origin; that he assigns to a violent act by A, which initiated a sequence A-B, B-A; A-B, B-A; etc. The difference in their perceptions can be illustrated as follows:

AS PERCEIVED BY PERSON A

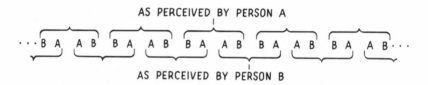

AS PERCEIVED BY PERSON B

The perception of a precipitating event is required only to launch such a sequence; once begun, it is fueled by the value of retributive justice. Both points are included in the following paradigm:

> Person X has committed violence (against me or some blameless other).
>
> Violence (unprovoked) deserves a violent response.
>
> Therefore, I (or some other person as agent) am justified in committing violence against person X.

Moreover, the likelihood that the first condition of the paradigm will be met is increased by the wide discrepancies among American men in respect to what acts are defined as violent. For example, white union members were more than twice as likely to think student protest or draft card burning violent than were college students (Chapter 4). Such discrepancies make it possible for the cycles of perceived violent provocation and justified violent response to be set in motion unintentionally. An initiating act may be nonviolent in the actor's terms, but violent in the eyes of some others.

We turn now to the means by which the value-orientation of retributive justice was measured, the background characteristics associated with this value, and its implications for the justification of violence as they appear in our data.

Measurement. The Retributive Justice Index is based on responses to the five value-oriented statements cited earlier and repeated in Table 1. The more the respondent agreed with these statements, the higher was his score on the Index. (For details of index construction see Appendix C.)

The greatest agreement was to the most specific of the five retributive statements, the proposition that murderers deserve capital punishment. The extent of the agreement is surprising in view of the specificity; it is often easier to get agreement to generalities and abstractions. Moreover, the large proportion of strong agreement (43 percent) and the substantial majority of agreement compared to disagreement (71 percent versus 29 percent) is in sharp contrast to present practice in the United States. The death penalty has been virtually suspended, even where it is law; a bill before the Senate would make suspension a legal requirement for two years, and serious questions of constitutionality have been raised against capital punishment (Nation 1971). Some surveys (Erskine 1970) have shown less support for capital punishment, partly because of the inclusion of women, who are more opposed to it than men. It is also possible that our question wording—"deserve capital punishment"—evoked positive responses from some men who would consider appropriate a lesser punishment than the one "deserved."

Table 1

Percentage Responses to Items Measuring Retributive Justice

(all respondents; N=1,374)

	Strongly Agree	Agree Somewhat	Disagree Somewhat	Strongly Disagree	Total
People who commit murder deserve capital punishment.	43%	28%	14%	15%	100%
When someone does wrong, he should be paid back for it.	23	44	22	11	100
It is often necessary to use violence to prevent it.	19	45	20	16	100
Violence deserves violence.	17	27	26	30	100
"An eye for an eye and a tooth for a tooth" is a good rule for living.	9	15	29	47	100

The next highest proportion of agreement was obtained for the broadest of the retributive statements, the assertion that a person who does wrong should be somehow "paid back for it." Neither the wrongdoing nor the punishment is specified, but the idea of retribution is clear and 67 percent of American men endorsed it. They were less willing to endorse the statements that insisted on an exact parallel between crime and punishment—violence for violence, eye for eye, tooth for tooth. The latter statement is the only one to which a large majority of men registered disagreement. It is a quotation from the Old Testament, but it may be one that many American men learned was wrong in Sunday school. If this is the case, the lesson does not appear to have generalized to other expressions of retribution.

Among the items in the Retributive Justice Index is the statement that it is often necessary to use violence to prevent violence. This is not retribution in the dictionary definition of the term, but, in a world in which the vocabulary of preventive strikes and deterrent actions has become common-place, the justification of "retribution" which precedes wrongdoing perhaps should not surprise us. In any case, 19 percent of all men agreed strongly to this view, and another 45 percent were somewhat in agreement.

On balance, the principle of retributive justice commands widespread agreement among American men. Moreover, they hold it as a value; the predicates in the five items make that fact quite unambiguous. "Deserves," "is a good rule," "should be paid back"—these phrases carry the quality of "oughtness" that is central to the value concept.

Background Characteristics. In general, one would expect an individual's background to affect his values. We think of values as formed out of early experiences, perhaps especially in the family, although in some degree the formation and reformation of values can be assumed to continue throughout life. Such assumptions are commonplace in the social sciences; in the present instance they are given only modest support.

Six major background factors (education, race, religion, age, town size and region) in combination generated a correlation of .30 with Retributive Justice and accounted for 9 percent of the variance in that index. Some of the six—age, for example—had virtually no explanatory power in relation to Retributive Justice. However, there are some relationships that merit attention.

Education. Education makes a difference in a person's belief in Retributive Justice; in general, this value was held most strongly among the least educated American men, and was rarely held in strength by the most educated. The relationship, however, is not linear, as Figure 1 illustrates. The curve is high and flat among men with less than high school education;

it begins to decline with graduation from high school, and among men with graduate-school education the proportion who strongly disavowed the value of Retributive Justice was four times greater (24 percent) than the proportion among men with only elementary school education. What combination of self-selection and educational experience is reflected in this pattern is uncertain, of course.

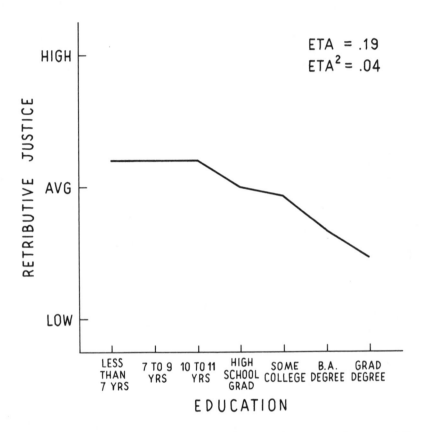

Figure 1. Mean Retributive Justice Index in relation to education (all respondents; N=1,374).

Race. Blacks expressed less belief in Retributive Justice than whites. Half again as many blacks as whites fell in the lowest categories (Table 2). Moreover, the direction of the difference was opposite to some of the current interpretations of black protest, which emphasize its retaliative implications. The small contribution of race to explaining the value-orientation of Retributive Justice was quite independent of other background factors to which race is related—education, region, etc.

Table 2

Percentage Responses to the Retributive Justice Index
in Relation to Race

Retributive Justice		Whites	Blacks
		(N=1,046)	(N=303)
Low	1-2	24	37
	3-4	48	43
High	5-6	28	20
	Total	100%	100%

Other Background Factors. Other background factors show lesser or less regular relationships to the value of Retributive Justice. Differences in religion, for example, contributed slightly to the explanation of differences in the Index of Retributive Justice. Jews and nonreligious respondents agreed less often with the principle of Retributive Justice than did people of other denominations; Catholics scored slightly lower than Protestants. Whether the respondent lived in a rural or urban location also showed a small irregular relationship to the value of Retributive Justice, that value being very slightly more characteristic of rural areas and towns than the cities. Age made no difference worth remarking, nor did region. Table 3 summarizes these relationships, singly and in combination:

Table 3

Region, Religion, Age, Race, Town Size and Education
in Relation to the Retributive Justice Index
(all respondents; N=1,374)

Predictor Item	eta	eta^2
Region	.07	.01
Religion	.13	.02
Age	.04	.00
Town size	.12	.01
Race	.10	.01
Education	.19	.04
Multiple R = .30	(population estimate = .26)	
Variation Explained (R^2) = 9%	(population estimate = 7%)	

Retributive Justice and the Justification of Violence. The core idea of retributive justice is that the punishment shall fit the crime. Literal-minded believers in this principle are therefore most likely to be satisfied when the punishment *resembles* the crime—when, to take the most extreme example, the killer is killed. The law is sometimes quite explicit in this regard; retributive damages require that the guilty person pay back to the victim an amount equal to that which was taken.

The retributive turn of mind is conducive to overzealousness, and we expected that the justification of violence for social control would increase steadily with an increased belief in the value of retributive justice. That is the case; as the scores on the Retributive Justice Index moved from low to high, the level of Violence for Social Control increased as shown in Figure 2.

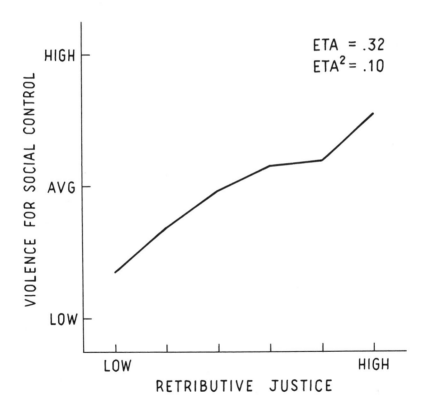

Figure 2. Mean Violence for Social Control in relation to the Retributive Justice Index (most consistent respondents; N=747).

The substantial relationship of Retributive Justice to Violence for Social Control was not repeated for Violence for Social Change. Among American men in general, a belief in retributive justice had no apparent implications for accepting or rejecting the idea of using violence to produce social change. This may mean that most men do not see violence for social change as retributive. Justified or not, it does not involve for them the concept of paying back.

However, the pattern was different for blacks. Like other consistent respondents, blacks who believe in Retributive Justice advocated higher levels of Violence for Social Control, although the tendency was less marked among blacks than among whites. Unlike most American men, blacks who believe in retributive justice tended to justify higher levels of Violence for Social Change than other blacks (Figure 3). A speculative interpretation would be that men who hold strongly to the value of retributive justice attempt to understand complex social situations by identifying aggressors and victims, or offenders and damaged. Having determined who has caused the damage, the course of retribution is clear.

If one accepts this interpretation, the pattern of racial differences described above can also be interpreted. It tells us that most men see protesters and rioters in the aggressive role and the police as agents of retribution. Many black men share this view, although both among believers and disbelievers in retributive justice, the absolute level of Violence for Social Control advocated by blacks was lower than that advocated by consistent respondents generally. However, black men are more likely than whites to see the white-dominated society as having committed the initial aggression. Acts of violence committed for the purpose of producing social change can then be justified in the name of retribution, and the stronger the belief in retribution, the higher the level of violence so justified.

We can now consider the evidence for the syllogism proposed earlier in this chapter, which involves a three-step sequence of perceived violence, asserted belief in retributive justice, and consequent justification of violent response. We would expect, for example, that men who defined student protest as violence and who believed strongly in retributive justice would be likely to advocate high levels of police force in the control of campus disturbances. Similarly, we would expect that men who were least retributive and who did not regard student protest as violence would be least likely to recommend high levels of violence in the control of campus disturbances.

Table 4 indicates that such is the case. Either factor by itself—the definition of student protest as violence or the belief in retributive justice—substantially increased the advocated level of violence for social control of student protest. The two factors in combination have a greater effect than either alone, although they are not wholly independent.

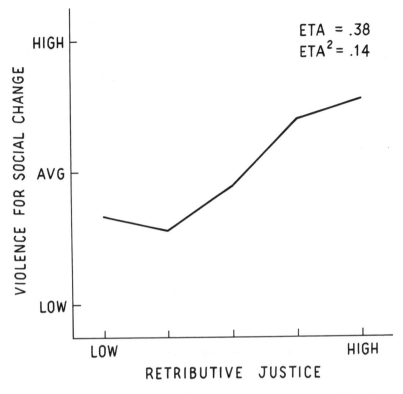

ETA = .38
ETA^2 = .14

Figure 3. Mean Violence for Social Change in relation to the Retributive Justice Index (black respondents; N=303).

Table 4

Mean Violence for Social Control of Student Protest in Relation to the Retributive Justice Index and the Definition of Student Protest as Violence

	High Retributive Justice		Low Retributive Justice	
	Mean	N	Mean	N
Student protest is violence	4.7	(290)	4.2	(207)
Student protest *not* violence	3.8	(286)	2.7	(363)

Self-Defense

"A man has a right to kill another man in a case of self-defense." "A man has the right to kill a person to defend his own family." "A man has the right to kill a person to defend his house."

These items are the basis of our inquiry into beliefs about self-defense, a value that could be considered a special case of retributive justice. The statements above have certain distinctive elements, however. All of them imply strongly an unprovoked attack on person or property; all ask for a response in terms of direct action by the person attacked; all stipulate the most extreme retaliation—killing rather than restraining or incapacitating. On the other hand, all make the action permissive rather than obligatory: "A man has the right to . . . " rather than "A man ought to . . . ."

Defense of self and family is a traditional masculine value in many cultures, including the American, where it is also the redundant and seemingly eternal theme of the western films that play some substantial role in the socialization of boys. We expected a strong endorsement of the value of self-defense, and our expectation was fulfilled. The overwhelming majority of American men agreed strongly to the right to kill in defense of self or family, and the majority agreed (though less strongly) that the right exists as well for the defense of one's house. The fact that over half agreed a man has a right to kill a person to defend his house raises questions as to the relative importance of human life and property in the minds of American men.

Table 5

Percentage Responses to Items Measuring Belief in Self-Defense

(all respondents; N=1,374)

	Strongly Agree	Agree Somewhat	Disagree Somewhat	Strongly Disagree	Total
A man has a right to kill another man in a case of self defense.	60%	29%	6%	5%	100%
A man has a right to kill a person to defend his family.	69	24	4	3	100
A man has a right to kill a person to defend his house.	23	35	25	17	100

Percentage distributions for all three items are shown in Table 5. The Self-Defense Index was constructed from them. The more the individual agreed with the right to self-defense, the higher was his score on the Index. (For details of index construction see Appendix C.)

Background Characteristics. Background factors were only slightly predictive of beliefs in Self-Defense; this value-orientation was common to black men and white, old and young. Six background characteristics (region, religion, age, town size, race and education) explained only 7 percent of the variation in attitudes toward Self-Defense. Of the elements that contributed to that bit of explanation, region was most important; the value of self-defense was held most strongly in the South. Thirty-three percent of the men interviewed in the South expressed strong agreement with all the statements of Self-Defense, thus getting the highest possible score on the index. In the rest of the country, the percentage was only about half as large.

Some small differences among religious groups can be seen with respect to the value of self-defense. It was endorsed less strongly by Protestant fundamentalists, Jews, Roman Catholics, and nonreligious groups than by the major Protestant denominations.

Table 6 summarizes the relationships between background factors and the Self-Defense Index.

Self-Defense and the Justification of Violence for Social Control. One might expect that men who hold strongly to the value of self-defense would justify relatively high levels of Violence for Social Control. The social control measures describe situations in which the police are acting against

Table 6

Region, Religion, Age, Race, Town Size and Education
in Relation to the Self-Defense Index

(all respondents; N=1,374)

Predictor Item	eta	eta^2
Region	.19	.04
Religion	.15	.02
Age	.08	.01
Town size	.11	.01
Race	.03	.00
Education	.09	.01
Multiple R = .27	(population estimate = .22)	
Variation Explained (R^2) = 7%	(population estimate = 5%)	

possible threats to property and to persons. Such situations have at least something in common with the more direct threats incorporated in the self-defense items, and many people think of the police as their agents. For these reasons it seems plausible that the justification of force by the police might be argued by many of the same people who believe in the use of extreme force in more personal circumstances. This is indeed the case; as the Self-Defense value-orientation moves from low to high, the average level of violence seen as justifiable rises. Self-Defense accounted for 11 percent of the variation in attitudes toward Violence for Social Control. Figure 4 illustrates these findings. Data are not shown separately here for black men, but the association between the indices of Self-Defense and Violence for Social Control is similar for the consistent black respondents, although the trend was less marked. The self-defense orientation for them implies less support of force by police, perhaps because blacks are less inclined to regard the police as their agents than are whites.

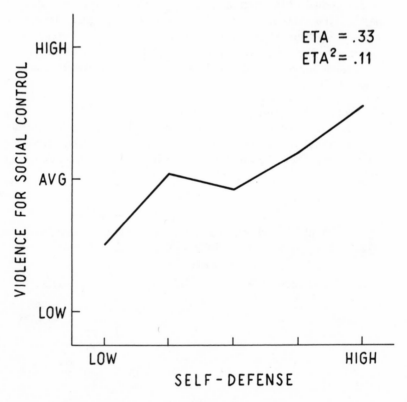

Figure 4. Mean Violence for Social Control in relation to the Self-Defense Index (most consistent respondents; N=747).

Self-Defense and the Justification of Violence for Social Change. Among American men in general, there was no relationship between the Self-Defense value-orientation and the justification of Violence for Social Change. Among blacks there was a positive relationship (eta=.23). The complementarity of these findings with those for social control is interesting: Self-Defense for blacks was associated primarily with social change; for American men in general it was associated with social control.

Humanism

In the course of the interview on violence, respondents were presented with a card on which were printed six values: equality; human dignity; respect for property; respect for law; freedom; financial security. The interviewer then said, "For the kind of world you want to live in, which of these do you think is *most* important?" And after the respondent had chosen, the process was repeated: "Now which do you think is the next most important?" The result of course was a rank order from each man in the sample.

Two of these values—equality and freedom—are among the concepts proposed by Rokeach (1968) as terminal, that is, as end-states of existence that the individual considers personally and socially preferable. Others of the six values could be considered either terminal or instrumental; financial security, for example, is perhaps more plausibly understood as a means than as an end in itself. In any case, the presentation of the six values to the respondent did not require him to discuss his frame of reference or interpretation of "importance"; he had only to rank the values from one to six.

The values had been chosen to represent two presumably different and identifiable points of view, one of which might be called liberal-humanistic and the other conservative-materialistic. The labels may be unfair, but there seems an undeniable contrast between the values of equality, freedom, and human dignity on the one hand, and on the other the values of respect for property, law, and financial security.

If a man gave his first three ranks to equality, freedom, and human dignity—in any order—he was coded as humanistic. If he gave his first three ranks to respect for property, respect for law, and financial security—in any order—he was coded as materialistic. He was also coded as material-ialistic if he ranked equality fifth or sixth. If he ranked the six values in any other way he was coded as mixed. Thus, the ranking of these values was reduced to a three-point scale, ranging from materialistic to humanistic. This scale is called the Humanism Index.

As Table 7 indicates, preferences among these six values were by no means equally distributed. Freedom was rated first by a near majority of men; human dignity, which was the next most frequent first choice, was so named by only 24 percent, and no other value came near these two. Interestingly enough, equality was ranked last by 20 percent of American men.

Respect for property was seen as the least of the values; virtually no one ranked it first, and a majority ranked it fifth or sixth. The accusation that Americans are "hung up" on property may have some validity, but the response pattern suggests that it also has some limits. The materialistic syndrome expresses the value of order and security more than property.

Table 7

Percentage Responses of Rank Order Preference
on the Humanism Index Items
(all respondents; N=1,374)

Humanism Index Items	Rated 1st	2nd	3rd	4rd	5th	Rated 6th	Total
Equality	9%	23%	21%	15%	12%	20%	100%
Human dignity	24	21	22	13	13	7	100
Respect for property	1	6	11	20	33	29	100
Respect for law	7	15	20	27	22	9	100
Freedom	48	20	13	9	6	4	100
Financial security	11	14	15	17	14	29	100

Background Factors in Relation to the Humanism Index. There is substantial evidence that values comprising the Humanism Index are taught in school, at home, and at church. The effect of education on these values is clear, and it is on the humanistic side (Table 8). Some question of confounding with socio-economic factors might be raised; financial security, for example, may well appear more important when one lacks it than after one has attained it. Nevertheless, the humanistic value syndrome increased quite regularly with increasing education (eta = .27), and was six times more frequent among the college-educated than among men with only an elementary school education.

The next most important determinant of the Humanism Index was age (eta = .22). It is a truism that materialism increases with years, and the data bear it out. The proportions of unmixed humanistic and materialistic values change symmetrically with age, as Table 9 illustrates. For example, less than one-fifth of the very young were materialistic; more than half of the elderly were so.

Table 8

Percentage Responses to the Humanism Index in Relation to Education

(all respondents; N=1,374)

Humanism Index		Education						
		Less than 7 Yrs.	7 to 9 Yrs.	10 to 11 Yrs.	High School Grad.	Some Coll.	BA Degree	Grad. Degree
Materialistic	1	51	50	38	31	24	30	28
	2	41	37	35	32	27	24	33
Humanistic	3	8	13	27	37	49	46	39
	Total	100%	100%	100%	100%	100%	100%	100%
	N	(86)	(255)	(225)	(431)	(202)	(120)	(52)

Table 9

Percentage Responses to the Humanism Index in Relation to Age

(all respondents; N=1,374)

Humanism Index		Age					
		16-19	20-29	30-39	40-49	50-59	60-64
Materialistic	1	19	24	39	37	47	51
	2	39	32	33	32	29	31
Humanistic	3	42	44	28	31	24	18
	Total	100%	100%	100%	100%	100%	100%
	N	(144)	(280)	(310)	(283)	(234)	(123)

The single survey on which these data are based cannot, of course, show the dynamics underlying the pattern just described. We do not know whether aging brings with it a sort of pervasive drift toward materialism or whether some men are transformed from strong humanists to strong materialists, while the center remains relatively constant. Nor can we say whether the greater humanism of the young today is a generational difference which will persist as this cohort grows older, or a stage in their lives. Such questions will be resolved only when recurrent studies are done on the same populations.

Background factors other than age and education had only very minor explanatory power in relation to the Humanism Index. Differences of statistical significance occurred, but none of them accounted for more than a few percentage points of the variation in attitudes toward Humanism. For example, the proportion of materialists (in terms of their ranking of values) was highest in the Southern and Border states, while the proportion of humanists was highest in the mountain and Pacific states. Jews were most humanistic (52 percent), Orthodox Christian and fundamentalist denominations least so. Rural residents were slightly more materialistic than urban, although the differences were small and irregular. Racial differences also accounted for only small amounts of the variation in attitudes toward Humanism, although the proportion of "materialists" among black men was about half of that among whites (19 percent compared to 37 percent).

All these relationships are summarized in Table 10. Education and age were the most important predictors of the Humanism Index. In combination, the background factors we have examined produced substantial prediction to the Humanism Index. The multiple correlation was .39, accounting for 16 percent of the variation in the value rankings.

Table 10

Region, Religion, Age, Race, Town Size and Education
in Relation to the Humanism Index
(all respondents; N=1,374)

Predictor Item	eta	eta^2
Region	.15	.02
Religion	.15	.02
Age	.22	.05
Town size	.15	.02
Race	.09	.01
Education	.27	.07

Multiple R = .39 (population estimate = .37)
Variation Explained (R^2) = 16% (population estimate = 14%)

The Humanism Index and the Justification of Violence. One would expect persons holding the materialistic value-orientation to support relatively strong measures for social control by police. They tended to do so, although the relationship was by no means pronounced. Scores on the Index of Violence for Social Control increased as values moved from humanistic to materialistic value rankings. Figure 5 illustrates these data for all consistent respondents; the tendency among blacks was less pronounced than among all consistent respondents but the direction of the association was the same.

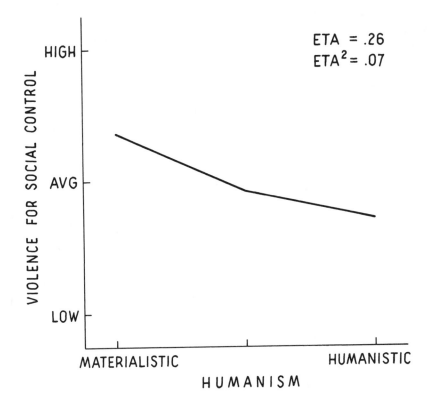

Figure 5. Mean Violence for Social Control in relation to the Humanism Index (most consistent respondents; N=747).

No relationship of strength existed between the Humanism Index and the belief that violence is necessary to produce social changes "fast enough," either among Americans as a whole or for whites and blacks separately. However, there was such a relationship among men with some college education (Figure 6). Among this group, the more humanistically inclined individuals scored higher on Violence for Social Change. In a sense it seems contradictory that men who are both educated and humanistically inclined should be more likely to think that violence may be necessary for social change. After all, violence is destructive of persons or property, irrespective of the cause in which it is used. It may be that education makes more apparent some of the unmet human needs in American society and so increases a feeling of need for social change. A less encouraging possibility is that the well-educated are more skeptical about the readiness of American society to apply itself to contemporary problems. Either or both possibilities could explain the association between humanistic values and the justification of violence to produce social change.

One might speculate that for other groups in the population the *goal* of social change would be strongly related to the humanistic ranking of the Humanism Index, but that the justification of violence as a means to social change obscures that relationship. Most people who find social change desirable do not condone violence for achieving it, and most people find it

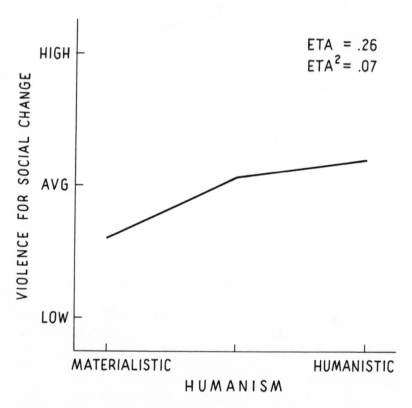

Figure 6. Mean Violence for Social Change in relation to the Humanism Index (high education respondents; N=374).

easier to accept the use of force by the police than by dissident groups. Thus, the proposition of violence for social change is unacceptable to some because of their opposition to change, and to others because of their opposition to violence.

Property/Person Priority

The relative value that a man puts on property and person, or more specifically the negative value that he attaches to property loss as compared to personal injury, could be regarded as a special and important manifestation of the general hierarchy of values discussed in the preceding section. The issue of person versus property was posed in terms of two questions, asked about midway during the interview on violence:

> *Some people say that stealing or damaging property is as bad as hurting people. Others say that damaging property is not as bad as hurting people. What do you think?*

> *Do you think it would be worse to become a permanent cripple, or to lose an uninsured home through fire, or are they equally bad?*

The response patterns to these two questions were rather different, as Table 11 indicates. A scant majority of American men considered that hurting people was worse than stealing or damaging property, and a nearly

Table 11

Percentage Responses to Items Comprising the
Property/Person Priority Index

	All Respondents (N=1,374)	Whites (N=1,046)	Blacks (N=303)
Stealing bad as hurting?			
Stealing as bad	46	47	43
Hurting worse	54	53	57
Total	100%	100%	100%
Lose home or crippled worse?			
Home loss a lot worse	2	2	2
Home loss somewhat worse	2	1	2
Both equally bad	20	19	31
Being crippled somewhat worse	7	6	11
Being crippled a lot worse	69	72	54
Total	100%	100%	100%

equal number thought that one was as bad as the other. Black men and white responded similarly to this question. However, when a case was posed in more specific terms—loss of home versus permanent crippling injury—a large majority of blacks and a larger majority of white men considered the injury to be worse, most of them a lot worse.

These two questions were combined to form the Property/Person Priority Index. The more person-oriented the individual, the higher was his score on the Index. (For details of index construction see Appendix C.)

Background Factors. This evaluation of person versus property was not strongly predicted by background factors. Only education showed significant effects, with a steady increase in the person-orientation beginning with junior high school and continuing through graduate school (Figure 7).

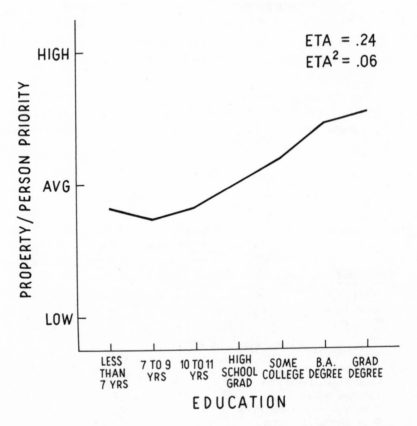

Figure 7. Mean Property/Person Priority Index in relation to education (all respondents; N=1,374).

There were some minor and irregular differences by region, with the person-orientation being most characteristic of the Border and Pacific states. Other background factors, including race, were near the vanishing point in their effects on this value orientation. These relationships are summarized in Table 12.

Table 12

Region, Religion, Age, Race, Town Size and Education
in Relation to the Property/Person Priority Index
(all respondents; N=1,374)

Predictor Item	eta	eta^2
Region	.12	.01
Religion	.09	.01
Age	.07	.01
Town size	.05	.00
Race	.09	.01
Education	.24	.06

Multiple R = .30 (population estimate = .26)
Variation Explained (R^2) = 9% (population estimate = 7%)

Property/Person Priority and the Justification of Violence. The apparent effects of the property-versus-person value-orientation are plausible in direction but trivial in magnitude. People who scored high on the evaluation of property also found justifiable relatively high levels of Violence for Social Control (Figure 8). People whose orientation was mixed or clearly person-over-property found the use of force for social control less justifiable. The relationship was expected, especially since the measures of Violence for Social Control are cast in terms of threats to property and the police are generally regarded as protectors of property.

It does not follow, however, that person-oriented values lead to a greater readiness to justify violence for social change, at least in the population as a whole. Among black men there was a small tendency in that direction, consistent with the pattern of racial differences that has emerged repeatedly in this analysis (Figure 9).

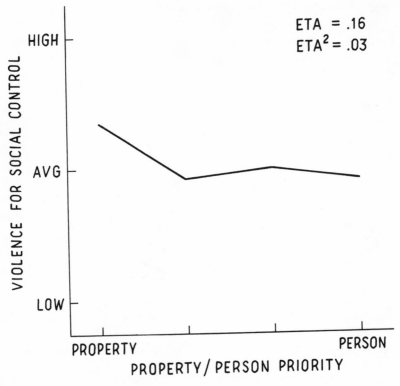

Figure 8. Mean Violence for Social Control in relation to the Property/Person Priority Index (most consistent respondents; N=747).

Kindness

"It's important to be kind to people even if they do things you don't believe in." "When a person harms you, you should turn the other cheek and forgive him." "Even if you don't like the person, you should still try to help him."

The agreement or disagreement of American men to these statements was taken as a measure of a value orientation toward kindness. There is a problem inherent in the measurement of values that is especially conspicuous in this instance: the tendency to answer in a socially acceptable way. Since *oughtness* is intrinsic to the concept of values, it becomes difficult to distinguish between the value and the bias toward socially acceptable responses. Nevertheless, there is a difference between really believing that something is good for oneself and others and saying that one so believes for extraneous reasons.

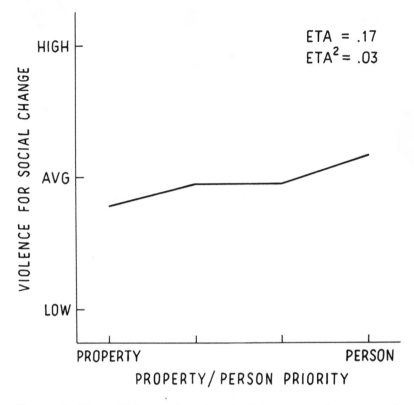

Figure 9. Mean Violence for Social Change in relation to the Property/Person Priority Index (black respondents; N=303).

It is difficult also to distinguish between hypocrisy and compartmentalization. If a man tells us that he believes in the value of kindness, but other evidence suggests that he does not act kindly, is he consciously deceiving us or subconsciously deceiving himself?

Such questions are appropriate to any of the value orientations. The questions arise with special sharpness in the case of kindness because social etiquette and religion so clearly enunciate the "right" answers, and because the actual responses are so little predicted by background factors and in turn predict so little to the justification of violence.

The responses to the three kindness items leaned toward the side of virtue. However, the majority of men did not propose to turn the other cheek—even though the question was posed in that Bible-reminding language. These findings are shown in Table 13.

Table 13

Percentage Responses to Items Measuring Belief in Kindness

(all respondents; N=1,374)

	Strongly Agree	Agree Somewhat	Disagree Somewhat	Strongly Disagree	Total
It's important to be kind to people even if they do things you don't believe in.	44%	43%	11%	2%	100%
Even if you don't like a person you should still try to help him.	46	48	5	1	100
When a person harms you, you should turn the other cheek and forgive him.	10	36	35	19	100

These three questions were combined into the Kindness Index. Higher scores on the Index reflect greater professed belief in kindness. (For details of index construction see Appendix C.)

Background Factors and the Value of Kindness. The six background factors that we have considered as predictors of value orientations accounted for about 8 percent of the variation in the Kindness Index. The factors contributed about equally to this modest explanation, with the exception of race, which was unrelated to the responses. With respect to the other factors, there was some tendency for expressed kindness responses to increase as one moves south and west from New England, as one moves from younger to older age groups, and as one moves from metropolitan to small-town and rural populations. Education showed a curvilinear tendency, with the least-educated and the most-educated groups expressing the greatest attachment to the value of kindness. These relationships are summarized in Table 14.

Kindness and the Justification of Violence. One might expect that a strongly held value of kindness would lead to a generalized opposition to violence, either for social control or social change. It could be argued to the contrary, of course. Even violent revolutionaries or violent repressors of social change are unlikely to equate their violence with unkindness. The actual data showed only faint relationships between Kindness and the justification of violence. For consistent respondents, there was a slight tendency for those lowest in Kindness to be highest in the justification of Violence for Social Control; there was absolutely no relationship between Kindness and the justification of Violence for Social Change.

Table 14

Region, Religion, Age, Race, Town Size and Education
in Relation to the Kindness Index
(all respondents; N=1,374)

Predictor Item	eta	eta^2
Region	.17	.03
Religion	.15	.02
Age	.12	.01
Town size	.13	.02
Race	.02	.00
Education	.13	.02

Multiple R = .29   (population estimate = .25)
Variation Explained (R^2) = 8%   (population estimate = 6%)

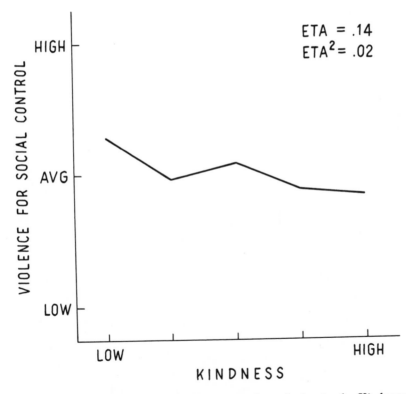

ETA = .14
ETA^2 = .02

Figure 10. Mean Violence for Social Control in relation to the Kindness Index (most consistent respondents; N=747).

The responses of black men are worth noting separately, however, because they showed complementary and distinctive patterns in relation to the Kindness Index. Among all consistent respondents—who were largely white—the value-orientation of kindness was associated with lower levels of violence deemed justifiable for social control, but had no association with the justification of Violence for Social Change. Among black men, the value-orientation of kindness had no association with the justification of Violence for Social Control, but was associated with lower levels of Violence for Social Change (Figure 11). It is as if the men of each race, to the extent that they respond to the kindness value, do so by inhibiting that type of violence which they see as more "their own."

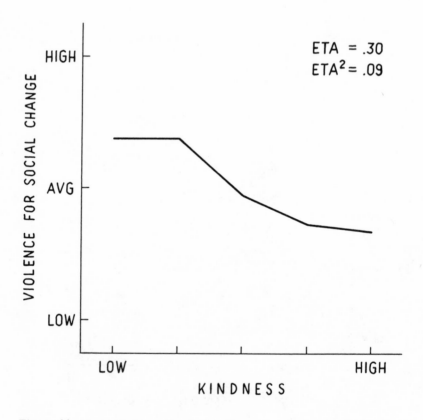

Figure 11. Mean Violence for Social Change in relation to the Kindness Index (black respondents; N=303).

Values and Violence: Combined Effects

We have been examining five values—retributive justice, self-defense, humanism, property/person priority, and kindness. We have thought about these values as determinants of attitudes toward violence and have looked for their effects in terms of two indices, one measuring the tendency to justify violence for the sake of social control and the other measuring the tendency to justify violence for social change. The patterns of relationships between these values and these attitudes toward violence were so different for black men than for American men as a whole that we have often discussed the results for black men separately. We can now examine the overall pattern that emerges from this consideration of five values, two races, and attitudes toward the two types of violence.

Violence for Social Control. To begin with, among American men in general, values appear to relate primarily to the justification of violence for social control. In respect to this attitude, the most potent values appear to be Self- Defense and Retributive Justice, the least potent, Kindness. Taken jointly, Retributive Justice and Self-Defense accounted for 16 percent of the variation in the Index of Violence for Social Control, nearly as much as all five values taken together.

One is tempted to say that the values that justify violence are more important in the determination of attitudes than the values that oppose it. The apparent importance of retributive justice and the unimportance of kindness as determinants of attitudes toward violence are perhaps a commentary on our measures, but perhaps also a commentary on our society. We can speculate on how the value of kindness might be taught more successfully, and what the social consequences of such teaching might be.

In general, however, the more a man believes in retributive justice, in self-defense, in material rather than humanistic values, in the value of property as compared to persons, and the less he believes in kindness—the higher will be the level of violence he finds justifiable by the police against hoodlums, protesting students, or rioting blacks.

Having said that much, we must add several qualifications having to do with the magnitude of these relationships, with consistency and inconsistency of response, and with differences associated with education and race. None of the values generated a very high correlation with Violence for Social Control; all five combined showed a multiple correlation of .45 with that index, explaining about 21 percent of the variation in such attitudes (Table 15). American men were influenced by their values, but values were hardly the dominant influence in determining the amount of violence they advocated for social control.

Table 15 shows the association between the Index of Violence for Social Control and all five values taken jointly. The table presents data separately for all respondents and for those who gave logically consistent scores on the Violence for Social Control measure, both for the general population of American men and for blacks. We have taken the data for the consistent scorers to provide the clearest test of the hypothesis that the level of violence advocated for social control is influenced by the individual's values. Data for all respondents are, of course, more descriptive of the relationship between values and attitudes towards this type of violence among men in the United States, and provide a safer basis for generalization to that population.

Table 15

Five Values (Combined) in Relation to Violence for Social Control

		Multiple R		Variation Explained	
All races	N	R	(Pop. Est.)	R^2	(Pop. Est.)
Consistent respondents	(747)	.45	(.43)	21%	(18%)
All respondents	(1,374)	.41	(.39)	17%	(15%)
Blacks only					
Consistent blacks	(157)	.51	(.39)	26%	(15%)
All blacks	(303)	.34	(.23)	12%	(6%)

A further qualification in respect to the relationship between values and Violence for Social Control has to do with race. While the data show that the relationship between values and attitudes toward Violence for Social Control was not very different for all American men than for those who responded consistently on this measure, this was not true for blacks. Those black men who responded consistently show about the same association between values and Violence for Social Control as did consistent respondents as a whole, but among all black men the association was greatly attenuated. Black men in general not only found Violence for Social Control less justifiable than did most American men; their attitudes on this subject were less related to the five values studied.

The subpopulation of college-educated men deserves special attention for several reasons. Among men who have had at least some college training, the relationship between values and attitudes toward Violence for Social Control was stronger than for the population at large or even for "consistent respondents." Among the college-educated, who are predomi-nately whites, the individual values (except for property/person priority) related more strongly to Violence for Social Control, and the five values in combination explained a larger proportion of the variation in that index (27 percent, Table 16). Perhaps there is something about the process of education which forces the individual to become more consistent in his attitudes, or which calls attention to inconsistencies in personal philos-ophies. If this is a correct interpretation, it is also a hopeful one, for it implies that consistency in belief and value systems is already being taught in college to some extent and that it might be taught more widely and more successfully at other educational levels.

Table 16

Five Values (Combined) in Relation to
Violence for Social Control
(high education respondents; N=374)

Predictor Item	eta	eta^2
Retributive Justice Index	.39	.15
Kindness Index	.24	.06
Self-Defense Index	.42	.17
Property/Person		
Priority Index	.08	.01
Humanism Index	.22	.05

Multiple R $= .52$ (population estimate = .48)
Variation Explained (R^2) = 27% (population estimate = 23%)

Violence for Social Change. Violence for Social Change presented a pattern essentially complementary to that for Violence for Social Control, with race as the key explanatory factor in the interaction. Among American men in general, none of the values showed significant effects on the justification or condemnation of violence for social change. Indeed, all five values in combination produced a multiple correlation of only .07. An over-whelming majority of American men found violence for social change unjustifiable, and to the extent that opinions differed on this subject, the differences were not explainable in terms of the values we have measured.

Among black men, however, values did predict to the amount of violence found tolerable for social change. Belief in Retributive Justice and Kindness were strong predictors. Next was the belief in Self-Defense. The valuation of property as compared to person, and humanistic as compared to materialistic considerations were less influential. The multiple correlation of the five values in relation to the Index of Violence for Social Change was .49 among black men, a correlation similar to that for the prediction of Violence for Social Control among the predominately white consistent respondents. Only the value of Kindness breaks this mirror image; it correlated .30 with Violence for Social Change for black respondents. The more strongly blacks believed in the value of Kindness, the less were they willing to justify Violence for Social Change. Table 17 summarizes the relationships between values and Violence for Social Change for blacks.

Table 17

Five Values (Combined) in Relation to
Violence for Social Change
(black respondents; N=303)

Predictor Item	eta	eta^2
Retributive Justice Index	.38	.14
Kindness Index	.30	.09
Self-Defense Index	.23	.05
Property/Person Priority Index	.17	.03
Humanism Index	.14	.02

Multiple R = .49 (population estimate = .43)
Variation Explained (R^2) = 24% (population estimate = 18%)

A current vogue in social criticism makes much of alleged polarizations in American society, between black and white, old and young, men and women. Such generalizations are often overdone, although racial differences in the relationship of values to the justification of violence are important.

Moreover, we have seen that subgroups other than race showed patterns of value-responsiveness different from the population at large. The relationship of values to the justification of Violence for Social Control was greater among the highly educated; this tendency was present in modest degree for Violence for Social Change. The multiple correlation of values and Violence for Social Change was .29 among highly educated men, and only .06 for men as a whole.

Values and Rhetoric

One might suspect that a person's values would influence his rhetoric and language. It seems reasonable to suppose that the more humanistically inclined the individual, the more likely he would be to call police acts such as shooting looters or beating students violence, and the less likely he might be to define protest and other acts of dissent as violence. Table 18 shows that such is the case. Table 18 also shows that the more retributive the individual, the more likely he was to call protest-related activities violence and the less likely he was to call police activities violence.

As one might have expected, those who set a relatively high value on property compared to persons were somewhat more inclined to call acts of protest violence and less inclined to view police behaviors in this fashion. Attitudes toward Self-Defense and Kindness did not appear to play a role in determining how the language of violence was used. The five values taken together explained 11 percent of the variation in whether or not police actions are called violence. The influence of values on the respondent's definition of violence is significant but overlapping.

Table 18

Five Values in Relation to What Acts
Are Called Violence
(all respondents; N=1,374)
(gammas)

Value Indices	Is Protest Violence? Index	Are Police Acts Violence? Index
Humanism Index	-.29	.30
Retributive Justice Index	.21	-.24
Property/Person Priority Index	-.19	.14
Self-Defense Index	.11	-.13
Kindness Index	.03	.01

Nevertheless, there is an important point here. We have seen that values are associated with attitudes toward violence, and presumably play a role in determining such attitudes. Now it also appears that values are associated with how the language is used, and presumably are important in determining whether or not certain acts are defined as violence. If so, values act both to define a situation as violent and to determine how that perceived violence should be handled. Thus, the more materialistic, property-oriented, retributive individuals apparently saw more violence in acts of protest and also recommended higher levels of police force in handling real violence. The tendency of people with certain values to define the meaning of specific acts and behaviors in such a fashion that those values can be more easily rationalized deserves study. As an unintended human tendency, it is dangerous; as an intentional device, it would be Orwellian.

Values and Violent Behavior

We have been looking at values as they relate to attitudes toward violence. More specifically, we have sought to determine the extent to which a man's values lead him to condone or condemn violence for social control and violence for social change.

In discovering such relationships, we have assumed that they have much to do with the quality of life in our society. The climate of opinion in these matters, the common and shared beliefs about what is good or bad, necessary or unnecessary for a society, tell much about what it is and what it is in process of becoming. On the whole, a common and shared structure of values and beliefs has the effect of changing the probabilities of certain behaviors by members of the group or society in which that normative structure exists. The lack of such a structure, or the simultaneous existence of different and opposing belief systems, permits behaviors that might otherwise be controlled by individuals and those nearest to them. These propositions, while relevant to our research, are not directly testable by it.

There is, however, another and more direct way in which we expect values to affect behavior. We expect each individual to act in ways that express his own values, as well as his needs and other motives. The kindly person should be less likely to commit acts of violence as well as less likely to approve their being committed by others. The strong believer in retributive justice should be more likely to take revenge as well as to approve retributive acts by others. Such assumptions are almost axiomatic; we would consider suspect any measure of values that turned out to have no relationship whatsoever to the behavior of the people who profess them. In this sense, the investigation of connections between values and behavior becomes a study in validation.

In connection with the national survey, an adjunct study was made of a group of students who participated in a street disturbance (Chapter 3). These students might be regarded as having acted in the interests of social change. It therefore becomes relevant to ask whether they differed in their values from other young people of similar background. We attempted to answer this question by comparing the responses of those arrested with the answers given by all college students in our national sample. The results are shown in Table 19.

Table 19

Percentage Responses to the Five Value Indices for the Students
Participating in the Ann Arbor Street Disturbance and
for College Students in General

Retributive Justice Index

	N	Low 1	2	3	4	5	High 6	Total
Student Arrestees	(29)	58	23	15	4	--	--	100%
College Students	(63)	26	13	23	24	8	6	100%

Kindness Index

	N	Low 1	2	3	4	High 5	Total
Student Arrestees	(29)	15	11	22	30	22	100%
College Students	(63)	15	14	25	22	24	100%

Self-Defense Index

	N	Low 1	2	3	4	High 5	Total
Student Arrestees	(29)	59	21	10	7	3	100%
College Students	(63)	33	19	15	19	14	100%

Property/Person Priority Index

	N	Property 1	2	3	Person 4	Total
Student Arrestees	(29)	--	--	8	92	100%
College Students	(63)	7	10	24	59	100%

Humanism Index

	N	Materialistic 1	2	Humanistic 3	Total
Student Arrestees	(29)	3	--	97	100%
College Students	(63)	8	25	67	100%

In comparison with other college students, those arrested showed a value pattern which is consistent with, and exaggerates, the pattern for people who found violence for social change relatively easy to justify. Those arrested were relatively low in retributive justice and self-defense. They were almost undeviatingly high on the value of persons as compared to property and on humanistic as compared to materialistic values. On the value of kindness they did not differ significantly from college students as a whole.

The data of this chapter only begin to answer some of the complex questions of value formation, the influence of values on social perception and cognition, and their effect on the justification of violence by others. Their effect on violent behavior can be only hinted at, on the basis of data from the adjunct study of students. The relationships obtained, in spite of their limitations, contribute to explaining the phenomena of violence and suggest some means for their reduction.

Summary

Among the psychological factors one might think important in determining attitudes toward violence are the values around which the individual seeks to organize his behaviors. Values may be regarded as statements of how the individual feels he ought to behave, and carry the implication that others also ought to behave in this fashion. Five values were measured in this survey: the extent to which the individual believes in retributiveness; kindness, that is belief in the principles embodied in the Golden Rule; the right to self-defense; how people are valued relative to property; and how humanistic values are regarded in comparison to more materialistic ones.

Altogether, these values accounted for about one-fifth of the variation in attitudes toward the use of violence in pursuit of social control. Retributiveness and self-defense were most closely related to such attitudes, while kindness was almost totally unrelated. Not only were the two "pro-violent" values (retributiveness and self-defense) closely related to attitudes about how much force the police should use in the control of disturbances, but there was a high degree of agreement with such values among American men. So it would seem that there are strong values in our country favoring violence for social control, and only weak values that act against it.

For the population in general, values were unrelated to the extent to which the individual thought violence necessary to produce social change, but this was not true for black men, among whom there was somewhat more support for such violence. For blacks, the more retributive the individual and the more he believed in self-defense, the more likely he was to believe that violence was required to produce social change. Moreover, the more person-oriented and the more humanistic the black man, the more likely he was to feel violence necessary to bring about social change; perhaps this indicates a despair on the part of some blacks that racial equality can be attained by less drastic means. The value of kindness, which showed little or no effect among whites, was influential among blacks. The more a black man expressed a belief in kindness, the less likely he was to advocate violence of either kind.

In summary then, values are related to attitudes toward violence and probably influence such attitudes. Belief in the values measured tended to augment rather than to diminish the justification of violence, and to provide moral support for violence, especially violence for social control.

Chapter 6

IDENTIFICATION

In-groups and Out-groups. The traditional metaphor calls the United States a melting pot for many peoples. In the past immigrants have landed on these shores by the millions—white, black and yellow; Protestant, Catholic, and Jew; peasant and professional; fugitives from famine and from tyranny. Each of these groups draws from a separate history and tradition; each brings its own culture. To some extent, all have been assimilated, but some have found their way into the mainstream of American life more easily and completely than others. As a result, the boundaries of this country contain an extraordinary mixture of peoples, including many who for one reason or another stand apart sufficiently to form recognizable subgroups within the larger culture.

Members of such groups recognize their membership and are so recognized by others. Indeed, membership in such groups may be ascribed by outsiders even when the individual in question does not admit or claim it. For example, people with certain names are often considered Jews irrespective of their religion, or Italians irrespective of their birthplace. Often there are stereotypes about such subgroups in the population; the mere recitation of certain adjectives brings to mind the people to whom they are so often applied and misapplied—hard-drinking, inscrutable, aggressive, lazy, dumb, shrewd, and so on through an endless list.

Group memberships—wanted or unwanted, owned or disowned—have social consequences. Groups are defined in terms of differences, and people seen as different are treated differently. But what do these truisms imply with respect to violence? Do attitudes toward violence differ in accordance with stereotypic notions of people and groups of people? Is there a relationship between the level of violence justified, and beliefs about the people against whom violence is used? Is violence more tolerable when it is used by someone you might regard as a friend than when it is used by someone you might think an enemy? These are the questions to which this chapter is addressed.

One might think that it would be easier to justify violence when it is used against people who are seen as different from oneself, and more difficult to justify violence against those who are perceived as one's peers. It is known, for example, that people who commit repetitive violent acts are often characterized by the lack of ability to form meaningful relationships with others (Wolfgang and Ferracuti 1967, p. 216). This inability of the psychopath to form meaningful connections with other persons can be viewed as a failure to see others as people like himself, vulnerable to the same aches and pains which form his own reactions to unpleasantness. But such attitudes toward others are not restricted to psychopaths; they may be held by members of one group about members of another. Smelser (1962, p. 101) has pointed out the importance of hostile belief systems in justifying outbursts of scapegoating and rioting. He asserts that groups which have been the target of collective violence are often regarded as the personification of evil in the belief systems of the aggressor. Such belief systems exclude the victims from those moral considerations usually extended to peers, and make it possible for aggressors to think of themselves as highly moral individuals even as they are committing violent acts.

Excluding people from having the status of peers or even of human beings probably serves as an important rationalization for acts of violence (Sanford and Comstock 1971). For example, William Manchester (1970, p. 540) points out that during the inception of brutal treatment of slave labor by the House of Krupp, the enslaved laborers ceased to be referred to as people or workers and began to be termed "stucke" (cattle). Empathic considerations which are normally extended to people of "our own kind" may be perceived as unnecessary or inappropriate in relation to inferior species. Such mechanisms are not unique to the German treatment of the Jews. In the early history of our own country, similar rationalizations were used to justify the slaughter of Indians. In 1755, the Boston Council Chamber was moved to proclaim:

> . . . the Penobscot Tribe of Indians to be enemies, rebels and traitors to his Majesty . . . and . . . hereby require his Majesty's subjects of the Province to embrace all opportunities of pursuing, capturing, killing and destroying all and every one of the aforesaid Indians.
>
> And whereas the General Court of this Province have voted . . . the premiums of bounty following viz:
>
> For every scalp of a male Indian brought in as evidence of their being killed as aforesaid, forty pounds.

> For every scalp of such female Indian or male
> Indian under the age of twelve years that shall be killed
> and brought in as evidence of their being killed as
> aforesaid, twenty pounds (Deloria 1970, p. 14).

Similarly, in contemporary times, in reference to charges of murder against a Black Panther on trial in Berkeley, David Hilliard stated:

> The brother is charged with four counts of attempted
> murder of four pigs. And I don't think that's wrong.
> Because everybody knows that pigs are depraved tra-
> ducers that violate the lives of human beings and that
> there ain't nothing wrong with taking the life of a
> mother----ing pig (Burnstein 1970, p. 9).

And in another area of contemporary violence, *Newsweek* (December 1, 1969, p. 37) states:

> Many U.S. fighting men under the stress of combat
> display a profound contempt for the people of South
> Vietnam. With hearty distaste, GI's commonly refer to
> the South Vietnamese—allies and enemies alike—as
> "dinks." And in the view of many longtime observers of
> the war, it is not unreasonable to conclude that the
> strong antipathy underlying such epithets—or the "dink
> syndrome" as it is known in Vietnam—sometimes plays a
> part in the casual killing of civilian bystanders. "Psycho-
> logically and morally," says a U.S. civilian official, "it's
> much easier to kill a 'dink' than it is to shoot a 'Viet-
> namese.' "

The examples cited illustrate that excluding people from groups to which one feels related can serve as a rationalization justifying violence toward them. But there is another aspect to the problem, that is, the extent to which feelings of relatedness and identification with a group lead one to justify its actions, even its violent actions, and to find unjustifiable any violence committed against the group.

Such partisan responses are not limited to those individuals who define themselves as being members of a particular group. Many groups are surrounded by a larger population of individuals who see themselves as having some likeness or commonality of goals and interests. This percep-tion of similarities we term "identification," and we suggest that it typically includes both cognitive and affective aspects. For example, statements such as "the Democrats have always helped the working man"—"the police are waging a war against crime in the streets"—might illustrate the former, and statements such as—"blacks are friendly people"—"Southerners are warm and hospitable"—might illustrate the latter. Our measures of identification were designed to tap both cognitive and affective components.

In the course of the interview, respondents were asked how the police should handle three kinds of disturbances, those caused by "hoodlum gangs," those occurring in ghettos, and those occurring on college campuses. Respondents were also asked how much violence they thought necessary to bring about changes desired by students, changes desired by black people, and change in general. In four of these six scenarios the contenders are the police on the one side, and student demonstrators or black protesters on the other. By investigating the respondents' identification with these groups, we could test the hypothesis that identification with the contenders modifies attitudes toward violence.

On the basis of this hypothesis, we would expect that the more an individual is identified with white student demonstrators and black protesters, the less likely he will be to justify high levels of police force in disturbances involving such groups and the more likely he will be to justify violence in behalf of causes advocated by such groups. We would also expect that the more the individual identifies with the police, the more likely he will be to justify high levels of police force, and the less likely he will be to justify violence for social change, which can be interpreted as action against the police.

Measuring Identification

To assess the extent of their identification with three "contender" groups in our scenarios of violent conflicts, respondents were asked a series of four identical questions about "white student demonstrators," "black protesters," and "police." For each group, the items were in the following form:

1. On the whole, would you say that *most* white student demonstrators are *trying to be helpful,* or that they are *looking for trouble,* or they aren't one way or the other?
2. Think of how white student demonstrators think of people like yourself. Do you think that *none* dislike people like yourself, *only a few, many,* or *almost all* dislike people like yourself?
3. Would your say that *most* white student demonstrators *can*

be trusted, or that you *can't be too careful in dealing with them?*

4. If white student demonstrators get the things they want, do you think *your* life will change? . . . (IF "WILL CHANGE"): Do you think *your* life will change for *better* or *worse?*

Of the four identification stems, two (the first and third) address themselves to the intentions of the contenders; one addresses itself to the question of whether or not there is a commonality of goals between the respondent and the contender (item four), and one assesses the affective relationship between the respondent and the contender (item two).

Table 1 shows how American men responded to these questions in respect to the three groups. On the whole, the police were highly regarded by Americans. The vast majority of American men regarded them as helpful, trustworthy, and not hostile. In addition, of those respondents who felt that their lives would change if police achieved their goals, the vast majority thought life would change for the better.

American men were not nearly so favorably inclined toward black protesters and white student demonstrators. Moreover, attitudes toward the white student group were almost as unfavorable as attitudes toward the black dissidents. It is difficult to know whether attitudes have changed since these data were collected in the summer of 1969. The episodes at Kent State University and Jackson State College, and the conclusions of grand juries in both cases that shooting the students was justified, may well have affected attitudes toward student demonstrators. In both cases, the law enforcement officers who shot students were absolved of blame by local grand juries, and the blame for the deaths was laid squarely on the shoulders of University officials, faculty, and the students themselves. It seems quite possible that the attitudes of American men toward such students are less favorable in 1971 than they were in 1969, especially since more publicity was given to the grand jury indictments than to the differing conclusions reached subsequently by the federal courts, or to the finding of the National Commission on Campus Unrest that the killings on both campuses were "inexcusable."

To the extent that the four items cited above do indeed measure how respondents identify with the contenders, we would expect different subgroups in the respondent population to respond differentially to the items. If membership is one important determinant of identification, and if among the blacks in our sample there were some who would classify themselves as black protesters, then blacks should score higher than whites on the items measuring identification with black protesters. In addition, it

Table 1

Percentage Responses to Items Measuring Identification with White Student Demonstrators, Black Protesters, and Police

(all respondents; N=1,374)

On the whole, would you say that *most* _____ are *trying to be helpful,* or that they are *looking for trouble,* or that they aren't one way or the other?

	White Student Demonstrators	Black Protesters	Police
Looking for trouble	40	45	4
Not one way or the other	30	23	13
Trying to be helpful	30	32	83
Total	100%	100%	100%

Think of how _____ think of people like yourself. Do you think that *none* dislike people like yourself, only *a few, many,* or *almost all* dislike people like yourself?

	White Student Demonstrators	Black Protesters	Police
Almost all	14	17	4
Many	18	29	5
A few	58	49	52
None	10	5	39
Total	100%	100%	100%

Would you say that *most* _____ *can be trusted,* or that you *can't be too careful in dealing with them?*

	White Student Demonstrators	Black Protesters	Police
Can't be too careful in dealing with them	54	68	14
Don't know	12	9	2
Can be trusted	34	23	84
Total	100%	100%	100%

If _____ get the things they want, do you think *your* life will change? If "WILL CHANGE": Do you think *your* life will change for *better* or *worse?*

	White Student Demonstrators	Black Protesters	Police
Worse	23	34	7
Won't change	60	41	58
Better	17	25	35
Total	100%	100%	100%

seems reasonable to suppose that in general blacks would be more identified with black protesters than would whites. We would also expect that whites who in the course of the interview expressed fears of being discriminated against by blacks would score lower on black identification items than would whites in general. Finally, we might expect that college students, some of whom have become active in the civil rights movement during the last decade, would score higher on these identification items than would whites in general.

Figure 1 shows that the data bear out these expectations. A higher proportion of blacks than of any other group responded positively to the identification items dealing with black protesters. A lower proportion of those expressing fears of being discriminated against by blacks responded positively to such items than any other group. The identification of college students compares as expected with the general population of men.

Following a line of reasoning similar to that outlined above for blacks, we would expect that there would be a larger proportion of college students than of other population groups who would identify themselves as being white student demonstrators or as sharing some of their goals. We would therefore expect a relatively smaller proportion of college students to agree with the negative end of the identification items that refer to white student demonstrators and a larger proportion to agree with the positive end. Figure 2 shows that this is generally the case, although blacks were more apt than students to state that life would change for the better if the white student demonstrators achieved their goals. Blacks are more likely to be poor and in urgent need of change and it may be that questions about a change in their way of life are more salient for them than for the usually affluent college student.

Figure 2 also shows that blacks were less likely to agree with negative statements about student demonstrators than were whites, and that whites who fear reverse discrimination were more likely to agree with such items than were whites in general. These findings seem reasonable when one recalls the identification of student activists with the civil rights movement.

These data support the notion that the items used to measure identification do have some validity and that commonality of goals, motives, and affective ties with groups are actually components of "identification" with such groups.

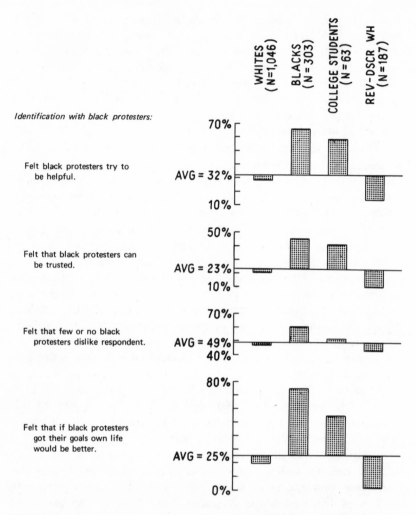

Figure 1. Percentage responses to black protester identification items for whites, blacks, college students, whites who fear reverse discrimination, and for American men as a whole.

Black men in the United States were less trusting in their orientation to other people (Table 2) than were whites. (For details of construction of the Trust Index, see Appendix C.) This may reflect the personal experiences of blacks with discrimination and with the treatment that often accompanies poverty and lack of education. Such experiences might well make a person less trusting and more suspicious. It is also true that when

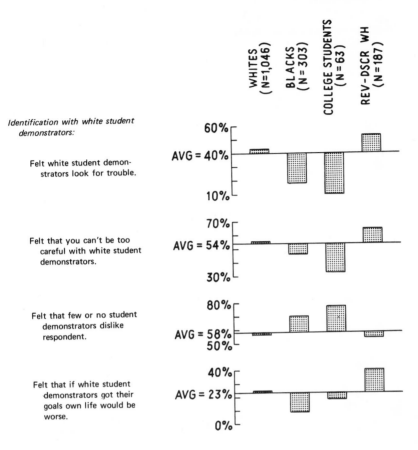

Identification with white student
demonstrators:

Felt white student demon-
strators look for trouble.

Felt that you can't be too
careful with white student
demonstrators.

Felt that few or no student
demonstrators dislike
respondent.

Felt that if white student
demonstrators got their
goals own life would be
worse.

Figure 2. Percentage responses to white student demonstrator identification items for whites, blacks, college students, whites who fear reverse discrimination, and American men as a whole.

blacks respond to questions about the trustworthiness of "people in general," they are speaking in terms of a society which is predominantly white. Nevertheless, it seems likely that lack of trust for people in general could influence the extent to which blacks identify with other groups. Consistent with this view, blacks who scored high on the Trust Index were more likely to feel that student demonstrators are helpful than blacks who scored low (Figure 3).

It is interesting that the subgroup of blacks who showed higher than average trust for people in general were more highly identified with white student demonstrators than were college students themselves. This finding

Table 2

Percentage Responses to the Trust Index[a]
for White and Black Respondents

Trust		Whites (N=1,046)	Blacks (N=303)
Low	1	10%	27%
	2	19	33
	3	26	19
High	4	45	21
Total		100%	100%

[a] This index is based on three questions inquiring into whether the respondent thought "people in general" were trustworthy. For details of index construction see Appendix C.

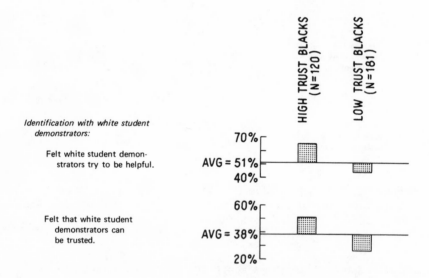

Figure 3. Percentage responses to black protester identification items for high trust and low trust black respondents and for black men as a whole.

may indicate something about the relative importance of cognitive and affective components in identification with a group. Blacks, who as a group are probably more apt to think of social change as a desirable goal than are most college students, identify highly with the white student contender group, despite differences in color and cultural background.

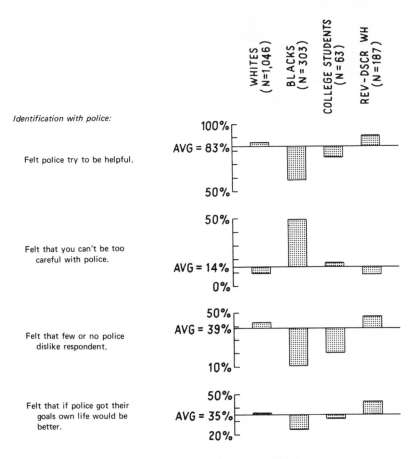

Figure 4. Percentage responses to police identification items for whites, blacks, college students, whites who fear reverse discrimination, and American men as a whole.

Nevertheless, the relatively low level of trust displayed by blacks toward people in general should be taken into account in the interpretation of their responses regarding identification with any specific groups. Low levels of trust appear to diminish identification with those who might otherwise be highly regarded for cognitive reasons.

Figure 4 shows how whites, blacks, college students and men who feared reverse discrimination compared to the general population in their identification with the police. The major difference among these groups is the fact that black men were far less likely than others to believe that the police are helpful and far more likely to believe that one "can't be too careful" in dealing with them. Very few blacks subscribed to the belief that no police are apt to dislike people like themselves. A larger proportion of students than other American men felt that policemen are apt to dislike people like themselves. Otherwise, college students appear to be much like white American men in their beliefs about the police.

Background Characteristics and Identification

The preceding analysis suggests something of the impact of broad experiential and cultural differences on attitudes toward the three contender groups. The issue deserves further investigation, however. For example, do educated men respond differently to the identification items than those who are less educated? Do the young feel differently about dissenters and the police than the old? Do people who live in the South have different attitudes from those who live elsewhere?

Six demographic variables relate to the identification items more or less consistently. These are race, education, age, region, town size, and religion. Table 3 shows the strength of the association between these variables, taken together, and the identification items. In general, the two items dealing with the intentions of the contenders (whether they are trustworthy and are trying to be helpful) are most likely to be related to the demographic characteristics of the respondents (Table 3). Background factors explain from 13 to 21 percent of the variation in such attitudes.

The question dealing with the commonality of goals between the contenders and the respondents is variably related to demographic characteristics, showing a high degree of association when asked for black protesters and almost no association when asked in respect to the police. The items dealing with the affective component of identification (the extent to which the respondent feels that people in each contender group are apt to dislike people like himself) appear to be quite independent of demographic characteristics, except for responses about the police.

Because the data did not justify combining the identification items into indices, it is necessary to examine separately the association of demographic characteristics with each item. From the rather large number of resulting analyses, only associations of meaningful size will be discussed.

Race and Identification with Contenders. Of the demographic characteristics considered, race accounts for the largest part of the variation in identification with the three contender groups (Table 4). Moreover, the relationship between race and the identification items is in the direction expected on *a priori* grounds. Blacks were more apt to identify positively with black protesters than were whites, and they were less likely to identify with the police. Race alone accounts for almost as

Table 3

Race, Religion, Region, Town Size, Education and Age Combined in Relation to Each Identification Item

(all respondents; N=1,374)

White student demonstrators:	Multiple R		Variation Explained	
	R	(Pop. Est.)	R^2	(Pop. Est.)
Helpful	.41	(.38)	17%	(14%)
Trustworthy	.35	(.32)	13	(10)
None dislike respondent	.16	(.03)	3	(0)
Better life	.34	(.29)	12	(9)
Black protesters:				
Helpful	.45	(.43)	21%	(19%)
Trustworthy	.36	(.33)	13	(11)
None dislike respondent	.29	(.25)	9	(6)
Better life	.49	(.47)	24	(22)
Police:				
Helpful	.34	(.31)	12%	(9%)
Trustworthy	.43	(.40)	18	(16)
None dislike respondent	.36	(.33)	13	(11)
Better life	.23	(.16)	5	(2)

much of the variation in attitudes about whether or not the police are trustworthy as did all six background factors combined. To the extent that race accounts for any part of the variation in identification with white student demonstrators, blacks were more apt to identify with this group than were whites.

Education and Identification with Contenders. Next to race, the demographic characteristic which explains the largest part of the variation in identification with the contender groups is education (Table 5). The more educated the respondent, the more likely he was to identify with black protesters and white student demonstrators (Figures 5 and 6). All the items relating to these two groups show this association except for the items which dealt with the affective component of identification, which appear unrelated to education. It is possible that the association between education and more tolerant attitudes is due to factors not directly related to the educational process such as self-selection. However, it may be that continued education ameliorates some of the negative attitudes which

Table 4

Race in Relation to Each Identification Item
(all respondents; N=1,374)

Identification with:	Helpful		None Dislike R		Trustworthy		Better Life	
	eta	Variation explained	eta	Variation explained	eta	Variation explained	eta	Variation explained
Police	.26	7%	.26	7%	.38	15%	.13	2%
Black protesters	.30	9	.24	6	.20	4	.39	15
White student demonstrators	.20	4	.04	0	.05	0	.16	3

Table 5

Education in Relation to Each Identification Item
(all respondents; N=1,374)

Identification with:	Helpful		None Dislike R		Trustworthy		Better Life	
	eta	Variation explained	eta	Variation explained	eta	Variation explained	eta	Variation explained
Police	.08	1%	.10	1%	.19	4%	.09	1%
Black protesters	.23	5	.08	1	.21	4	.13	2
White student demonstrators	.21	5	.05	0	.21	5	.12	1

seem to be such a characteristic human response to people who are not members of one's own peer group. One could explain the more positive attitudes of the educated toward white student demonstrators by postulating that educated people are more likely to see these students as members of their own peer group, but this explanation could not apply to the greater identification of the educated with black protesters. Indeed, since blacks are less educated than whites, one might have expected the opposite effect. However, greater education is associated with more positive attitudes toward both minority groups. The associations are not large, but they suggest that education might be a useful tool for dealing with

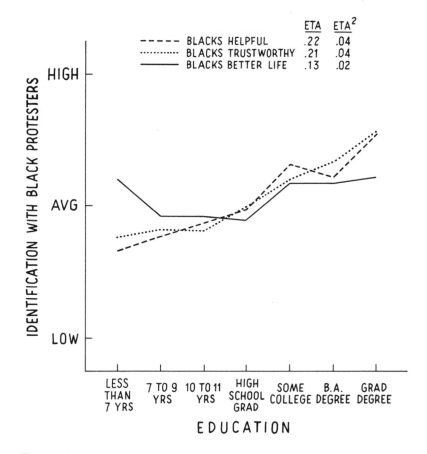

Figure 5. Mean identification with black protesters in relation to education (all respondents; N=1,374).

some of the fears and hates which, as we will later show, are related in a substantial way to attitudes toward violence. Moreover, if college education produces more favorable attitudes toward minorities and increased tolerance for dissent in the absence of specific programs to produce such effects, it seems reasonable to suppose that secondary school education could be modified to produce similar results.

Attitudes toward the police are not consistently related to education. The only identification item which shows such an association is the one inquiring whether police are trustworthy or not; the more educated the respondent, the more likely he was to trust the police (Figure 7).

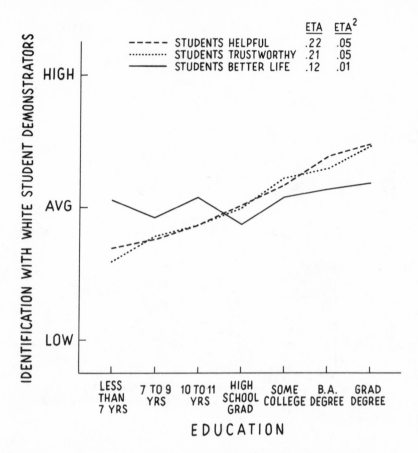

Figure 6. Mean identification with white student demonstrators in relation to education (all respondents; N=1,374).

Town Size and Identification with Contenders. Table 6 shows the associations between identification with the contender groups and the size of the town in which the respondent lived. In general, the larger the town, the more highly identified the respondent was with black protesters and white student demonstrators (Figures 8 and 9). As before, the item asking whether the respondent thought the black and student contenders disliked him did not show such associations.

Associations between town size and measures of identification with the police are small and variable. To the extent that such associations exist, it appears that people living in large cities were less apt to regard the police as trustworthy and more inclined to think that the police are apt to dislike people like themselves.

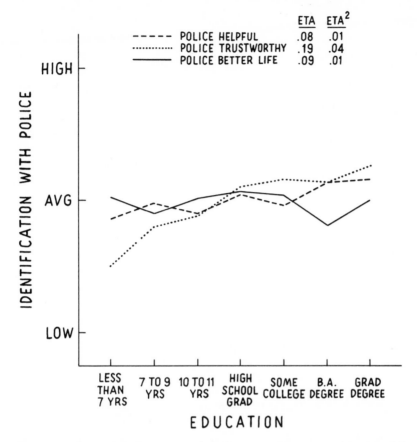

Figure 7. Mean identification with police in relation to education (all respondents; N=1,374).

Table 6

Town Size in Relation to Each Identification Item

(all respondents; N=1,374)

	Helpful		None Dislike R		Trustworthy		Better Life	
Identification with:	eta	Variation explained	eta	Variation explained	eta	Variation explained	eta	Variation explained
Police	.16	2%	.15	2%	.12	1%	.05	0%
Black protesters	.19	4	.07	0	.14	2	.18	3
White student demonstrators	.22	5	.05	0	.18	3	.16	3

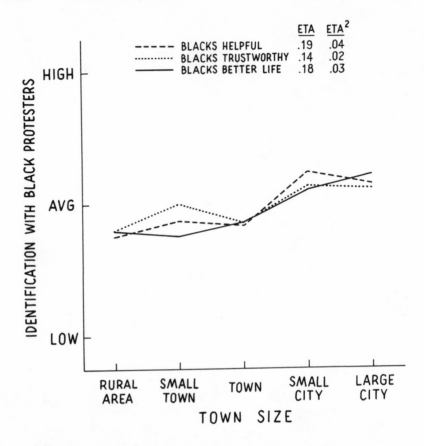

Figure 8. Mean identification with black protesters in relation to town size (all respondents; N=1,374).

Age and Identification with Contenders. Table 7 shows the association between age and identification with the contender groups. One might have expected such associations to be relatively large. Much is written of the generation gap, and one might think that college students and black dissidents speak with the voice of the young. Indeed, the effects are in this direction—the younger the respondent, the more likely he was to believe that black protesters and white student demonstrators are trustworthy, trying to be helpful and likely to improve life. However, the associatons are small; age does not appear to be important in determining identification with the contenders. Moreover, even the small relationships with age disappear in respect to identification with the police. The only association

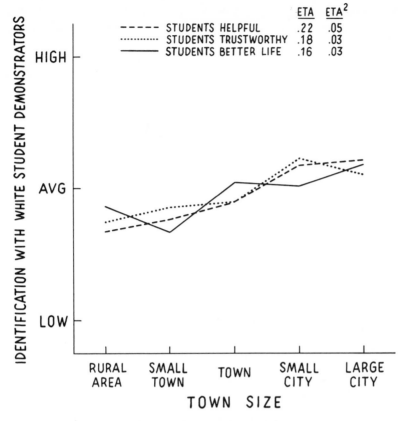

Figure 9. Mean identification with white student demonstrators in relation to town size (all respondents; N=1,374).

Table 7

Age in Relation to Identification

(all respondents; N=1,374)

Identification with:	Helpful		None Dislike R		Trustworthy		Better Life	
	eta	Variation explained	eta	Variation explained	eta	Variation explained	eta	Variation explained
Police	.14	2%	.19	4%	.09	1%	.03	0%
Black protesters	.11	1	.05	0	.10	1	.16	2
White student demonstrators	.15	2	.07	0	.14	2	.17	3

worth mentioning is that the younger the respondent, the more apt he was to believe the police are likely to dislike people like himself.

Region and Identification with Contenders. There are some associations between the region in which respondents lived and their identification with white student demonstrators. Those living in the Plains states and in the South were less identified with such groups. That is, they were more likely to feel that white student demonstrators are "looking for trouble," that "one can't be too careful" in dealing with them, and that life would be apt to take a turn for the worse if such demonstrators achieved their goals. Men living in the mid-Atlantic and New England states were least likely to express such opinions.

Religion and Identification with Contenders. On the whole, associations between the religious preference of respondents and their attitudes toward the three contender groups are small. The *etas* range from .08 to .19, with most of the smaller *etas* occuring in relation to the police identification items. However, there are some consistent trends in the data. Jews, people who indicated no religious preference, and those who classified themselves as atheists or agnostics were most identified with both black protester and white student demonstrator groups. The only exception to this pattern occurs for the question asking how many black protesters are apt to dislike people like the respondent.

The religious groups which most consistently were low in identification with the two dissenter groups are the Fundamentalist Protestants, followed closely by the Protestants who did not specify any particular denomination and the Pietistic Protestants.

The "Reformation Era" Protestants were most likely to identify with the police; no group consistently responded with low scores on the police identification items.

Identification and Attitudes Toward Violence

In the introductory chapter we suggested that the more an individual identified with the victim of an act of violence, the lower the levels of such violence he is likely to justify, and the more he identified with the aggressor in an act of violence, the higher the levels of such violence justified. Now, in any given episode of violence, the role of victim and aggressor is constantly interchanged. In fact, as we pointed out in the preceding chapter, a sequence of events involving a series of violent actions and responses to such actions may be viewed very differently by the participants, or by others observing them. It is possible and even commonplace for each of two human beings involved in such an episode to claim in all sincerity that the other "started it" and to explain their own actions as responsive rather than instigatory.

In the interview, however, it was possible for us to specify the protagonist and the opponent in the action. By "protagonist" we mean the contender group which initiates the violent action, and by "opponent" we mean the contender group which either explicitly or implicitly opposes the protagonist's action. The assumption is made that the protagonist is likely to be viewed as the aggressor, and that the opponent is likely to be viewed as the recipient or victim of the action.

The roles of protagonist and opponent are reversed if the focus is on Violence for Social Control rather than Violence for Social Change. For example, when the respondent is asked to consider how the police should handle campus disturbances, he is being asked what level of violence he would suggest the police use against student demonstrators. This query tends to place the police in the role of protagonist and the students in the role of opponent. On the other hand, when the respondent is asked how much violence is necessary for students to bring about social changes, the question casts the students in the role of protagonists, and, by implication, the police (as agents of the larger society) in the role of the opponent. The same definition and reversal of roles holds true for the questions dealing with the control of ghetto disturbances and the amount of violence necessary to bring about social changes for blacks.

According to our model, persons with above average identification with white student demonstrators should advocate lower levels of Violence for Social Control in the case of campus disturbances.[1] Such persons should also justify above average levels of violence to bring about changes needed by students.[2] Similarly, one would expect that persons who identify more than the average with the police would justify higher levels of Violence for Social Control and lower levels of Violence for Social Change in the student disturbance situation. Analogous expectations obtain in respect to identification with blacks and the use of force in ghetto

---

[1] This variable is known as Violence for Social Control: Students. It is based on the respondents' answers to the question about how the police should handle campus disturbances. The analogous variables for the scenario involving ghetto disturbances and hoodlums are known as Violence for Social Control: Blacks; and Violence for Social Control: Hoods. In each case, the higher the score, the higher the level of force advocated. (For details of index construction see Appendix D.)

[2] This variable is known as Violence for Social Change: Students. It is based on the respondents' answers to how much force is necessary to bring about changes fast enough. The analogous variables dealing with the level of violence needed to bring about change for blacks and change in general are called Violence for Social Change: Blacks; and Violence for Social Change: General. (Details of index construction are given in Appendix D.)

disturbances, and the amount of violence deemed necessary to bring about change for blacks.

As was true for the analysis of the relationship between values and Violence for Social Control, the analysis between this variable and the identification items was conducted on the most consistent data. The consistent subset is most appropriate for testing the model, but the results cannot be generalized to all American men. Those data will be presented in a subsequent section.

Identification and Violence for Social Control

Identification with the Police and Violence for Social Control. According to the model, people who are more identified with the police should justify higher levels of Violence for Social Control than those who are not. This is indeed the case for each of the three situations in which the respondent was asked how much force the police should use, and for the summary measure of social control (Table 8 and Figure 10).

The relationships between the individual identification items and the summary measure of Violence for Social Control are shown in Figure 10. Increased identification with the police is associated with an increase in the level of Violence for Social Control justified. There is nothing *a priori* which necessitates such an association. It is not necessary to justify the use of force because you feel positively about some person or some group. The

Table 8

Identification with the Police in Relation to
Violence for Social Control

(most consistent respondents; N=747)

	Multiple R		Variation Explained	
	R	(Pop. Est.)	R^2	(Pop. Est.)
Violence for Social Control: Hoods	.29	(.27)	8%	(7%)
Violence for Social Control: Students	.24	(.22)	6	(5)
Violence for Social Control: Blacks	.24	(.22)	6	(5)
Violence for Social Control	.32	(.29)	10	(8)

Note: Further analysis shows that the individual identification items behaved in an additive though greatly overlapping fashion. These analytic characteristics of the items allowed us to combine the items in Multiple Classification Analysis (MCA), the results of which are given in this and the following tables.

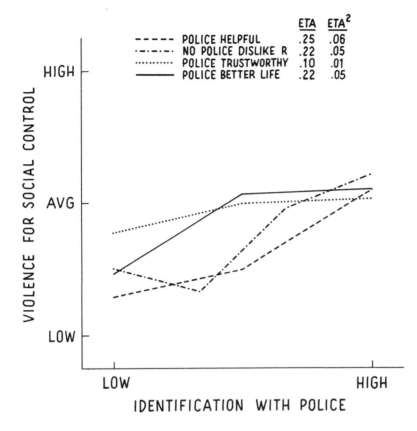

Figure 10. Mean Violence for Social Control in relation to identification with police (most consistent respondents; N=747).

British are said to think well of their police, and the latter are rarely assaulted or killed. Nevertheless, in England the police are not routinely allowed to carry guns. Presumably a lower level of Violence for Social Control is justified in that country than we seem willing to allow here.

Identification with Black Protesters and Violence for Social Control. According to the model, we would expect that people who were more identified with black protesters would be less likely to justify high levels of Violence for Social Control against such groups. This is the case. Table 9 shows the magnitude of the association for each of three scenarios and for Violence for Social Control in general. Identification with black protesters accounts for 13 percent of the variation in attitudes about how

Table 9

Identification with Black Protesters in Relation to
Violence for Social Control

(most consistent respondents; N=747)

	Multiple R		Variation Explained	
	R	(Pop. Est.)	R^2	(Pop. Est.)
Violence for Social Control: Blacks	.36	(.34)	13%	(12%)
Violence for Social Control: Students	.30	(.28)	9	(8)
Violence for Social Control: Hoods	.32	(.29)	10	(9)
Violence for Social Control	.40	(.38)	16	(14)

the police should handle ghetto disturbances, and for a somewhat smaller amount of the variation in attitudes about how the police should handle campus disturbances and those caused by hoodlum gangs.

Figure 11 shows the relationships between each of the four identification items and the summary measure of Violence for Social Control. In each case, the more the individual identified with black protesters, the lower the level of Violence for Social Control justified.

The fact that identification with black protesters is related to the amount of force advocated for controlling campus disturbances and hoodlum gangs is interesting, and permits several interpretations. One might speculate that people have certain sets with which they view marginal or dissenting groups. If a person is apt to sympathize with one out-group, perhaps he is more likely to sympathize with another; conversely, if a person tends to regard one such group with suspicion, he may be likely to regard other groups similarly. The items measuring identification with black protesters are positively correlated with the items measuring identification with white student demonstrators with an average gamma of .3, indicating some tendency for people to answer the items about student demonstrators and black protesters similarly. Whether those who are more inclined to feel positively about student demonstrators and black protesters would also tend to be more sympathetic toward hoodlums we do not know, since no such measurements were made, but it seems plausible that people who feel more positively about the former might be more likely to find extenuating circumstances to explain the behavior of the latter. It also seems reasonable to suppose that people who find the two groups of dissenters untrustworthy and looking for trouble might be even more likely to have such negative feelings about hoodlum gangs.

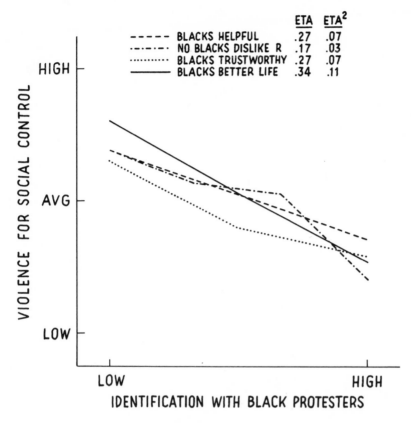

Figure 11. Mean Violence for Social Control in relation to identification with black protesters (most consistent respondents; N=747).

Identification with White Student Demonstrators and Violence for Social Control. The model explaining the justification of attitudes toward violence proposed would lead one to expect that positive attitudes toward white student demonstrators would be associated with decreased justification of Violence for Social Control, particularly in the case of campus disturbances. Such associations do exist, and Table 10 shows their magnitude. As is the case for identification with black protesters, identification with white student demonstrators also shows associations with the level of police force advocated to control disturbances caused by hoodlum gangs and those occurring in the ghettos.

Figure 12 shows the relationships between the summary measure of Violence for Social Control and identification with white student demonstrators. The more identified the respondent was with the students, the lower the level of Violence for Social Control he considered justified.

Table 10

Identification with White Student Demonstrators
in Relation to Violence for Social Control
(most consistent respondents; N=747)

	Multiple R		Variation Explained	
	R	(Pop. Est.)	R^2	(Pop. Est.)
Violence for Social Control: Students	.33	(.31)	11%	(10%)
Violence for Social Control: Blacks	.31	(.29)	10	(9)
Violence for Social Control: Hoods	.36	(.34)	13	(11)
Violence for Social Control	.39	(.37)	16	(14)

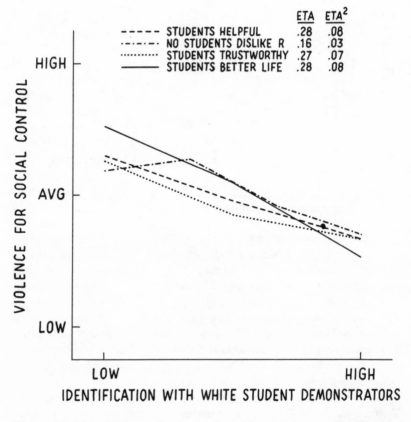

Figure 12. Mean Violence for Social Control in relation to identification with white student demonstrators (most consistent respondents; N=747).

For identification with white student demonstrators as with black protesters, the single item which relates most strongly to the level of Violence for Social Control justified is the question which asks whether the respondent's own life would change for the better or the worse if the contenders achieved their goals. Similarly, the item which was least powerful in its associations with such attitudes was the one concerned directly with affect—that is, whether the respondent felt that the people in question were apt to like or to dislike people like himself. This may be taken to imply that the most important component of identification in determining attitudes toward violence is perceived commonality of goals with the contenders. Whether or not one perceives the contenders as pleasant people has less to do with it. If their goals are seen as bad, the level of violence justified is higher than average; if their goals are perceived as good or desirable, lower levels of police force are justified.

These data also imply that the less highly regarded the members of a particular group, the more likely American men are to justify high levels of police force is to be used against them. More specifically, police violence is something to be used more readily against people whose goals you don't approve of, who can't be trusted, and who are "looking for trouble."

These response patterns contradict some of the propositions on which the government of our nation is based—equality before the law, right of due process, no punishment without such process, and the presumption of innocence until guilt has been proved.

Identification with two contenders and Violence for Social Control. Having shown that each set of identification items is related to the justification of Violence for Social Control as the model predicted, we can explore the relationships between identification and Violence for Social Control when attitudes toward two or more contending groups are considered simultaneously. *A priori,* it seems reasonable to suppose that if identification with the police were combined with identification with one of the contender groups, there should be a stronger association with attitudes toward Violence for Social Control. In other words, if the respondent identifies with the police and also thinks that black protesters are untrustworthy, looking for trouble, hostile, and likely to change his life for the worse, he would be apt to justify higher levels of police force than if he identified postively with black protesters as well as with the police. This is the case, and Table 11 shows the relevant correlations. Similarly, identification with the police and with white student demonstrators when taken together explain a larger part of the variation in attitudes toward Violence for Social Control than either one of these can account for alone. The order of magnitude of the associations in Table 11 is conspiciously larger than that for the single-group data presented in Tables 8-10.

Table 11

Identification with Contender Groups (Paired)
in Relation to Violence for Social Control
(most consistent respondents; N=747)

Predictor Group	Multiple R		Variation Explained	
	R	(Pop. Est.)	actual (R^2)	possible[a]
Black and Police Identification	.47	(.42)	22%	26%
Student and Police Identification	.46	(.42)	21	26
Black and Student Identification	.48	(.44)	23	32

[a] This number represents the sum of the variation explained by two sets of four predictors when each set is used to predict Violence for Social Control independently. It represents the maximum possible variation that the two sets could explain when acting jointly.

Table 11 also shows that when identification with the police and identification with one of the two opponent groups are combined, the amount of variation in attitudes toward Violence for Social Control explained approximates the maximum amount possible, that is, the sum of the variation that each set can account for independently. In other words, there is very little overlap in explanatory power of these two sets of variables. However, this is not the case when identification with the two opponent groups is combined. Here there is substantial overlap between the two sets of items. This is not surprising, since these items tend to be correlated, as was mentioned earlier. Moreover, it seems reasonable to suppose that identification with dissenters, whether they be white and student or black and non-student, might be part of a general set of attitudes toward deviant groups. Such a generalized attitude may relate consistently to opinions about the use of violence against such groups. For example, if the generalized attitude is to regard dissenters as alien and dangerous, it seems likely that one would justify higher levels of violence against such people than if the generalized attitude were one of sympathy with the problems of the underdog. However, it is clear that the overlap between identification with white student demonstrators and black protesters is not complete and that there is a distinct component in identification with white student demonstrators which is not common to identification with black protesters.

Identification with all contenders and Violence for Social Control. The fact that each of the three sets of identification items has some independent explanatory power makes it reasonable to test the combined effect of all twelve identification items on the Index of Violence for Social Control. The results of this analysis are presented in Table 12.

Table 12

All Identification Items Combined in Relation
to Violence for Social Control
(most consistent respondents; N=747)

Predictor Item	eta	eta^2
Students helpful	.28	.08
No students dislike R	.16	.03
Students trustworthy	.27	.07
Students better life	.28	.08
Blacks helpful	.27	.07
No blacks dislike R	.17	.03
Blacks trustworthy	.28	.08
Blacks better life	.34	.12
Police helpful	.25	.06
No police dislike R	.22	.05
Police trustworthy	.10	.01
Police better life	.22	.05

Multiple R = .56 (population estimate = .48)
Variation Explained (R^2) = 27% (population estimate = 23%)

Table 12 shows that the combination of all twelve identification items accounts for a larger part of the variation in attitudes toward Violence for Social Control than any pair of item sets. In all, 27 percent of the variation in such attitudes can be explained by attitudes toward the contender groups. To this extent the model postulating that identification with the contenders modifies attitudes toward violence is substantiated in respect to attitudes toward Violence for Social Control.

A number of questions are raised by this analysis. First, it seems appropriate to ask to what extent race influences the outcome. We have already suggested that membership, or ascribed status, is one of the most important determinants of identification, and we know that there are substantial differences between blacks and whites in respect to the extent to which they identified with the contending groups. Could it be that much of the apparent relation between identification and our criterion measures might be attributable to racial differences?

Second, since the analysis has been conducted only on the most consistent data, one must ask whether the association between identification and Violence for Social Control holds for American men in general. Table 13 answers both these questions.

Table 13

All Identification Items in Relation to Violence for Social Control for All Respondents, Whites and Blacks

	N	Multiple R		Variation Explained	
	N	R	(Pop. Est.)	R^2	(Pop. Est.)
All Respondents	(1,374)	.44	(.40)	20%	(16%)
Whites	(1,046)	.45	(.40)	20	(16)
Blacks	(303)	.53	(.38)	28	(14)

A comparison of Table 13 with Table 12 shows that when the analysis includes all men, rather than just those who were consistent in their responses to questions measuring attitudes toward Violence for Social Control, the relationships remain substantial, although the magnitude of the associations is somewhat smaller. Moreover, the associations between identification with the contenders and attitudes toward Violence for Social Control are not greatly different in white and black populations. The association between identification and the endorsement of Violence for Social Control is not an artifact of race, but a real association between attitudes toward certain groups and the use of violence in situations involving such groups.

Identification and Violence for Social Change

In measuring attitudes about how much property damage and personal injury was necessary to produce social change, the questions in one scenario implied that protest involving such violence would be initiated by students, and in another scenario by blacks. In both cases the students and the blacks are protagonists rather than opponents in the action. In these scenarios the police are implicit opponents in the action rather than explicit protagonists, as they are in the situation measuring attitudes toward violence for maintaining social control. In other words, the scenarios that deal with measuring attitudes toward the use of violence to produce social change reverse the roles of the police and the protesters from the roles these groups occupied in the scenarios that measured attitudes toward Violence for Social Control.

The model predicts that those who are more identified with white student demonstrators or black protesters would be likely to recommend higher levels of Violence for Social Change than those who are less identified with these groups. Similarly, it predicts that those who are more identified with the police would be less likely to recommend high levels of Violence for Social Change than those who were not. Table 14 shows that the predicted associations exist, and the accompanying Figures 13, 14 and 15 show the direction of the association to be as anticipated; the more the respondent identified with black protesters or white student demonstrators and the less he identified with the police, the more likely he was to see high levels of violence as necessary for social change.

Table 14

Identification with Each of the Contender Groups
in Relation to Violence for Social Change
(all respondents; N=1,374)

Contender Group	Multiple R		Variation Explained	
	R	(Pop. Est.)	R^2	(Pop. Est.)
White student demonstrators	.30	(.28)	9%	(8%)
Black protesters	.33	(.32)	11	(10)
Police	.36	(.34)	13	(12)

In respect to attitudes about Violence for Social Change, identification with the police seems to account for a slightly larger proportion of the variation in such attitudes than can be accounted for by either of the other contender groups, whereas identification with the police accounted for the smallest part of the variation in attitudes toward Violence for Social Control. This finding suggests that it may be attitudes toward the opponents (or victims) of a violent action which are most important in determining the level of violence justified. Further data would be required before such speculation could be accepted, but if this were the case, it might be a hopeful sign, since education appears to be associated with a decrease in negative attitudes toward out-group members, as we have already seen.

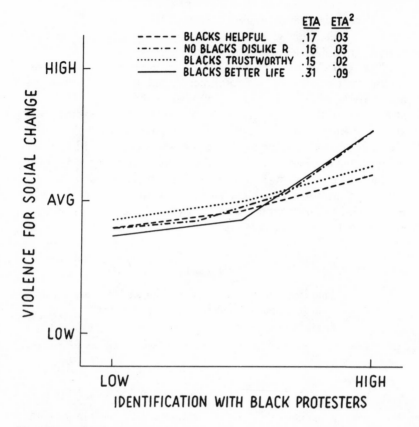

Figure 13. Mean Violence for Social Change in relation to identification with black protesters (all respondents; N=1,374).

Identification with two contenders and Violence for Social Change. Table 15 shows that for attitudes toward Violence for Social Change, as for attitudes toward Violence for Social Control, a larger part of the variation can be explained when pairs of the contender groups are combined in the analysis. Again, when these figures are examined in combination, there appears to be more overlap in explanatory power between identification with white student demonstrators and black protesters than is the case when either of these two groups is combined with the police in an analysis.

Identification with all contenders and Violence for Social Change. Table 16 shows that the combined association of all twelve identification items with attitudes toward Violence for Social Change provides only a small gain in explanatory power over the paired data shown in Table 15.

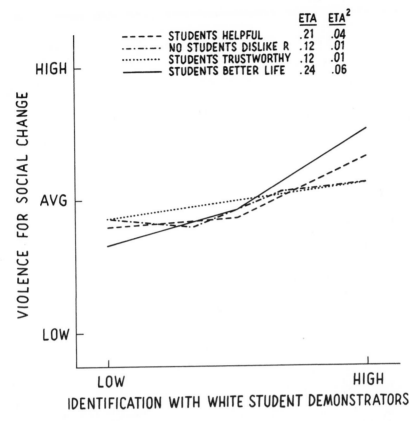

Figure 14. Mean Violence for Social Change in relation to identification with white student demonstrators (all respondents; N=1,374).

Table 15

Identification with Contender Groups (Paired)
in Relation to Violence for Social Change
(all respondents; N=1,374)

Predictor Group	Multiple R		Variation Explained	
	R	(Pop. Est.)	actual (R^2)	possible
Black and Police Identification	.45	(.42)	20%	24%
Student and Police Identification	.42	(.40)	18	22
Black and Student Identification	.39	(.36)	15	20

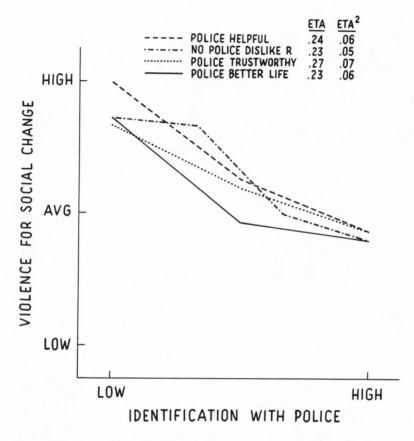

Figure 15. Mean Violence for Social Change in relation to identification with police (all respondents; N=1,374).

Identification, Definitions and Values

Identification with Contenders and What Acts Are Called Violence

Because of the relationship between the identification items and attitudes toward violence, it seems reasonable to ask how these items relate to some of the variables previously shown to be important determinants of attitudes toward violence. For example, we found a substantial relationship between the respondent's definition of certain acts of protest as violence and his attitudes toward white student demonstrators and black protesters. The more negatively inclined the respondent was toward these two groups, the more likely he was to call sit-ins, draft card burning, and "student protest" violence. Altogether, attitudes toward the

Table 16

All Identification Items (Combined) in Relation to
Violence for Social Change
(all respondents; N=1,374)

Predictor Items	eta	eta^2
Students helpful	.21	.04
No students dislike R	.12	.01
Students trustworthy	.12	.01
Students better life	.25	.06
Blacks helpful	.17	.03
No blacks dislike R	.16	.03
Blacks trustworthy	.16	.03
Blacks better life	.31	.09
Police helpful	.24	.06
No police dislike R	.23	.05
Police trustworthy	.27	.07
Police better life	.23	.06

Multiple R = .47 (population estimate = .44)
Variation Explained (R^2) = 22% (population estimate = 19%)

contenders can explain 22 percent of the variation in whether or not the respondent called protest activities violence and 26 percent of the variation in whether or not he called police acts such as "shooting looters," "beating students" and "frisking people" violence (Table 17).

Table 17

All Identification Items in Relation to Whether or Not
Protest and Police Acts Are Labeled Violence
(all respondents; N=1,374)

	Multiple R		Variation Explained	
	R	(Pop. Est.)	R^2	(Pop. Est.)
Is Protest Violence?	.47	(.43)	22%	(19%)
Are Police Acts Violence?	.51	(.48)	26	(23)

It is not possible to say from these data whether the respondent's attitude toward the dissident groups and police determined whether or not he called protest and police acts violence, or whether his opinion about such actions tended to determine his attitudes toward dissidents and the police. Both statements, or neither, may be true. It is clear that respondents' use of language is related to their opinions about participants in social action, whatever the causal relations.

Identification with Contenders and Values

It also seems reasonable to ask what sorts of relationships exist between a person's values and how he identifies with the contenders in campus disturbances and ghetto uprisings. One might think, for example, that a person who valued human dignity, equality, and freedom above respect for law, property and financial security, might be sympathetic toward black protesters and white student demonstrators.

Because the relationships between identification items and values differed substantially for blacks and whites, the analysis pertinent to this issue was conducted separately for the two races. Moreover, of the five values studied, only a few were related to identification. For whites, attitudes toward the contenders were related to the Retributive Justice and the Humanism Indices. For blacks, identification with the contenders related to Kindness and the Property/Person Priority Indices.

Table 18 shows the associations for white respondents between identification with the two groups of dissidents and the Retributive Justice Index. Almost all the items account for part of the variation in attitudes toward Retributive Justice. Moreover, the nature of the association is what one might have expected; the more retributive the individual, the less likely he was to identify positively with the black protester and white student demonstrator groups. As the reader may recall, men who were high on retributiveness were more likely to define acts of protest as violence, and the police actions inquired about as not violence.

When one examines these bits of information together, an interesting picture begins to emerge. The individual white respondent who is high on Retributive Justice is apparently more likely to regard student demonstrators and black protesters as untrustworthy, looking for trouble, and likely to change his life for the worse. In addition, he is more likely to define their behaviors as violence (so that he is more likely to find something to be retributive about). Moreover, he is less likely to consider police actions such as "shooting looters" or "beating students" to be violence, a fact that may make it easier for him to rationalize the use of such methods in the service of his retributiveness.

Table 19 shows the associations for white respondents between the

Table 18

Identification with Black and Student Contenders
in Relation to the Retributive Justice Index
(white respondents; N=1,046)

Predictor Item	eta	eta^2
Students helpful	.20	.04
No students dislike R	.07	.01
Students trustworthy	.23	.05
Students better life	.24	.06
Blacks helpful	.29	.09
No blacks dislike R	.13	.02
Blacks trustworthy	.26	.07
Blacks better life	.26	.07

Multiple R = .40   (population estimate = .36)
Variation Explained (R^2) = 16%   (population estimate = 13%)

Table 19

Identification with Black and Student Contenders
in Relation to the Humanism Index
(white respondents; N=1,046)

Predictor Item	eta	eta^2
Students helpful	.22	.05
No students dislike R	.11	.01
Students trustworthy	.22	.05
Students better life	.23	.05
Blacks helpful	.26	.07
No blacks dislike R	.12	.02
Blacks trustworthy	.23	.05
Blacks better life	.26	.07

Multiple R = .40   (population estimate = .36)
Variation Explained (R^2) = 16%   (population estimate = 13%)

Humanism Index and identification with the student demonstrator and
black protester groups. The more humanistically inclined the individual,
the more likely he was to identify positively with the black protesters and
white student demonstrators. The only items which did not show this
relationship were those inquiring whether the respondent thought the

contender hostile. Altogether, identification with the dissident groups accounts for 16 percent of the variation in the attitudes of white respondents measured by the Humanism Index.

For black men, the identification items were most closely associated with the Kindness Index. Identification with black protesters and police served as the best predictors of this value. Altogether, identification with these two groups of contenders accounts for 21 percent of the variation in the kindness value among blacks (Table 20).

Table 20

Identification with Black Protesters and
Police in Relation to the Kindness Index
(black respondents; N=303)

Predictor Item	eta	eta^2
Police helpful	.25	.06
No police dislike R	.32	.10
Police trustworthy	.15	.02
Police better life	.26	.07
Blacks helpful	.17	.03
No blacks dislike R	.07	.00
Blacks trustworthy	.22	.05
Blacks better life	.12	.02

Multiple R = .46 (population estimate = .34)
Variation Explained (R^2) = 21% (population estimate = 12%)

The nature of the relationship between kindness and identification with the two contender groups can be stated as follows: the more the individual black respondent believed in kindness, the more he identified with the police and the less he identified with black protesters. What can this mean? One interpretation would argue that kindness and forgiveness have implied for the black the adoption of a passive life style and the acceptance of abuse with meekness. One can hardly have more explicit instruction in this regard than that conveyed by the statement included in the Kindness Index: "When a person harms you, you should turn the other cheek and forgive him." The adoption of this value by blacks during slavery and the period thereafter has been criticized by militants as facilitating their continued exploitation. The development of militancy among some blacks and an increasing emphasis on the right of self-determination and equal opportunity have brought with them a rejection of the passive life style. When one considers this background it is not surprising that blacks who scored high on a value index which embodies a passive concept of kindness should be more identified with the police and less identified with black protesters than their fellows.

There is an additional piece of information which tends to substantiate the notion that blacks scoring high on Kindness are conservatively oriented. Blacks who were relatively more oriented to property than to persons were also more identified with the police and less willing to countenance violence for social change than their more person-oriented fellows. All this is tenuous, but it is saddening to think that the kindness value may for some blacks be experienced as inconsistent with their efforts to attain equal opportunity.

Identification with Contenders and Police/Court Power

One might expect the respondent's identification with contenders to be related to his notions about the police need and the courts. Respondents were asked a series of questions about how the courts should deal with agitators and criminals, and how much power was needed by the police:

> *People who make speeches stirring people up should be put in prison before they cause serious trouble.*
>
> *Police are getting so much power the average citizen has to worry.*
>
> *Courts nowadays are much too easy on criminals.*
>
> *Recent Supreme Court decisions have made it more difficult to punish criminals.*
>
> *Police nowadays should have more power (authority) to enforce the law adequately.*

How the respondents answered such questions can be seen in Table 21.

Fifty percent of American men thought that agitators should be imprisoned before they caused any trouble, 79 percent thought the courts too easy on criminals, 84 percent felt that recent Supreme Court decisions had made it more difficult to punish criminals, and 75 percent felt the police needed more power in order to be able to enforce the law adequately. Altogether, one might take the responses of American men to these items to convey a rather punitive message. It was surprising to us to find so many Americans willing to imprison agitators *before* they caused trouble. The administrative endorsement and the passage of bills such as the preventive-detention section of the Omnibus Crime Acts suggest that

Table 21

Percentage Responses to Questions about How the Courts Should Deal
with Criminals and How Much Power Is Needed by the Police

(all respondents; N=1,374)

	Agree a Great Deal	Agree Some-what	Dis-agree Some-what	Dis-agree a Great Deal	Total
People who make speeches stirring people up should be put in prison before they cause serious trouble.	24%	26%	32%	18%	100%
Police are getting so much power the average citizen has to worry.	6	11	32	51	100
Courts nowadays are much too easy on criminals.	45	34	15	6	100
Recent Supreme Court decisions have made it more difficult to punish criminals.	51	33	11	5	100
Police nowadays should have more power to enforce the law adequately.	44	31	17	8	100

the executive and legislative branches of government share such attitudes.

To analyze the relationships of such attitudes as these to the indices of violence and the identification with contending groups, we combined the last three items of Table 21 into an index, the Police/Court Power Index. (The first two questions were not sufficiently stable in their relationships to the other items to justify their inclusion.) The higher the score on the Index, the more the respondent agreed that the police needed more power and the courts were too easy on criminals. (For details of index construction see Appendix C.)

Figures 16 and 17 show how the Police/Court Power Index relates to Violence for Social Control and Violence for Social Change. It can be seen that such attitudes are powerful predictors of Violence for Social Control. The more the individual believed that the police should have more power and that the courts are too easy on criminals, the higher the levels of

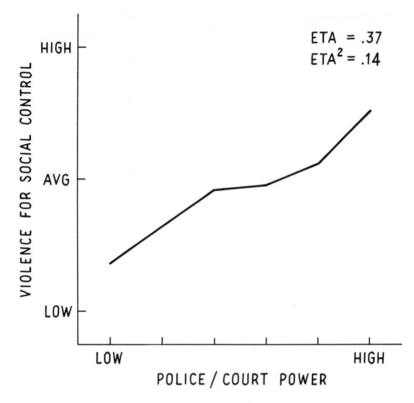

ETA = .37
ETA^2 = .14

Figure 16. Mean Violence for Social Control in relation to Police/Court Power (all respondents; N=1,374).

police force he was apt to advocate in the control of disturbances. As one might have expected, the opposite relationship holds in respect to Violence for Social Change; the higher the individual scored on Police/ Court Power, the less likely he was to score high on Violence for Social Change.

Individuals who had high scores on the Police/Court Power Index also were strongly identified with the police and were inclined to view white student demonstrators and black protesters rather negatively (Table 22). Taken altogether, the respondent identification with the contender groups accounts for 26 percent of the variation in the attitudes measured by the Police/Court Power Index. The more the respondent identified with the two dissident groups, the less likely he was to score high on

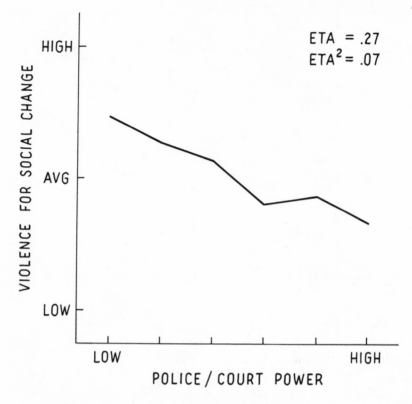

Figure 17. Mean Violence for Social Change in relation to Police/Court Power (all respondents; N=1,374).

Police/Court Power. Conversely, the more he identified with the police, the more likely he was to recommend the police have more power and the courts be less lenient.

Summary

The concept of identification refers to an individual's perception of himself as related to other people or groups. A person may regard himself as being a member of a group, as sharing some of its goals, or as having some other likeness with members of the group. The more an individual relates himself to a group in these ways, the more he is identified with it. One can also think in terms of negative identification, in which a person sees himself as entirely dissimilar or having goals antithetical to those of the person or group in question.

Table 22

All Identification Items in Relation to
the Police/Court Power Index

(all respondents; N=1,374)

Predictor Item	eta	eta^2
Students helpful	.25	.06
No students dislike R	.13	.02
Students trustworthy	.24	.06
Students better life	.28	.08
Blacks helpful	.27	.07
No blacks dislike R	.12	.02
Blacks trustworthy	.28	.08
Blacks better life	.30	.09
Police helpful	.21	.04
No police dislike R	.26	.07
Police trustworthy	.17	.03
Police better life	.30	.09

Multiple R $= .51$ (population estimate $= .48$)
Variation Explained $(R^2) = 26\%$ (population estimate $= 23\%$)

One of the important determinants of attitudes toward violence is the extent to which the individual identifies with the individuals or groups that are party to that violence. The more the contenders in violence are seen as basically helpful, trustworthy and likely to change life for the better, the more likely the individual is to justify violence used by them, and the less likely he is to justify violence directed against them. This is true both in respect to violence for social control and in respect to violence for social change.

In the scenarios of violence which were presented to the respondent, three contending groups appear: white student demonstrators, black protesters, and the police. The extent to which the individual identifies with each of these groups is related not only to his attitudes toward violence, but also the acts he chose to regard as violence. The more the individual identified with the black and student dissidents, the less likely he was to regard student protest, sit-ins or draft card burning as "violence." The more the individual identified with police, the less likely he was to view police actions such as beating students or shooting looters as violence.

As one might have expected, values also relate to identification with these groups. The more a person believes in retributive justice, the more likely he is to hold negative opinions about student and black protesters.

The more humanistically inclined, the more likely he is to identify with black and student protesters.

How the individual identified with black protesters, white student demonstrators and the police reflected to some extent his demographic characteristics. Of these, race and education are the most important. Black men tended to be more identified with the dissident groups than were whites, and less identified with the police. The well educated were also more likely to identify with the dissidents, although education did not seem to influence attitudes toward the police.

Chapter 7

PACIFISTS, ANARCHISTS, VIGILANTES, AND WARRIORS

Americans differ widely in their feelings about violence and the purposes for which it is appropriate. Some people are prepared to damage property, inflict injury, or kill to achieve what they think are needed changes. Others feel that those who use such tactics should be forcibly constrained. While pacifists deplore the use of any violence, others seem to revel in the fray, whatever the setting.

Our survey of American men was designed to measure people's views about the use of violence to achieve social control and social change. From the survey, it is possible to identify respondents who adhered to extreme ideological positions about the use of violence. The purpose of this chapter is to describe how these contrasting types differed in background characteristics and psychological makeup.

The Violence Typology

Four Contrasting Ideological Positions

Previous chapters have dealt with two distinct kinds of violence: that used by the police to achieve social control, and that used to produce social change. People's views about using violence for one of these purposes were only weakly related to their views about using violence for the other (gamma = -.2). Thus, it becomes meaningful to consider the various possible *combinations* of views about the appropriate uses for violence. Four extreme positions are logically possible:

1. A person might believe that violent means should never be used to achieve either social control or social change.

2. Alternatively, one might justify violence when used for producing social change, but not for achieving control.

179

3. Or conversely, one might justify forceful police methods, including use of clubs and guns to maintain social control, but feel violence should not be used to bring about social change.

4. Finally, some people may support violence for both social control and social change.

The first position—to use no violence for whatever purpose—can be identified as that of the "pacifist."

The second position, which would use violence only to bring about social changes, is that of the anarchist, terrorist, or political extremist. (Hereafter "anarchist" will be used to refer to adherents of this position.)

Naming the third position presents a problem. There seems to be no word in English which refers to the use of violence for maintaining social control while at the same time proscribing its use for social change. This is part of the fascist ideology, but "fascism" includes heavy emphasis on dictatorship, which we wish to avoid. "Hawk" and "super-patriot" are terms sometimes associated with this position, but these names tend to be restricted to discussions of war. "Vigilante" refers to a person who uses violence to achieve social control without the legitimate authority to do so. (But in Spanish, the original source of the English word, *vigilante* means watchman or guard.) For lack of a better term, we shall use "vigilante" to refer to people who accept violence when used for social control by the police, but reject it when used for social change. We recognize, however, that this use of the term differs somewhat from the dictionary definition.

Finally, we shall refer to the fourth position, which advocates using violence to produce both social control and social change, as that of the "warrior."

Classification of Respondents

As described in Appendix D, each person responding to the questionnaire was assigned a score on a summary measure of Violence for Social Control and a score representing a summary of their feelings about the use of violent means to achieve social change. Based on these two scores, each respondent could be classified in one of the nine categories depicted in Figure 1.[1]

---

[1] A small percentage of respondents (4 percent) could not be so assigned because they had failed to supply data needed to determine their views on the use of violence for social control and/or social change.

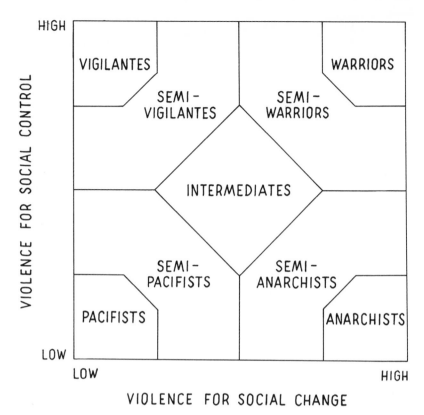

Figure 1. Schematic representation of nine "types" of respondents based on their views about the use of violence.

Four of the categories correspond to the four extreme or "pure" ideological types described previously: pacifists, anarchists, vigilantes, and warriors. Four other categories also correspond in an approximate and less extreme way to these four positions. These each carry the prefix "semi." The final category refers to an "intermediate" situation, and is composed of people who—compared to others in the sample—held intermediate views with respect to violence used for social control and social change.

Given the nature of the actual data, the coding scheme by which respondents were assigned to one of the categories only approximated the symmetry of Figure 1. Figure 2 shows the assignment procedure actually used. The breaks between various groups were determined on the basis of two considerations: 1) the actual answer patterns given by respondents to the original items from which the violence values were constructed, and 2) the frequencies with which the various combinations of answers

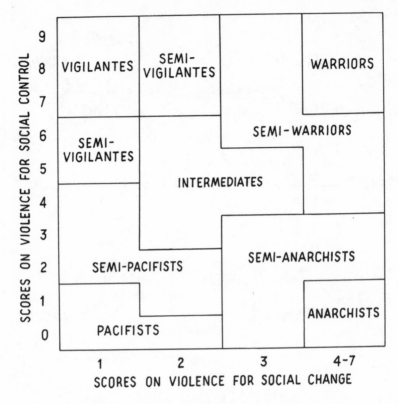

Figure 2. Assignment scheme for classifying respondents into violence "types."

occurred in the data. Figure 2 shows, for example, that a respondent falling in category #0 on Violence for Social Control and category #1 on Violence for Social Change would be classified as a pacifist.

Since the two summary indices used for coding respondents into these categories were themselves based on a dozen different questions in the interview, it is not a simple matter to show all possible patterns of answers which could result in a person being classified as a pacifist, warrior, anarchist, or vigilante. Nevertheless, for each of the categories shown in Figures 1 and 2 it is possible to determine the more common answer patterns. Figures 3 and 4 indicate these for five of the violence types. Typical answers to the eight items involving black protesters are shown in Figure 3 and to the eight items involving white student demonstrators in Figure 4.

Violence Type	How Should the Police Handle Big City Riots Involving Blacks?				How Much Violence Is Necessary for the Blacks to Bring About Change?			
	Make Arrests Without Clubs or Guns	Use Clubs	Shoot But Not to Kill	Shoot to Kill	Some People Get Hurt	Some Property Damage	Much Property Damage	Some People Get Killed
Pacifists	Almost Always	Hardly Ever	Never	Never	Disagree Strongly	Disagree Strongly	Disagree Strongly	Disagree Strongly
Anarchists	Almo t Always	Sometimes to Hardly Ever	Never to Hardly Ever	Never	Agree	Agree	Disagree Somewhat	Agree Somewhat to Disagree Somewhat
Vigilantes	Sometimes	Sometimes	Sometimes	Sometimes	Disagree Strongly	Disagree Strongly	Disagree Strongly	Disagree Strongly
Warriors	Sometimes to Hardly Ever	Sometimes	Sometimes	Sometimes	Agree Somewhat	Agree	Agree Somewhat to Disagree Somewhat	Agree Strongly to Disagree Strongly
Intermediates	Sometimes	Sometimes	Sometimes	Never to Sometimes	Disagree	Disagree	Disagree Strongly	Disagree Strongly

Figure 3. Common answer patterns relevant to black protesters from respondents classified as designated violence types.

Violence Type	How Should Police Handle Student Disturbances Involving a Lot of Property Damage?				How Much Violence Is Necessary for the Students to Bring About Change?			
	Make Arrests Without Clubs or Guns	Use Clubs	Shoot But Not to Kill	Shoot to Kill	Some People Get Hurt	Some Property Damage	Much Property Damage	Some People Get Killed
Pacifists	Almost Always	Never to Sometimes	Never	Never	Disagree Strongly	Disagree Strongly	Disagree Strongly	Disagree Strongly
Anarchists	Almost Always	Never to Sometimes	Never	Never	Agree Somewhat	Agree Somewhat	Agree Somewhat to Disagree Somewhat	Agree Somewhat to Never
Vigilantes	Sometimes	Sometimes	Sometimes	Sometimes	Disagree Strongly	Disagree Strongly	Disagree Strongly	Disagree Strongly
Warriors	Sometimes	Sometimes	Sometimes to Almost Always	Sometimes to Never	Agree Somewhat	Agree Somewhat to Disagree Somewhat	Agree Strongly to Disagree Somewhat	Agree Strongly to Disagree Somewhat
Intermediates	Sometimes	Sometimes	Never to Almost Always	Never to Hardly Ever	Disagree	Disagree	Disagree Strongly	Disagree Strongly

Figure 4. Common answer patterns relevant to white student demonstrators from respondents classified as designated violence types.

Figures 3 and 4 are almost identical, indicating that the particular referent (black protester or white student demonstrator) made little difference with respect to how people in a given category felt about using violence for social control or change.

Prevalence of Violence Types

It is of considerable interest to know how American men were distributed across the nine violence types. It should be stressed, however, that the proportion of people falling into each category is arbitrarily determined by the way the particular boundaries between categories were drawn (as shown in Figure 2) and does not indicate how many avowed pacifists, for example, exist in the United States. Shifting the boundaries would shift the percentage figures. The present data, however, will take on added significance when it becomes possible to compare them with comparably derived figures at some future date. Then it will be possible to say whether the United States is moving toward greater espousal of pacifism, anarchism, or other views.

Figure 5 shows the percentage of American males (aged 16-64) falling into each category in 1969. Among the pure types, the vigilantes were most common (13 percent). These were people who, as shown in Figures 3 and 4, expressed the belief that the police should "sometimes" make arrests without using clubs or guns and should also shoot to kill "sometimes," while "strongly disagreeing" that any injury to persons or property was necessary to bring about social change. However, 3 percent of the respondents expressed a diametrically opposite view about appropriate uses for violence. Typically, such respondents, labelled anarchists, said the police should "never" shoot, either to maim or kill, and should "almost always" make arrests using neither clubs nor guns; they also felt that some damage to people and property—maybe even much damage—would be necessary to bring about desired social change.

Six percent of American men fell in the pacifist category, believing little or no violence was ever appropriate, while 4 percent were identified as warriors. Altogether, more than a quarter of American men were classified as belonging to one of these pure types.

While percentages such as 4, 6, and 13 sound small, a small percentage can represent a very significant number of people. Four percent of our sample represents approximately two million men. Hence our scheme would classify some two million men as anarchists, another two million as warriors, about three million as pacifists, and roughly six million as vigilantes. These are substantial numbers of people with opposing views about when it is appropriate or necessary to inflict physical damage on persons and property.

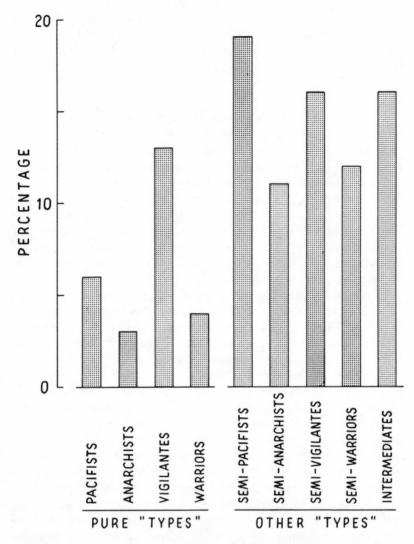

Figure 5. Percentage of respondents classified as designated violence "types" (all respondents; N=1,374).

Some Special Groups

It is of interest to observe how some of the special groups discussed in previous chapters were classified by this typology. The results support the validity of the classification scheme. Table 1 shows how six subgroups selected from respondents in the national sample and two groups of

Table 1

Percentage of Designated Groups Classified as "Pure" Types

Group	N	Pacifist	Anarchist	Vigilante	Warrior
			Violence Type		
All respondents	(1,374)	6%	3%	13%	4%
Students involved in confrontations with police	(29)	15	59	0	0
College students	(63)	3	9	11	3
Men with at least some college education	(374)	7	5	12	2
Blacks	(303)	8	10	2	9
Whites who feared discrimination by blacks	(187)	2	0	20	4
White union members	(279)	3	1	18	4
High scorers on Police/ Court Power Index	(330)	3	0	29	3
Prisoners in a federal prison	(52)	6	8	0	4

supplementary respondents compared to American men in general in terms of the violence typology.

More than half (59 percent) of a group of college students who were involved in a confrontation with police over "liberation" of a city street fell in the anarchist type, according to the answers they provided to our interview. This is very much higher than the 3 percent of American men in general who gave such answers. This group of students also included a higher proportion of pacifists, (15 percent) and a much lower proportion of vigilantes (zero percent) than the population at large.

The students involved in confrontation with the police, of course, are an unusual group, and Table 1 provides information on two other high-education groups which are more representative. College students in our national sample included 9 percent classified as anarchists and 3 percent as pacifists. While closer to figures for the general population than the students involved in confrontation with the police, this represents more than double the proportion of anarchists and half the proportion of pacifists that occurred in the general population. If one considers *all* men who had at least some college education (including the college students but mainly men well past student age), one finds a distribution of violence types rather similar to that of the general population.

Table 1 shows that blacks in the national sample include higher proportions of people classified as anarchists and warriors, and a lower proportion of vigilantes than the population at large.

Conversely, among whites in the national sample who expressed fears of being discriminated against by blacks there is a lower proportion of anarchists and a higher proportion of vigilantes. This "reverse discrimination" group also was less likely to include pacifists than the general population. Two other groups showed the same pattern: white union members and respondents who scored high on the Police/Court Power Index—indicating a feeling that police and/or the courts should have more power.

Finally, a representative sample of the prisoners in the federal prison at Milan, Michigan, proved to include a higher proportion of anarchists and a lower proportion of vigilantes than did American men in general.

Background and Psychological Characteristics of Pacifists, Anarchists, Vigilantes, and Warriors

In this section, the characteristics of people who were classified in each of the four extreme types are described, contrasted, and compared to American men (aged 16-64) in general. The analytic strategy was to see how people of the four violence types differed in personal background (age, education, race, etc.), and in certain psychological characteristics. Subsequently we consider the extent to which the psychological characteristics might account for the observed differences in background characteristics, and (conversely) the extent to which the background factors might account for the relationships with the psychological factors.

Personal History Characteristics

Long before a person becomes an adult, he has a variety of experiences which may shape his views about appropriate uses for violence. Table 2 examines six such factors—his age, his parents' country of birth, his race, where he grew up, how much formal education he obtained, and his military service.

A general observation, supported by the results shown in Table 2, is that none of the four types—pacifists, anarchists, vigilantes, and warriors—comes from a single background. Each violence type included people of all ages, all education levels, all regions of the country, and the like. (The nearest exception occurred for the vigilantes, of whom 98 percent were white—compared to 86 percent of American men in general.) There are, nevertheless, some interesting differences in backgrounds among the four violence types.

Table 2

Violence Types in Relation to Six Background Characteristics

	All Respondents (N=1,374)	Violence Type			
		Pacifists (N=77)	Anarchists (N=54)	Vigilantes (N=168)	Warriors (N=60)
Age					
16-19 years	14	19	13	3	19
20-29 years	20	17	40	17	20
30-49 years	41	34	35	53	37
50-64 years	25	30	12	27	24
	100%	100%	100%	100%	100%
Parental background					
Both parents born in USA	83%	77%	90%	89%	91%
Race					
White	86%	83%	60%	98%	73%
Childhood region					
Mid-Atlantic states[a]	19	33	16	15	4
Southern states[b]	33	19	40	41	57
All other	48	48	44	44	39
	100%	100%	100%	100%	100%
Education					
Less than high school graduate	40	36	43	41	50
High school graduate	31	29	13	32	34
Some college or more	29	35	44	27	16
	100%	100%	100%	100%	100%
Military service					
In service, combat duty	21	13	13	23	18
In service, no combat duty	27	34	18	39	31
Never in service	52	53	69	38	51
	100%	100%	100%	100%	100%

[a] Includes: Delaware, New Jersey, New York, Pennsylvania, West Virginia.

[b] Includes: Alabama, Arkansas, Florida, Georgia, Louisiana, Mississippi, North Carolina, South Carolina, Texas, Virginia, Kentucky, Maryland, Oklahoma, Tennessee, Washington D.C.

Age. With respect to age, pacifists closely matched the overall distribution of American men. Anarchists, however, tended to be younger than average (with 40 percent of all anarchists between 20 and 29 years of age). Among vigilantes, the teens and 20's were under-represented while people in their 30's and 40's were over-represented. Warriors, like pacifists, were not distinctly different from the general population.

Any attempt to interpret the observed age differences between anarchists and vigilantes raises at least two possibilities. One line of reasoning is that younger people, especially those in their 20's, have established less stake in the existing society. In contrast, those in their thirties and forties may be more committed to the status quo because of family, business, and civic activities, and hence are more likely to appear as vigilantes. This approach would predict that the typical maturational trend involves a shift toward conservatism, though most individuals would not change all the way from one extreme to the other.

A competing explanation would be that the experiences of one generation differ from those of another, and that respondents who were in their 20's will continue to remain more "anarchistic" than those somewhat older. In support of this view, one might recall that World War II and the Korean conflict are within the direct memory of respondents in their 30's and 40's, but largely absent from the experience of respondents in their teens and 20's. They are the generation of the war in Vietnam.

Unfortunately, the competing hypotheses of maturation versus differential cohort experiences cannot be tested with the present data. We can only speculate as to where the boundary lies between the effects of individual and national history.

Parental Background. Turning next to parental background, we find (Table 2) that pacifists were slightly less likely to have had both parents born in the United States than was typical, while anarchists, vigilantes, and warriors were all more likely to have been born into native American families.

Race. There were substantial racial differences between the groups. Vigilantes included a substantially higher proportion of whites than the general population, while whites were sharply under-represented (though still a majority) among anarchists and warriors. Pacifists were very similar to the general population in respect to race.

Region. Table 2 also shows differences associated with the region in which a person grew up. (The questionnaire had asked "In what state did you live longest during the first ten years of your life?") Pacifists were almost twice as likely to have grown up in the mid-Atlantic states as the population at large (33 percent as compared to 19 percent), while anarchists, vigilantes, and warriors all included over-representations of men who had grown up in the South.[2] The data for warriors are particularly striking, with more than half (57 percent) of this group having grown up in the South. (Although Table 2 combines other regions of the country into a single "all other" category, five other geographic regions were separately examined and no sharp contrast among the violence types was found.)

If where a person grew up makes a difference, is there also a difference according to where he lived at the time he was interviewed? The answer is yes: at the time we interviewed them, pacifists included a disproportionate number of people living in mid-Atlantic states; vigilantes, anarchists, and warriors all had disproportionate numbers of southerners. The differences, however, were less sharp than those in Table 2, and we suspect the region in which respondents lived during their formative years had more to do with their psychological development and attitudes about the use of violence than where they happened to be when interviewed.

The fact that men reared in the South were more likely to be positively oriented toward violence of both types is interesting in view of the unique traditions of this region of the country. It has often been pointed out that the South has its own violent history; moreover, this region of the country suffers from higher rates of violence than other sections (Hackney 1969, p. 387). If violent behavior is based on pro-violent attitudes such as those we have measured, one would expect to find a higher proportion of Southerners to hold such attitudes, as, indeed, they appear to do.

Education. Data for education indicate that pacifists tended to have completed more schooling than average and warriors less. It is not true, however, that pacifism was an ideology of the educational elite. Table 2 shows that a majority of pacifists (64 percent) had no college experience. Among the warriors, however, a full 50 percent had not even completed high school, and only 16 percent had any college experience. Anarchists were split into two groups in terms of education—44 percent had some college experience (a higher proportion than any other violence type), but almost as many (43 percent) had not completed high school. The vigilantes, educationally, closely matched the general population.

Military Experience. Last in Table 2 comes the matter of military experience. One of the places many young men come into contact with certain forms of violence is through military service. A simple series of questions inquired whether a respondent had had military service, and if

---

[2] During analysis the states of the traditional South were kept separate from the bordering states of Maryland, Kentucky, Tennessee, Oklahoma and the District of Columbia. Since results for both groups were similar, they were combined in Table 2.

so, whether he had been assigned to combat duty.[3] Pacifists were no less likely to have been in the service than American men in general, though were less likely to have been assigned combat duty. Anarchists were *less* likely to have had military experience than other men, while vigilantes were both *more* likely to have had service and more likely to have had combat duty. The military experience of warriors was typical of that of the population in general.

Comments and Summary. Of course, the various background factors just described are not independent of each other. For example, the finding that anarchists were relatively low in the proportion with military service is undoubtedly related to the finding that among this group was a disproportionate number of men in their 20's. This age group has not been extensively called upon to serve in a major war. Similarly, the racial differences between the violence types are undoubtedly related to the educational and regional differences. Such overlapping effects receive detailed consideration later in this chapter.

In summary, each violence type had some members from each age group, each education level, each region of the country, each race, both native and foreign parents, and various levels of military experience. Compared to American men as a whole, pacifists tended to have more education, more foreign parental background, less experience with combat duty, and were more likely than average to have grown up in a mid-Atlantic state. Anarchists included over-representations of men in their 20's, of southerners, of non-whites, of people with native-born parents, of men with college experience (but also of men who had not completed high school), and were less likely than average to have been in the military service. Like the anarchists, vigilantes included an over-representation of men from native American families and of men who had grown up in the South. Unlike the anarchists, however, they also included more than proportionate numbers of whites, men in their middle years and men with military service (with and without combat duty). Warriors differed from the general population by their relatively low educations, the predominance of southern backgrounds, a higher-than-average proportion of non-whites, and of native-born parents.

Psychological Characteristics

Finding that people's attitudes about the appropriate uses for

---

[3] Of course, not all people assigned to combat duty actually participated in active combat. The questionnaire also permitted separation of those with combat duty into those with and without actual combat experience. (Most had had such experience.) This contrast, however, proved not to be fruitful in the present analysis.

violence were related to several demographic and experiential variables, as shown in Table 2, does not—by itself—*account* for the relationships. Aspects from a person's past must be somehow represented in his present life before there can be a satisfactory psychological explanation for a set of attitudes. It becomes reasonable to ask, then, about the psychological makeup of pacifists, anarchists, vigilantes, and warriors. We have done so in terms of basic value orientations, identification with certain groups, definitions of what constitutes violence, and reactions to the notion of violence in general.

Values. Figure 6 shows how the four extreme violence types differed from the general population (and each other) with respect to five basic values. Pacifists tended to score lower than average on two of the value indices. They were less likely than the general population to believe in retributive justice and in the right of a man to kill another in self-defense. They scored about average in the emphasis they gave to the humanistic concerns about equality-freedom-human dignity as compared to property-law-financial security, and they also closely matched the American average on the Property/Person Priority Index. Pacifists scored just slightly higher than average with respect to the importance of kindness, forgiveness, and helpfulness.

Like the pacifists, anarchists tended to give lower than average endorsement to Retributive Justice and Self-Defense. Anarchists tended to give more humanistic and more person-oriented responses than men in general.

Vigilantes differed from the general population, and stood in marked contrast with the pacifists and anarchists on three values. They gave greater than average endorsement to Retributive Justice and Self-Defense, and lower than average endorsement to Humanism. They were close to the average with respect to the valuation of people relative to property and the importance of being kind to people.

Warriors tended to hold to the same values as vigilantes. The only exception came in the area of the relative value of people versus property. Here the warriors gave relatively more emphasis to property—and were distinctive among the four violence types in this respect.

From the results shown in Figure 6, it is clear that men of these four violence types held sharply differing views about several fundamental values prescribing how one ought to respond to certain situations and what kinds of concerns deserve highest priority.

It is interesting that the four violence types, with their sharply differing views about appropriate uses for violence, were *not* very different in their scores on the Kindness Index. An examination of the underlying data (not shown) indicates that the explanation is not that everyone gave

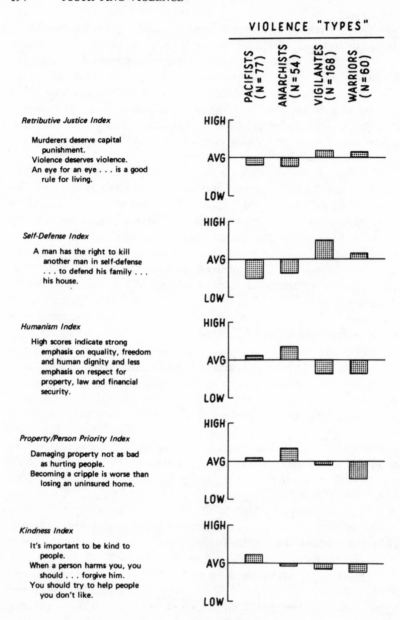

Figure 6. Mean position of value orientations of designated violence types compared to the average for American men.

Note: The "average" score is based on our sample of 1,374 American men aged 16-64. About two-thirds of these men had scores falling between the points marked "high" and "low."

maximal endorsement to values having to do with kindness, helpfulness and forgiveness. On the contrary, what information is available indicates that endorsement of these often-talked-about virtues was largely irrelevant to people's beliefs about when it is appropriate to injure, kill, break and burn.

Identification with Police, White Student Demonstrators and Black Protesters. A second psychological area which the study investigated concerned respondents' feelings about groups which have sometimes used violence. As described in previous chapters, three such groups were chosen for detailed examination—white student demonstrators, black protesters, and police. A series of parallel questions measured respondents' sense of identification with each group. A different set of items explored people's views about the power and authority of the police/court system.[4]

Figure 7 and Table 3 show how respondents identified as "pacifists," "anarchists," "vigilantes," and "warriors" felt about these users of violence and about the police/court system. As is immediately apparent, there are sharp differences among the violence types in how they identified with these several groups.

As expected, respondents tended to feel more highly identified with groups that used violence for purposes the respondents approved of or felt were necessary, and relatively little identified with those who used violence for other purposes.[5] Of course, an alternative way of reporting the same finding would be to say that respondents approved of using violence for those purposes for which groups with which the respondent felt identified actually used it. Examples of the association between violence types and group identification are abundant in Figure 7, particularly in the sharp contrasts between anarchists and vigilantes.

Anarchists, who were defined as those who felt it was necessary to use violence for achieving social change but not for social control, showed much higher than average identifications with both black protesters and student demonstrators, and lower than average identification with police. Vigilantes, defined as people with opposite beliefs about appropriate uses for violence, showed just the opposite pattern of feelings toward these contenders.

---

[4] Table 3 includes those five identification items of the original 12 which individually showed the largest unique effects.

[5] This basic notion is a classic one in social psychology and has been explored under the name of "Balance Theory." In the abstract, the theory states that if A (a person) is positively associated with X (an act), and if B is also positively associated with X, then A and B can be expected to have a positive relationship. Newcomb (1956) and Heider (1958) have developed and explored this theory.

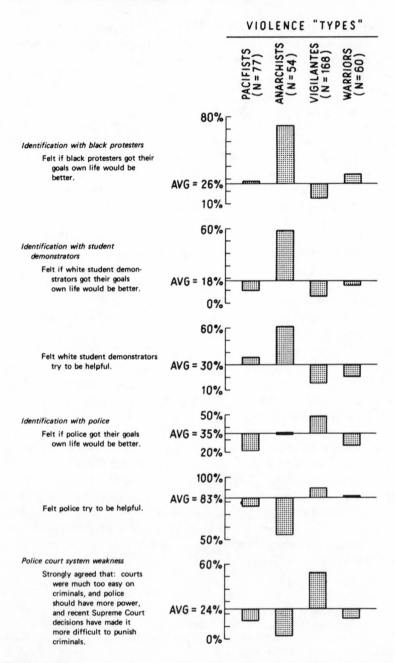

Figure 7. Percentage responses of designated violence "types" in relation to identification with black protesters, white student demonstrators, police, and attitudes toward the courts.

Table 3

Violence Types in Relation to Feelings about Black Protesters, Student Demonstrators, Police and Courts

	All Respondents	Violence Type			
		Pacifists	Anarchists	Vigilantes	Warriors
	(N=1,374)	(N=77)	(N=54)	(N=168)	(N=60)
Identification with black protesters					
Felt if black protesters got their goals own life would be better	26%	28%	73%	14%	34%
Identification with student demonstrators					
Felt white student demonstrators try to be helpful.	30	36	61	15	20
Felt if white student demonstrators got their goals own life would be better.	18	10	59	5	14
Identification with police					
Felt police try to be helpful.	83	76	53	92	85
Felt if police got their goals own life would be better.	35	21	35	49	25
Police/court system weakness					
Strongly agreed that courts are much too easy on criminals, police should have more power, and recent Supreme Court decisions have made it more difficult to punish criminals.	24	14	2	53	16

Anarchists were also less likely than men in general to feel that the police/court system was weak or being weakened, while vigilantes included a disproportionately high number of people who felt this way.

Neither the pacifists nor warriors showed marked deviations from the general population in their feelings about any of these matters. What trends there were suggested that pacifists tended to be slightly lower than average in their identification with police (and perhaps with student demonstrators), and warriors were atypically low in their identification with student demonstrators.[6]

Before we leave the discussion of people's feelings toward certain users of violence, it is appropriate to emphasize the magnitude of the differences in attitudes toward these groups by explicit reference to the percentage figures in Table 3. Almost three-quarters (73 percent) of the anarchists felt that their own lives would be better if black protesters achieved their goals, whereas only about one-seventh (14 percent) of the vigilantes felt this. Differences almost as large occurred in feelings about student demonstrators, police, and the police/court system. One cannot help but be concerned when respondents who disagreed profoundly on the appropriate uses for violence are also found to hold such disparate views about the underlying motives of groups which themselves sometimes turn to violence to achieve their ends, and about the operation of a formal system in society which is intended to ensure justice for all. While based on intentionally extreme subgroups, these data suggest how great the lack of consensus on some fundamental matters may be in contemporary American society.

Beliefs in what constitutes violence. In addition to disagreeing profoundly about appropriate uses for violence, and about the motives of groups which have sometimes used violent means, pacifists, anarchists, vigilantes, and warriors also held divergent views about whether certain activities even constituted "violence." In a real sense, people of different violence types spoke different languages, and an action which one type regarded as "violence," and hence provoking, another· may not have recognized as having such characteristics.

As described in Chapter 4, the questionnaire included a series of items which asked whether the respondent regarded specific activities as constituting "violence" in and of itself.

Figure 8 shows what acts the violence types defined as violence. Pacifists and anarchists were more likely than the general population to think that police activities constituted "violence," and were less likely than average to call protest activities, burglary, and looting "violence." By contrast, vigilantes were *less* likely to call police activities "violence" and *more* likely to think protest, burglary and looting were "violence." The warrior group gave answers closely approximating the national average.

---

[6] While results from "anarchists" and "vigilantes" supported the Balance Theory model nicely, data from the "pacifists" and "warriors" showed a mixed picture. The Balance Theory model would predict that "pacifists" would have been atypically low in their identification with *all* groups which use violence, and that "warriors" would have been atypically high. That these expectations were not supported by the data suggests that considerations other than how a group used violence also affected feelings toward the group.

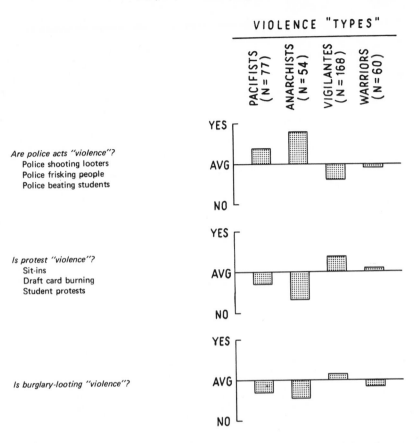

Figure 8. Mean position on definition indices for designated violence "types" compared to the average for American men.

Note: The "average" score is based on our sample of 1,374 American men aged 16-64. About two-thirds had scores falling between the points marked "yes" and "no."

Once again, the results provide ample leads for speculating about potential sources of civil strife. Here are several groups, defined on the basis of their distinctive views about the purposes for which it is appropriate to inflict damage on persons or property, and the data show that they disagreed sharply even with respect to what is "violence." Clearly, it would be inappropriate to assume that there would be a unanimity of purpose, even if all groups agreed that reducing violence was their goal!

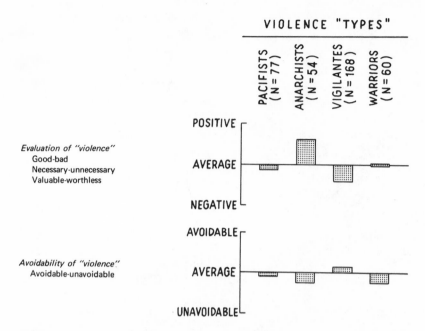

Figure 9. Mean position on semantic meaning of "violence" for designated violence "types" in comparison to the average for American men.

Note: The "average" score is based on our sample of 1,374 American men aged 16-64. About two-thirds had scores falling between the labelled points in the charts.

Reaction to the concept "violence." Still further evidence about the disparity in how the different violence types viewed violence is provided by a set of items which asked for people's feelings about the concept, however they defined it. Shown in Figure 9 are data derived from a general Evaluative Index[7] and a single item on which respondents rated the "avoidability" of violence.

One can see that anarchists reacted substantially more positively to what they meant by "violence," and vigilantes substantially more negatively than did the average man. When anarchists thought about

---

[7] The Evaluative Index is more fully described in Appendix C. It consists of three components which were seven-point scales ranging "good-bad," "necessary-unnecessary," and "valuable-worthless." The higher the score on the index, the more the respondent thought violence bad, unnecessary and worthless.

"violence," this was something they felt was relatively unavoidable, while vigilantes were more optimistic that *their* notion of "violence" could be avoided. Not only did these groups define different kinds of activities as constituting "violence," but we see here that they also evaluated the concept differently.[8]

Both the anarchists and vigilantes took optimistic viewpoints: anarchists were relatively positive in their evaluation of "violence" and also tended—more than the population at large—to think it would occur. But vigilantes were also optimists: they felt that a bad thing was avoidable. Pacifists, although not markedly different from the population at large, showed up as the pessimists: compared to the general population they felt worse about "violence" and also felt it was less avoidable.

Note on Intermediates

Before leaving this section, which describes and contrasts the various violence types, a brief word about the intermediate type is in order. This group fell midway between the four extreme types—pacifists, anarchists, vigilantes, and warriors—in their views about appropriate uses for violence.

We subjected the intermediates to an analysis similar to that related above, and found that they closely corresponded to the average for all men on all scales. Although there is no statistical necessity that such results should be obtained, they indicate that the intermediates, as a group, are a close approximation to the average American man on the dimensions examined.

Background and Psychological Characteristics Considered Jointly

Pacifists, anarchists, vigilantes, and warriors differ radically in what they feel are appropriate circumstances in which to injure or kill people or damage property, and also differ sharply in a variety of both background characteristics and psychological attributes. These findings raise a number of analytic problems, some of which will be explored in this section, others of which can only be speculated about with the present data.

One might ask about the extent to which one psychological (or background) characteristic shows results similar to another simply because it is related to the other. For example, warriors included an over-represen-

---

8 In another analysis of these data, our colleague Dean Runyan has explored the apparent inconsistency of respondents (such as anarchists) who evaluated violence positively, defined police activities as constituting "violence," and yet failed to identify positively with the police. Runyan's conclusion was that these respondents tended to think of the concept "violence" positively in terms of its role in effecting social change. However, they still tended to use the word as a pejorative, as most respondents did, when asked to relate it to certain activities of groups they did not like (Runyan 1971).

tation of people from Southern states and also an over-representation of people with low education. Education levels tend to be lower than average in the South. It might be that the region effect was attributable to differences in education. This kind of issue needs exploration in order to interpret the previous findings.

A related analytic problem is whether the relationships of background factors to violence ideology can be understood in terms of psychological characteristics assessed in the present study. *Some* psychological explanation is needed, since a background variable such as Region of Childhood does not by itself help us understand why a person holds certain attitudes about uses for violence, even long after he may have moved into another region. Similarly, one wonders whether differences in background might account for some of the psychological differences between the several violence types.

A third concern is the matter of causality—to what extent might the various differences in background and psychological characteristics, separately and jointly, *account for* a person's beliefs about appropriate uses for violence? Although the design of the study does not permit firm conclusions about cause and effect, the analysis reported below provides some upper bounds on how large such causal effects might be, given our measures.

To explore some of these matters four parallel analyses were conducted. One asked essentially what factors were related to whether a person held a pacifist view. In this analysis, pacifists plus semi-pacifists were contrasted with everyone else. The second analysis asked the same question for anarchism—contrasting anarchists and semi-anarchists with all others. The third did the same for vigilantes and semi-vigilantes, the fourth for warriors and semi-warriors.

The four analyses all started with the same set of background and psychological characteristics. Included were four demographic matters— age, childhood region, race, and education; five value indices; five items assessing identification with police, white student demonstrators, and black protesters; three indices assessing the respondents' own definitions of "violence," and two measures of their reactions to "violence." We have seen how people of the four *pure* violence types scored on each of these;[9]

---

[9]Three characteristics included previously were omitted from these analyses: parental background, military service, and attitudes about the police/court system. Parental background and military service seemed less fundamental than the other background factors of age, education, race, and childhood region. And we know from previous analysis that relationships between the violence measures and attitudes about the police/court system were heavily overlapped with other relationships involving attitudes about police, white student demonstrators and black protesters.

in general, inclusion of the "semi" categories in the present analysis did not greatly alter relationships described earlier. (Including the "semi" groups had the advantage of providing a somewhat less skewed distribution for use in multivariate analysis.)

Background Variables

Table 4 shows the extent to which each of four background factors could explain the variability in respondents' views about pacifism, anarchism, vigilantism, and the warrior orientation.

Table 4

Percentage of Variance (eta^2) in each of Four Violence Orientations
Explained by Designated Background Characteristics

| | Orientations | | | |
	Pacifism	Anarchism	Vigilantism	Warrior
Age	1	1	3	1
Region	2	1	1	2
Race	1	5	3	2
Education	3	0	1	2
(Sum of above)	7%	7%	8%	7%
All four jointly (R^2)	6%	8%[b]	8%	5%
(population estimates)	(4%)	(6%)	(6%)	(3%)
Multiple correlations[a] (multiple R)	.25	.28	.28	.23
(population estimates)	(.21)	(.25)	(.25)	(.19)

[a] For readers accustomed to thinking in terms of correlation coefficients, we present these figures. These multiple correlation estimates are derived from Multiple Classification Analysis and hence are not restricted by the usual assumptions of internal scaling and linearity of relations.

[b] In some instances the joint explanatory power of a set of variables may be greater than the sum of their individual effects. This phenomenon is akin to the "suppressor" effect, in which one variable "cancels out" the effect of another.

The explanatory power of the background factors, each taken by itself, is generally small—ranging from zero to five percent. However, the four background factors taken together explain almost as much of the variability in each of the violence orientations (5 to 8 percent) as the *sum* of the several background factors taken separately. This indicates that these background variables involve little duplication among themselves. On the contrary, that portion of the variation in, say, pacifism which one background factor could explain tends to be different from the portion explained by the others. One conclusion, then, is that on the whole, each of the four background factors shown in Table 4 operated differently from the others and hence was worthy of separate consideration.

Among the four background variables examined, education had most to do with respondents' espousal of pacifism, race was most strongly related to anarchism, both age and race were relevant to vigilantism, and no variable showed more than a very modest relationship to the warrior orientation.

Psychological Variables

Table 5 presents a similar analysis for fifteen psychological characteristics. Here, results are more complex and will be considered for each orientation separately.

Pacifism. With respect to pacifism, the strongest explanatory variable was how a person felt about Retributive Justice, which accounted for 4 percent of the variability. The lower a person's retributiveness, the more likely he was to espouse pacifism. Most other psychological characteristics had quite low relationships with pacifism. The fifteen variables taken jointly, however, accounted for 14 percent of the variation in feelings about pacifism, indicating that the 4 percent explained by Retributive Justice is by no means the whole story.

The moderate difference between the sum of the explanatory powers of the fifteen variables (19 percent) and the joint explanatory power (14 percent), indicates that there is only moderate duplication in explanatory ability.

Anarchism. Table 5 shows that several of the psychological variables show moderate relationships to the anarchism orientation, particularly identifications with black protesters, white student demonstrators, police, and whether police activities constituted "violence." The values included in this study, except for Retributive Justice, had little to do with espousal of the anarchist orientation. Reactions about how good, necessary, and valuable "violence" is (summarized in the Evaluative Index) explain four percent of the variability in "anarchism." Taken jointly, the pyschological variables accounted for about a fifth (22 percent) of the variability in this variable.

Summing the individual explanatory powers of the psychological characteristics yielded a sum more than double (49 percent) the actual

Table 5

Percentage of Variance in Each of Four Violence Orientations Explained
by Designated Psychological Characteristics

	Orientations			
	Pacifism	Anarchism	Vigilantism	Warrior
Values				
Retributive Justice	4	3	4	2
Self-Defense	2	2	5	1
Humanism	1	2	2	1
Property/Person Priority	0	1	0	1
Kindness	1	0	0	0
Group identification				
Black protesters better life	2	7	7	0
White student demonstrators helpful	1	3	6	0
White student demonstrators better life	1	7	5	0
Police helpful	0	5	2	0
Police better life	1	5	4	1
What constitutes "violence"				
Are police acts violence	1	7	6	0
Is protest violence	2	2	3	0
Is burglary looting violence	1	0	1	0
Reactions to "violence"				
Evaluation	1	4	4	1
Avoidability	1	1	3	2
(Sum of above)	19%	49%	52%	9%
All 15 jointly (R^2)	14%	22%	22%	9%
(population estimates)	(10%)	(18%)	(18%)	(5%)
Multiple correlations (multiple R)	.37	.47	.47	.30
(population estimates)	(.31)	(.42)	(.43)	(.22)

joint explanatory power of 22 percent, indicating that substantial overlap or "duplication of effort" occurred among these variables.

Vigilantism. The psychological variables showed more high relationships with vigilantism than with any of the other orientations. Almost without exception, the variables which related best here were the same as those which had related to anarchism. (Of course, the *direction* of the relationships, as shown earlier, is opposite in all cases except the Kindness Index, which bears little relationship to either anarchism or vigilantism.) Most of the group identification variables related strongly to whether a person espoused vigilantism, as did two of the values (Retributive Justice and Self-Defense), beliefs about whether police activities constitute "violence," and reactions to the concept "violence."

Warrior orientation. One of the more notable aspects of Table 5 is the consistently low relationships between the psychological characteristics and espousal of the warrior orientation. The psychological aspects we assessed, at least in the form we measured them, simply are not very relevant for distinguishing adherents of the warrior orientation from other respondents. The fifteen psychological variables jointly accounted for only 9 percent of the variability of the warrior orientation. A psychological understanding of the warrior orientation, clearly, awaits further study.

There are at least three alternatives as to why the relationships with the warrior orientation were not higher. One is that the kinds of psychological factors which distinguished warriors from others were not included in the study. A second is that people who held to the warrior orientation came to that set of viewpoints from a variety of directions, so that in a straightforward univariate or multivariate analysis these competing relationships cancelled out. Still a third alternative is that our measures were relatively unsuccessful in capturing the "true" position of these people. This group tended to be unusually low in education (shown in Table 2) and it may be that our interview worked poorly with them, or that they themselves were unclear or inconsistent in their views.[10]

Comment. A general comment about these results is in order. Table 5 shows that the joint explanatory power of the fifteen psychological factors is in all cases very substantially greater than the explanatory power of any one variable. This fact suggests that views about appropriate uses

---

[10] A subsequent analysis restricted to those respondents who gave logically consistent answers to the three sets of items used to measure Violence for Social Control showed relationships which were 30 to 60 percent stronger than those shown in Tables 5 and 6. While still not very strong (joint explanatory power reached 16 percent of the variance in the "warrior" orientations), this suggests that at least some of the reason for the low original relationships has to do with measurement problems.

for violence are *multi-determined:* it seems highly unlikely that any simple explanation involving just a few factors could provide a complete accounting of what appears to be a complex phenomenon.

Combining Background and Psychological Characteristics

The final stage in these analyses was to consider background and psychological characteristics simultaneously. This indicated the maximum ability of these variables to explain variation in the violence orientation and showed how well the observed relationships between background and violence orientation (the data of Table 4) could be accounted for by the psychological characteristics. Table 6 gives the results.

Data for anarchism present one extreme situation. Here, combining the background and psychological factors produced *no* increase in explanatory power over that shown by the psychological factors alone, a clear indication that the 8 percent explanatory power of the background factors was fully accounted for (and more) by the psychological characteristics of respondents. The same is also true, almost, with respect to vigilantism. Adding the 8 percent explanatory power of the background factors increased the total explanatory power by only 2 percentage points, to 24 percent. But with respect to the pacifist and warrior orientations, the background factors make a slightly larger addition to what could be explained by the psychological characteristics, suggesting that the effects of the background factors have not been fully accounted for by the particular psychological aspects assessed in the study.

Table 6 can also be viewed as a summary statement of how well these background and psychological factors account for espousal of the four different violence orientations. Total explanatory power for the combined background and psychological factors ranges from 12 percent (for the warrior orientation) to 24 percent (for vigilantism).

To know whether this is "good" or "bad" requires certain additional information. Clearly, nothing approximating 100 percent of the variability has been accounted for. But 100 percent is certainly the wrong criterion, since some (as yet unknown) part of the variability in the measures of the violence orientations was random perturbation and error, and hence of little intrinsic interest. Also, the explanatory power of our variables was likewise lessened by imprecisions in the measurement of the background and psychological factors themselves. Until better estimates of the intrinsic quality of these measures become available, it will be impossible to know how close the underlying concepts which the psychological measures attempted to tap come to providing the full story with respect to these violence orientations.

The issue of causality also remains unclear: did respondents endorse

Table 6

Percentage of Variance in Each of Four Violence Orientations
Explained by Background and Psychological Characteristics

| | Orientations | | | |
	Pacifism	Anarchism	Vigilantism	Warrior
Background factors jointly (from Table 4)	6	8	8	5
Psychological factors jointly (from Table 5)	14	22	22	9
(Sum of above)	20%	30%	30%	14%
Background and psychological factors jointly (R^2) (population estimates)	17% (12%)	22% (18%)	24% (20%)	12% (7%)
Multiple correlations (multiple R) (population estimates)	.41 (.35)	.47 (.42)	.49 (.44)	.35 (.27)

pacifism, anarchism, vigilantism, or the warrior orientation *because* of the factors tapped by our psychological variables and (ultimately) their experiences summarized in the background variables? This question also must wait for subsequent research.

The chapter has, however, provided a description of the backgrounds and certain psychological characteristics of people holding four sharply contrasting viewpoints about appropriate uses for violence. It has also described how most of these factors related to the corresponding orientations about the use of violence. Some substantial relationships were identified, which provide a start to understanding the possible reasons why people may espouse pacifism, anarchism, vigilantism, or a warrior orientation.

Summary

This chapter examines four contrasting groups of men who differed sharply in their views about appropriate uses for violence.

Those men who felt violence should be used neither for social control nor social change were called "pacifists." Those who supported its use for bringing about social change, but not for social control, were named "anarchists." "Vigilantes" were those who advocated its use for social control, but not for social change. The term "warriors" was assigned to those who would use violence for both social change and social control.

There were no simple and direct ties between orientations toward violence and background factors such as race, age, region, and education. These four background factors explained less than 10 percent of the variation in the violence orientations. This is in contrast to popular attempts to stereotype pacifists, anarchists, etc. Thus, despite our having defined the groups to include only those men who showed relatively extreme views, each group included some members from each age group, each education level, each region of the country, and each race.

There were some background differences among the four groups. Those that advocated violence for social change and/or social control—i.e., the anarchists, vigilantes, and warriors—included somewhat higher proportions of men born in the South and born of native American parents than was true of American men in general, and these groups also tended to have less than average education, although the anarchists provided many exceptions. The majority of anarchists and warriors were white, but they included a disproportionately high number of blacks. Vigilantes, by contrast, included an over-representation of whites. Men in their 20's were over-represented among the anarchists while men in their 30's and 40's were over-represented among vigilantes.

Psychological differences among the groups were more marked than background differences. These factors included several basic values, identification with police, student demonstrators, and black protesters, definitions as to what constitutes "violence," and reactions to "violence." Jointly, these factors explained from 9 to 22 percent of the variation in the violence orientations.

With respect to values and what was defined as violence, each of the four groups differed substantially from the general population. Pacifists and anarchists tended to be similar, and contrasted with vigilantes and warriors. Compared to the general population, pacifists and anarchists tended to be less retributive, less supportive of killing for self-defense, more person-oriented, and to give greater emphasis to equality, freedom, and human dignity. These groups also were less inclined to believe that protest acts were "violence" and more inclined to believe certain police acts were. Vigilantes and warriors showed opposite tendencies: These groups were more retributive and oriented toward self-defense than average, less concerned with humanistic and people-oriented values, and tended to feel that police acts were not "violence," but that protest acts were.

In respect to identificaton and how "violence" was evaluated, pacifists and warriors were rather similar to the general population.

Anarchists and vigilantes, however, differed sharply both from the general population and from each other. Anarchists showed above average identifications with student demonstrators and black protesters, below average identification with the police, and were more likely than the average American man to evaluate "violence" positively. Vigilantes showed just the opposite tendencies.

Chapter 8

PREDICTING ATTITUDES TOWARD VIOLENCE

To what extent can the personal characteristics and beliefs explored in this study explain the attitudes of American men toward violence? This chapter answers that question by pulling together the several themes described previously and showing how various combinations of them relate to attitudes toward violence. More specifically, the chapter shows how a person's background characteristics, his values, his identification with police and protesters, his definition of "violence," his perceptions of other people, and his views about social issues work together to explain the level of violence he advocates for social control and believes necessary for social change.

The analytic model that provides the basis for this study, and particularly this chapter, was described in Chapter 1 and is summarized on the following page as Figure 1. It provides a useful "road map" to the analysis. As the arrangement of Figure 1 makes clear, the many factors examined for their relationship to the violence indices can be thought of in terms of two very broad predictive categories—background characteristics and psychological characteristics. Moreover, the psychological characteristics can be considered as intermediary; one can imagine their being affected by a person's background and in turn influencing his attitudes toward violence.

Such inferences of causality must be very tentative. This study was designed to explore the relationship of many factors to attitudes about violence, rather than to demonstrate the causal power of any one. Moreover, if one hopes for a less violent society, one must hope also that some of the immediate social-psychological causes of violence can be reduced by means that take effect more quickly than changes in background and childhood experience.

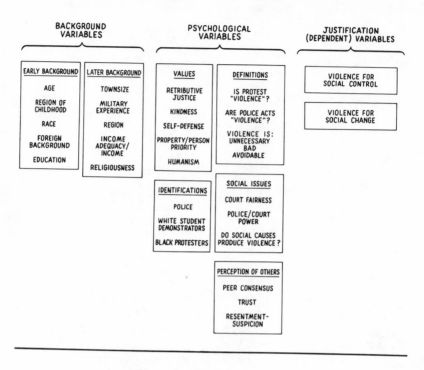

Figure 1. Analytic Model.

Before discussion of the specific results, one further comment is in order: None of the single variables, taken alone, showed a strong relationship to attitudes about violence. When the single variables were combined into sets, however, some of the sets showed moderate relationships to Violence for Social Control, Violence for Social Change, or both. When certain of the *sets* were themselves combined, very substantial relationships emerged. (Multiple correlations ranged up to .8.) This is perfectly in accord with the idea that attitudes about violence are multiply determined.

In one sense, the analysis about to be described combines many small building blocks to produce a larger structure of understanding and prediction. It does so primarily by considering each variable in terms of its ability to explain variations in the Index of Violence for Social Control or Social Change. For each variable this ability is expressed in percentage terms—the proportion of variance in the index accounted for by the variable being considered. These relationships are then combined to answer the corresponding question for each set of factors—early background, later background, values, identification, and the others. This structure of explanation is developed separately for the Index of Violence for Social Control and that for Violence for Social Change. It has been done separately also for two subpopulations—blacks and men with some college education. Where the pattern of results requires it, findings will be presented for both these groups as well as for American men as a whole.

Violence for Social Control

Background Characteristics

Early Background Factors. Table 1 shows the extent to which characteristics of respondents determined very early in their lives relate, separately and jointly, to attitudes toward Violence for Social Control. Among these characteristics education shows the strongest relationships, explaining 3 percent of the variance. Persons with higher education tended to advocate less violent police actions. Age also relates to attitudes toward Violence for Social Control; younger people tended to favor less police force than older people. (This relationship is absent among college-educated men.) The region of the country in which the respondent grew up is next in importance among factors of early background. American men who were raised in the South or the border states were more likely than others to advocate high levels of Violence for Social Control.

Table 1

Percentage of Variance in Violence for Social Control
Explained by Early Background Characteristics
(all respondents; N=1,374)

Age	2%
Region of childhood	2
Race	1
Foreign background	1
Education	3
All 5 jointly (R^2)	10%
Multiple correlations (Multiple R)	.32

Neither race nor nationality of background accounts for more than 1 percent of the variation in Violence for Social Control. In both cases, however, the tendency is for the minority to advocate less forceful police methods than the majority. Thus, blacks scored lower than whites on Violence for Social Control; men who had one or more foreign-born parents, or who were foreign-born themselves, were less likely to endorse forceful police methods than were men born of native American parents.

Table 1 also shows that these early background variables in combination account for only a small part of the variation in attitudes toward Violence for Social Control—10 percent for American men as a whole. (For blacks and men with college education these factors accounted for 6 percent.)

Later Background Characteristics. Table 2 shows how much of the variation in the Index of Violence for Social Control is explained by some of the current demographic characteristics of the respondents. On the whole, the amount of variation explained is small.

Table 2

Percentage of Variance in Violence for Social Control
Explained by Later Background Characteristics

(all respondents; N=1,374)

Town size	2%
Military experience	1
Region	1
Income adequacy	1
All 4 jointly (R^2)	5%
Multiple correlations (Multiple R)	.22

Men living in rural areas tended to advocate higher levels of police force than those in large cities. Men living in the southern and border states justified greater use of police force than others.

However, blacks did not fit this pattern. Black men in towns and small cities tended to advocate more Violence for Social Control than either those in rural areas or those in large cities. And black men living in the South were apt to advocate lower levels of Violence for Social Control than men elsewhere.

Other variables in Table 2 show weak or uninterpretable relationships to Violence for Social Control.[1]

---

[1] Income adequacy (family income relative to family size) showed similar trends to absolute family income.

Early and Later Background Factors Jointly. The figures presented in Table 3 indicate that background and demographic characteristics—including both the early and later factors—account for only a modest portion of the variation in attitudes toward the use of Violence for Social Control—12 percent among American men as a whole and 16 percent among blacks and men with college education. (Population estimates ranged from 6 to 9 percent.) This is an important finding: The major part of the variation in people's feelings about how forceful police should be seems not to be attributable to simple demographic differences, even when nine such factors are considered simultaneously.[2]

As we shall see next, psychological characteristics have much more to do with attitudes toward Violence for Social Control than do the background factors.

Table 3

Percentage of Variance in Violence for Social Control
Explained by Early and Later Background Characteristics

	All Respondents	Blacks	Men With Some College Education
	(N=1,374)	(N=303)	(N=374)
Early factors – 5 jointly	10%	6%	6%
Later factors – 4 jointly	5	12	13
Early and later factors jointly	12	16	16
Multiple Correlation (Multiple R)	.35	.40	.40

Note: Tables of this type, which combine sets of factors, will indicate the number of factors previously considered in each set. Because of limited computer capacity, however, variables which were known not to make an independent contribution were excluded from the computer runs.

Psychological Characteristics

As indicated in the analytic model in Figure 1, five sets of psychological characteristics were considered. These included a person's values, his group identifications, how he defined "violence," his views on several social issues, and his perception of other people. This last set,

---

[2] Strictly speaking, the truth of this statement depends not only on the data of Table 3, but it also requires demonstration of the validity of the measure and of the lack of statistical interaction. Preliminary checking leads us to believe these conditions were both present.

perception of others, proved to be virtually unrelated to Violence for Social Control, and hence was dropped from the analysis.

Values. Table 4 shows the extent to which the five values described in Chapter 5 explain attitudes toward Violence for Social Control among American men. Among all men, values in combination account for 17 percent of the variation, among blacks 12 percent, and among those who have had at least some college, 27 percent.

Of the values measured, Self-Defense and Retributive Justice account for the largest proportion of the variation. Men who believe most in the right of a man to commit homicide to defend himself, his family and his house were most likely to advocate violent police methods to achieve social control. This is hardly surprising; one might guess that many people regard the police as their agents, whose main purpose is to protect the citizen. If a person believes that he himself has the right to kill in self-defense, it seems reasonable that he would allocate such powers to his agents.

Table 4

Percentage of Variance in Violence for Social Control
Explained by Designated Values
(all respondents; N=1,374)

Retributive Justice Index	9%
Kindness Index	1
Self-Defense Index	9
Property/Person Priority Index	1
Humanism Index	5
All 5 jointly (R^2)	17%
Multiple correlations (Multiple R)	.41

Like Self-Defense, Retributive Justice explains 9 percent of the variation in attitudes toward violence; those who were most retributive advocated the largest amount of police force. This is true among whites, blacks, and the highly educated, as well as for the population in general. The data imply that for some American men the use of police force is associated with the idea of retribution. The data do not mean that police force is actually so utilized. Nevertheless, when one considers that the value of Retributive Justice accounts for 15 percent of the variation in attitudes toward the use of police force among the better-educated, who are most likely to be among those giving the orders and making decisions about the use of police force, one wonders if there might not be a real association between retributiveness and the use of police force as well as its verbal endorsement.

After Retributive Justice, the Humanism Index is next most important in explaining Violence for Social Control. Men who gave priority to freedom, human dignity, and equality justified lower levels of police force than men who put priority on respect for law, property, and financial security.

Neither Kindness nor the respondent's valuation of property as compared to persons contributes much to explaining advocacy of Violence for Social Control. Men with a high belief in Kindness were slightly less apt to advocate Violence for Social Control, as were those who expressed a relatively high valuation of persons over property.

There is some overlap in the explanatory power of these values; their joint relationship to Violence for Social Control is substantially less than the sum of their separate relationships. This is particularly true for men with some college education, among whom values are more related to each other than in the general population. A highly educated person who is retributive is more likely to fall toward the materialistic end of the Humanism scale, more likely to score high on Self-Defense, and so on. Indeed, it seems as though those with high educations have more integrated values and relate them more directly to their views on the use of force by the police. In the college-educated group, values explain over a quarter of the variation in attitudes toward this type of violence.

Identification. Table 5 shows the extent to which positive and negative attitudes toward black protesters, white student demonstrators, and the police explain variation in the Index of Violence for Social Control. On the whole, such attitudes account for a moderate amount of the variation in that index. For American men in general, attitude toward the contenders in the scenarios with which the respondent was presented explains one-fifth of the variation in Violence for Social Control; among black men, 28 percent; and among those who have had some college education, 31 percent of the variation is explained.

Among American men in general, the more a respondent saw student demonstrators and black protesters as being trustworthy, helpful, unlikely to dislike people like himself, and likely to change his life for the better, the less likely the respondent was to advocate high levels of Violence for Social Control. If he held such notions about the police, he was apt to advocate high levels of Violence for Social Control. However, among black men this pattern did not hold. Three of the four items measuring respondent identification with student protesters did not relate clearly to Violence for Social Control. Only the item in which the respondent was asked whether or not he thought the goals of student demonstrators would make his own life better or worse related linearly to the violence measure. The reason for this is not clear, although one might guess that some black people have highly ambivalent attitudes toward white college students, on the one hand identifying them with the civil rights movement and on the other identifying them with the American elite which has been responsible for much of the black man's disadvantaged situation. Such ambivalence might account for the lack of relatedness between three of the student identification items and Violence for Social Control. All other identification items are associated with this type of violence in the manner expected among blacks as well as other groups.

Table 5

Percentage of Variance in Violence for Social Control
Explained by Identification Items
(all respondents; N=1,374)

White student demonstrators helpful	7%
No white student demonstrators dislike respondent	1
White student demonstrators trustworthy	5
White student demonstrators better life	6
Black protesters helpful	6
No black protesters dislike respondent	2
Black protesters trustworthy	5
Black protesters better life	8
Police helpful	3
No police dislike respondent	4
Police trustworthy	1
Police better life	3
All 12 jointly (R^2)	20%
Multiple correlations (Multiple R)	.45

When one asks why the level of force advocated for the police varies with people's views of the groups being controlled, several possible reasons come to mind. One possibility is that, consciously or unconsciously, people want more than social control of groups they do not like; they wish to see them punished, and they see the police as convenient agents for wreaking social vengeance. It is consistent with this hypothesis that espousal of the value Retributive Justice is related to supporting the use of violence by the police.

The "vengeance hypothesis" is a disturbing one. It implies that a judgment of guilt or innocence is made on the basis of group membership prior to a fair hearing. It implies also the imposition of a sentence by police force, accidental or purposeful, which may be unjust, irreversible or both.

It seems unlikely that individuals advocating higher levels of Violence for Social Control against those whom they regard as untrustworthy and looking for trouble actually regard themselves as vengeful. The police are charged with maintaining order and apprehending those who act unlawfully, and people may believe that the minimal force necessary to restore order and apprehend those involved in a disturbance varies according to the nature of the disrupting group. The more untrustworthy or intractable the group, the more force is required. People adhering to this belief would be likely to feel that they were prudent rather than vengeful, that they advocate only "necessary" force.

How Violence is Defined. Table 6 shows the extent to which respondents' own definitions of "violence" are associated with attitudes toward the' use of force by the police. It can be seen that whether the respondent regarded protest and police acts as "violence" explains about 16 percent of the variation in attitudes toward the use of Violence for Social Control. People who thought protest actions, such as sit-ins or draft card burning, constituted "violence" were likely to advocate higher levels of violence to bring about social control than those who felt protest activities were not "violence." Also, people who regarded police activities involving "shooting looters," "beating students," and stopping people to frisk them as "violence" generally advocated below-average levels of Violence for Social Control.

The same relationships—at about the same strength—hold when blacks and men with college experience are considered separately. Furthermore, it is clear that the two definitional indices shown in Table 6 overlapped very little in their relationships to Violence for Social Control. The ability to predict a man's justification of violence by the police is significantly better if his views about whether both protest and police acts constitute "violence" are known, than if his views about only one of these matters are known.

These findings indicate that the rhetoric used to define situations for the public may exert a substantial effect on what the public will find justifiable by way of a police response. One step in the reduction of civil strife—the minimization of police violence—might be accomplished through encouraging greater awareness by the public of the non-violent nature of many protests and of the physical injuries sometimes inflicted by police.

Table 6

Percentage of Variance in Violence for Social Control
Explained by Definitions of "Violence"
(all respondents; N=1,374)

Is protest violence?	8%
Are police acts violence?	10
Both jointly (R^2)	16%
Multiple correlations (Multiple R)	.40

Perception of Social Issues. Table 7 shows the extent to which the beliefs of American men about certain social issues explain attitudes toward Violence for Social Control. It can be seen that such beliefs explain 16 percent of the variation in attitudes toward the use of police force. The most powerful of these beliefs is the extent to which the respondent believed that the police need more power and that the Supreme Court is making it more difficult to punish criminals. This variable alone explains 14 percent of the variation in such attitudes among all American men, and 17 percent of the variation among the well-educated. In all groups, the more the individual believed the police need more power, the more likely he was to advocate high levels of police force.

Table 7

Percentage of Variance in Violence for Social Control
Explained by Perceptions of Social Issues
(all respondents; N=1,374)

Social Causes Index	4%
Police/Court Power Index	14
Court Fairness Index	1
All 3 jointly (R^2)	16%
Multiple correlations (Multiple R)	.40

The extent to which American men believed that the social ills of poverty, poor education, unemployment and discrimination contribute to causing violence explains only 4 percent of the variation in attitudes toward the use of police force. The greater the belief that violence is caused by social problems, the less is the justification of Violence for Social Control.

The last variable in this set is our measure of Court Fairness—the extent to which the respondent thought the judicial system in the United States is apt to treat people equally, irrespective of their color or wealth. As one might expect, the more the respondent thought the courts are apt to be fair, the more likely he was to advocate high levels of police force, though relationships were weak.

These findings are quite uniform among blacks, the college-educated, and American men in general. In all three populations the Police/Court Power Index is the major explanatory variable. There is some tendency for perception of social issues to explain more of the variation in attitudes toward Violence for Social Control among college-educated men than among blacks or in the population at large.

Psychological Characteristics Considered Jointly. Having reviewed the associations between attitudes toward Violence for Social Control and each set of psychological variables which contributes to explaining such attitudes, we can now ask how well the different sets work together in explaining such attitudes. For example, if we combine values and the items which measure how the respondent identified with white student demonstrators, black protesters, and the police, can we explain more of the variation in attitudes toward Violence for Social Control than can be explained by either set alone? Moreover, we can ask whether there are similarities or differences in patterns of relationship among the three groups examined: the general population of American men, blacks, and those with college experience.

Table 8 presents a summary of the psychological factors discussed earlier in this chapter and shows how the different sets of factors act in combination. Although the magnitude of the relationships differs somewhat across the three groups (more educated respondents tended to have the most coherent attitudes and showed the highest relationships), the overall pattern is highly similar.

In the data for American men generally, one notes that each of the four sets of psychological factors explains from 16 to 20 percent of the variability in attitudes about the use of violence for achieving social control. When the identification set is combined with the values, there is an increase in explanatory power from 20 to 26 percent—about a one-third increase. Clearly the level reached is not as high as the sum of the separate relationships, but this would occur only if the sets acted entirely independently. And it seems reasonable that they should *not* be independent in their effects. On the contrary, one would expect values and identification with these contending groups to overlap. One would expect,

Table 8

Percentage of Variance in Violence for Social Control Explained by Psychological Factors

	Single Sets		
	All Respondents	Blacks	Men With Some College Education
	(N=1,374)	(N=303)	(N=374)
Values — 5 jointly	17%	12%	27%
Identifications — 12 jointly	20	28	28
Definitions — 2 jointly	16	15	17
Social issues — 3 jointly	16	14	22
	Combinations of Sets		
Values + Identifications	26%	28%	41%
Multiple correlations	.51	.53	.64
Values + Identifications + Definitions	29%	32%	43%
Multiple correlations	.54	.57	.66
Values + Identifications + Definitions + Social Issues	31%	36%	47%
Multiple correlations	.56	.60	.69

for example, a person's relative valuation of freedom, human dignity, equality, respect for law, property, and financial security to be related to whether he thinks white student demonstrators and black protesters helpful, and whether he thinks life would be better if goals of the white student demonstrators and black protesters were met.

Adding the definitional variables to the value and identification sets increased the explanatory power from 26 to 29 percent. The modest size of this gain indicates that most of the previously observed explanatory power of the definitional set (16 percent of the variance) could also be attributed to what we arbitrarily choose to regard as more basic psychological factors—values and group identifications. Nevertheless, what the respondent defines as "violence" does make a small unique contribution.

Finally, adding in the respondent's views about certain social issues results in another small increase. Altogether, from 29 to 31 percent of attitudes toward Violence for Social Control are explained. As with the definitions, views about these social issues make a small unique contribution, but most of what they do was already accounted for by values and identification.

Among blacks, one sees essentially the same pattern as for the general population. The most notable exception is that the values make no unique contribution to explaining variability in Violence for Social Control in addition to the identification items. Adding the value set to the identification set fails to push the explanatory power above 28 percent. How blacks defined "violence," and their views on the three social issues, however, each produce small gains in the explanatory power, yielding a final value of 36 percent.

The data for men who had at least some college experience tend to show the same pattern—values and identification account for most of the variation in attitudes toward Violence for Social Control, with the definition and social-issue sets each adding minor contributions. Notable in this group, however, is the substantially higher level of the relationships observed. Here, the four sets of psychological characteristics taken together can explain almost half the total variation in Violence for Social Control.

Three things may account for the higher explanatory power among the better educated. First, the data from these respondents may be somewhat better—questions better understood or answered more fully. To the extent that this occurs, there is less unexplainable "noise" or error to attenuate the size of the observed relationships.

Second, it may be that in the process of education at the college level, people are stimulated to develop more coherent and internally consistent sets of attitudes. It is commonly said that the early college years are marked by intense re-examination of personal beliefs with some resulting changes in attitudes (Newcomb 1943). If more educated respondents have more coherent belief systems, it seems entirely reasonable that attitudes about the use of violence should be more related to other attitudes (values, group identifications, etc.) among these people than in the general population.

A third possibility is that the views of men without college experience are affected by somewhat different factors and that the interview was not germane to as many of these as it was for the college-educated.

Background and Psychological Factors Jointly

The final step in understanding attitudes about the use of violence for achieving social control is to combine the explanatory power of the psychological factors with the explanatory power of the background factors. The results appear in Table 9. The table shows that background and psychological factors together can explain slightly more than a third of the variability of the attitudes of American men toward Violence for Social Control. (Multiple correlations range from .58 to .73.) In the black and college-educated populations, about half of the variation in such attitudes appears to be explained. It is possible to construct population estimates of the variance explained which attempt to compensate for capitalization on random variations in samples. In the present data, such estimates suggest that the explanatory power of the combined variables in the population as a whole would range from 27 to 37 percent, with the highest explanatory power occurring for the more educated respondents.[3]

It is also clear from Table 9 that the explanatory power of the background factors alone can be almost entirely accounted for by psychological factors. The combination of background and psychological factors has little more explanatory power than the psychological factors alone. This suggests that the psychological factors included in the present study mediated most (but not quite all) of the influences which can be attributed to demographic differences. Since there must be some psychological mediation to explain how a background factor, such as region of

---

[3] Analyses of this kind raise the question of how high the explanatory power might get. While an ability to explain 100% of the variance is the theoretical maximum, this is an unrealistic goal given measures that are less than perfect. Probably no measure in any science is perfect, and several sources of potential errors (unreliability) can be identified in the present study—the nature of the interview schedule, the respondents, the interviewers, and the various transcription steps needed to make data readable by a computer. No firm information is yet available about the overall reliability of these measures: Appendix A, however, presents figures on coding reliability, and generation of additional information is a current undertaking of the authors. A rough guess, based on data from other surveys, is that reliability might be in the range of .5 to .8. If one were dealing with only two variables of equal reliability (instead of the many predictors used here), and if one had explained *all* variation possible except for that attributable to unreliability, the strength of the observed relationship for given levels of reliability would be as follows:

reliability	% variance explained
.8	64%
.7	49
.6	36
.5	25

Given the suspected unreliability of measures in the present study and the observed magnitudes of the explanatory powers, the figures above suggest that the background and psychological variables working jointly may well be explaining a very large portion of the total variance which is theoretically explainable.

Table 9

Percentage of Variance in Violence for Social Control
Explained by Background and Psychological Factors

	All Respondents (N=1,374)	Blacks (N=303)	Men With Some College Education (N=374)
Background factors – 2 sets jointly	12%	16%	16%
Psychological factors – 4 sets jointly	31	36	47
Background and Psychological jointly (R^2)	34%	45%	54%
Multiple correlations (Multiple R)	.58	.67	.73

childhood, can relate to an adult's attitude toward how much violence should be used for social control, a psychologically complete study would be able to account for *all* background effects as psychological effects also. The present analysis approaches this goal, but does not quite achieve it.

A Composite Picture

From the preceding analysis, one can sketch the characteristics of an individual likely to endorse above-average levels of Violence for Social Control: He is a person who believes that his life will change for the worse if black protesters "get the things they want," and he believes with most Americans that few or no policemen dislike people like himself. He is a person who is likely to believe in retribution, and the right of a man to defend himself and his home with homicide. He probably thinks many forms of protest constitute "violence," and he is more likely than the average man to think that police activities such as shooting looters and beating students are not violence. He is more likely than most Americans to deny that violence has roots in such social problems as lack of jobs and poor education, and that poverty and discrimination cause violence. He is probably convinced that the courts treat everyone equally, that the Supreme Court has made it more difficult to punish criminals, and that the police need more power. Such an individual, compared to others who score lower on Violence for Social Control, is more likely to live in the South or in the border states, is more likely to be neither foreign-born nor of foreign parents, and is less likely to be well-educated.

Violence for Social Change

This section of the chapter presents results from a series of analyses parallel to those just described. for Violence for Social Control. The analytic model presented in Figure 1 again provides the guidelines for examining various sets of background and psychological factors to see how they operate, separately and jointly, to explain attitudes toward the use of violence for achieving social change.

As before, the data were separately analyzed for all men and for two subgroups—blacks, and men with some college experience. In contrast to the analysis of Violence for Social Control, where patterns of relationships tended to be rather similar for the different groups, regarding Violence for Social Change blacks sometimes show rather different patterns from whites, and more educated men show different patterns from those with less education. These differences sometimes mask each other when subgroups are combined. Instances of this will be noted in the text where appropriate.

Background Characteristics

Early Background Factors. Of the factors considered in this set of early experiences, race shows by far the largest relationship to attitudes toward Violence for Social Change (Table 10). Blacks expressed more conviction than whites that violence is necessary to bring about change fast enough. The region in which the respondent grew up is next in importance. People reared in southern or border states tended to be more supportive of Violence for Social Change than others. Age shows a small relationship—the young were slightly more radical in their views than their elders, but the differences are not of a magnitude to suggest the much-discussed generation gap.

Table 10

Percentage of Variance in Violence for Social Change
Explained by Early Background Characteristics
(all respondents; N=1,374)

Age	2%
Region of childhood	3
Race	12
Education	1
All 4 jointly (R^2)	15%
Multiple correlations (Multiple R)	.39

For American men as a whole, education is only slightly related to attitudes toward Violence for Social Change, with attitudes becoming less favorable as education increased. For blacks, however, the relationship is stronger and in the reverse direction: with increased education there is a tendency for blacks to see Violence for Social Change as more necessary. (This reversal explains in part why the relationship between education and attitudes toward Violence for Social Change is small in the population as a whole.)

One must ask why educated blacks were more likely to think violence necessary to bring about social change. Perhaps the more educated black men feel discrimination more keenly, are more impatient for an end of it, more discouraged with present efforts at improvement, and less hopeful that change can be brought about without property damage or injury.

Such feelings would be understandable. The past decade has seen some changes in the opportunity structure for blacks, but the rate of change has kept pace neither with the language of government nor the aspirations of the blacks themselves. Moreover, the principle of majority rule makes it extremely difficult for minority groups to further their position when there is a perceived conflict of interest with the majority, a condition which sometimes occurs for black people.

One might also guess that the more educated a black person becomes, the more he is apt to conclude that the exigencies of his existence are largely defined by the society in which he lives. The least educated blacks, who were least apt to see violence as necessary for social change, may be more inclined to believe that their lot in life is due to their own inadequacies. Indeed, there is evidence from other studies that black militancy increases to some extent with social status (Caplan 1970, p. 143).

For blacks, for the college-educated, and for the total population, the amount of variation explained by the early background variables considered jointly (7 to 19 percent) is nearly equal to the sum of their individual explanatory powers. This indicates that the explanatory ability of each variable is largely independent from that of the others.

Later Background Characteristics. Table 11 shows the relationships between some adult demographic characteristics and Violence for Social Change. The respondent's military experience, his pattern of church attendance, the size of town or city in which he lived, and his family income all show small associations with attitudes toward Violence for Social Change.[4]

---

[4] Absolute family income and family income relative to family size (called "income adequacy") show similar trends.

For the overall population, family income appears to have the largest association; men with larger incomes tended to score lower on Violence for Social Change. This is also true for those who are college trained. However, among black people those with higher incomes were likely to have *higher* scores on the Violence for Social Change measure, which calls to mind the finding that more educated blacks were also apt to have above average scores on Violence for Social Change.

Whether the respondent lived in a rural area, a town, or a large city plays the next largest role in this set of variables. In all cases, urban residence is associated with the belief that violence is necessary in order to bring about change fast enough. Whether this association occurs because city dwellers experience major social problems more directly than others is a matter for speculation. Certainly it must have been difficult to live in a metropolitan area in 1969 without becoming aware of poverty, crime, crises in schools, and the limited resources of municipal governments for coping with such problems.

Table 11

Percentage of Variance in Violence for Social Change
Explained by Later Background Characteristics
(all respondents; N=1,374)

Town size	3%
Military experience	2
Region	1
Family income	4
Religiousness Index	0
All 5 jointly (R^2)	8%
Multiple correlations (Multiple R)	.28

Military experience has a small effect in the general population and among those who were highly educated. Men who had never been in the armed forces scored slightly higher on Violence for Social Change than those who had served. For black men, however, the reverse was true; those who *had* served were a bit more likely to score high on Violence for Social Change. There is no evidence for an association between combat experience and attitudes toward violence.

As Table 11 shows, these later background characteristics, taken jointly, explain 8 percent of the variability in Violence for Social Change.

Early and Later Background Factors Jointly. When the early and later background factors are considered jointly (Table 12), the proportion of variation explained in attitudes toward Violence for Social Change rises to 18 percent for the population as a whole and for blacks, and to 31 percent for men with some college education. The population estimate for blacks (3 percent, not shown), however, casts doubt on the real explanatory power achieved for this subgroup; much of the 18 percent may be idiosyncratic to the particular sample of respondents being examined. With the exception of the blacks, however, it is clear that background factors do show a moderate relationship to attitudes about the use of violence for bringing about social change. Comparison of Table 12 with Table 3 indicates that background factors are more related to attitudes about Violence for Social Change than Violence for Social Control.

Table 12

Percentage of Variance in Violence for Social Change
Explained by Early and Later Background Characteristics

	All Respondents (N=1,374)	Blacks (N=303)	Men With Some College Education (N=374)
Early factors – 4 jointly (from Table 10)	15%	7%	19%
Later factors – 5 jointly (from Table 11)	8	13	15
Early and later factors jointly (R^2)	18%	18%	31%
Multiple correlations (Multiple R)	.42	.42	.56

Psychological Characteristics

To what extent are the five sets of psychological characteristics shown in the analytic model (Figure 1) related to Violence for Social Change? And to what extent do they act as mediators of the background relationships just examined? To answer these qustions we turn to the respondent's values, group identification, definitions of violence, views about social issues, and his perceptions of other people. These sets will be examined separately, then jointly. Then we will consider how well the psychological variables explain the observed relationships with the background factors.

Values. The values that were measured in this study—retributive justice, self-defense, attitudes toward kindness, the relative value of property and persons, and the extent to which humanistic values predominate over materialistic ones—explain almost none of the variation in attitudes toward Violence for Social Change in the general population (Table 13). However, they do account for 14 percent of the variation in such attitudes among the well-educated and 24 percent of the variation in such attitudes among blacks.

Among blacks and men with college experience, Retributive Justice is the value with the strongest relationship to Violence for Social Change. Among blacks, the more retributive the individual, the more likely he was to score high on Violence for Social Change. However, the reverse is true among the highly educated, most of whom were white. In this group, the higher the individual scored on Retributive Justice, the lower he was apt to score on Violence for Social Change.

Table 13

Percentage of Variance in Violence for Social Change
Explained by Values

	All Respondents	Blacks	Men With Some College Education
	(N=1,374)	(N=303)	(N=374)
Retributive Justice Index	1%	14%	7%
Kindness Index	0	9	2
Self-Defense Index	0	5	2
Humanism Index	0	2	7
Property/Person Priority Index	1	3	2
All 5 jointly (R^2)	2%	24%	14%
Multiple correlations (Multiple R)	.14	.49	.37

This interesting finding might be explained as follows: many black people have feelings of resentment and grievance against white society. Some may view that society as having committed violence against them and these people may also view violence as a means of redressing their grievances. Such considerations would generate a positive association between Violence for Social Change and Retributive Justice among blacks. On the other hand, one might speculate that whites are more likely to see violence for social change as initial disruption rather than retaliation.

Indeed, whites who are retributive may be least apt to see the justice of the movement for social equality, and most likely to resent actions to bring about such equality. Our data show that people who scored high on Retributive Justice were more apt to define protest as violence than were others. Hence, it is consistent for whites who are high on Retributive Justice to score low on Violence for Social Change. These relationships, which are opposite in direction for whites and blacks, are partly responsible for the failure of this value to account for any of the variation in attitudes toward Violence for Social Change in the total population.

For blacks, Kindness and Self-Defense are next in explanatory power. As one would expect, those professing more belief in Kindness were less apt to advocate Violence for Social Change. However, contrary to what one might expect, the more black men valued persons over property, the higher they scored on Violence for Social Change. At first this appears paradoxical; surely, if one values people, one would abhor that which injures them. Nevertheless, it seems tenable that if one places a high value on people, if one believes that they ought to be free and treated with respect and dignity, and if one also believes that there is no non-violent way to achieve such an estate for all people, one might espouse violence as a means of bringing about social change.

For those who were highly educated, Humanism is as important as Retributive Justice. Those who favored the humanistic values scored above average on Violence for Social Change, a finding very similar to the relation between Property/Person valuation and Violence for Social Change observed for blacks.

Identification. Table 14 shows the relationships between the twelve identification variables and Violence for Social Change. As expected, the more the respondent identified with white student demonstrators and black protesters, the more likely he was to score high on Violence for Social Change. The more the respondent identified with the police, the less likely he was to score high on Violence for Social Change. Jointly, the identification items explained from 22 to 44 percent of the variation in such attitudes, with the greatest explanatory power among the well-educated. However, the amount of variation explained is considerably less than the sum of the explanatory powers of the individual items, indicating extensive overlap among them.

Unlike the values measured in this study, identification is related in a very substantial way both to the index of Violence for Social Control and Violence for Social Change. Among the well-educated, it accounts for over a quarter of the variation in the former index and almost half of the variation in the latter. Clearly, the identifications which an individual

Table 14

Percentage of Variance in Violence for Social Change
Explained by Identification Items

	All Respond- ents	Blacks	Men With Some College Education
	(N=1,374)	(N=303)	(N=374)
White student demonstrators helpful	4%	3%	17%
No white student demonstrators dislike respondent	1	3	4
White student demonstrators trustworthy	1	2	11
White student demonstrators better life	6	3	13
Black protesters helpful	3	3	7
No black protesters dislike respondent	3	1	3
Black protesters trustworthy	2	2	9
Black protesters better life	9	3	18
Police helpful	6	4	10
No police dislike respondent	5	8	10
Police trustworthy	7	1	8
Police better life	6	4	12
All 12 jointly (R^2)	22%	26%	44%
Multiple correlations (Multiple R)	.47	.51	.66

makes may well be of considerable importance in determining attitudes toward violence. Moreover, as an individual becomes better educated and develops a more integrated belief system, the role of identification appears to increase in importance in relation to such attitudes. With respect to the social utility of the research, both these findings offer much hope. It may very well be that identifications can be changed by education, and identification could presumably be modified in such a fashion as to reduce the level of violence that the individual is willing to justify. Moreover, the data indicate that the principle probably has some generality. If individuals were taught to understand and appreciate their contrasts and commonalities with many different groups, a generalized decrease in the willingness to justify violence might well follow.

How Violence is Defined. Table 15 shows the extent to which attitudes toward Violence for Social Change are related to the respondent's definition of police actions and protest activities as "violence," and to his semantic conceptualization of violence (the extent to which he thought "violence" good or bad, necessary or unnecessary, avoidable or unavoidable). These variables, taken together, explain 16 percent of the variation in attitudes toward Violence for Social Change in the general population and considerably more among the college-educated.

Table 15

Percentage of Variance in Violence for Social Change
Explained by Definitions and Semantic Variables

	All Respondents	Blacks	Men With Some College Education
	(N=1,374)	(N=303)	(N=374)
Is Protest Violence? Index	0 %	2%	3%
Are Police Acts Violence? Index	6	3	9
Violence is:			
Necessary-Unnecessary	7	11	16
Good-Bad	7	10	14
Avoidable-Unavoidable	3	5	3
All 5 jointly (R^2)	16%	21%	30%
Multiple correlations (Multiple R)	.40	.46	.55

The most important variables in this set are the respondent's perception of violence as "good or bad" and "necessary or unnecessary." The more a respondent saw "violence" as necessary and good, the more likely he was to score high on Violence for Social Change.

Next most important is the extent to which the respondent regarded certain police actions as violent. The more he regarded shooting looters, beating students, and frisking people as "violence," the more likely he was to think Violence for Social Change necessary. This finding makes a good deal of sense: it seems reasonable that the more a person sees police behaviors as "violence," the more he might feel that counter-violence is necessary to produce change.

Perception of Social Issues. Table 16 shows how much of the variation in attitudes toward Violence for Social Change can be explained by the respondent's beliefs about certain social issues. The explanatory power of such beliefs varies from 9 percent for men in general to 19 percent among the highly educated. Of the three beliefs under considera-tion, the measure of Police/Court Power, summarizing the extent to which the respondent believed that the police need more power and that the Supreme Court is making it more difficult to punish criminals, is the most

Table 16

Percentage of Variance in Violence for Social Change
Explained by Perceptions of Social Issues

	All Respondents	Blacks	Men With Some College Education
	(N=1,374)	(N=303)	(N=374)
Social Causes Index	2%	2%	3%
Police/Court Power Index	7	2	12
Court Fairness Index	2	7	7
All 3 jointly (R^2)	9%	10%	19%
Multiple correlations (Multiple R)	.30	.32	.44

powerful explanatory variable. The less the respondent endorsed such beliefs, the more likely he was to advocate Violence for Social Change.

Next in explanatory power, particularly for blacks and for men with some college education, is the extent to which the respondent believes that the courts are fair. The less blacks and the better-educated believed that courts treat people equally, the more likely they were to advocate Violence for Social Change. This association is consistent with the notion that a government must maintain legitimacy in order to engender support. The courts are by definition places of appeal from unfair and illegal treatment. To the extent that an individual believes the courts themselves are arbitrary and unfair, he may question their legitimacy and that of the larger structure of government which they represent. In any case, it appears that disenchantment with the court system is a factor in justifying violence to bring about social change.

Perceptions of Others. Table 17 shows how three variables having to do with the respondent's perception of other people relate to his attitudes about Violence for Social Change. The explanatory power of variables in this set is modest, but cumulates to 12 percent for all men and for the subgroup of more educated men. For blacks explanatory power is only 6 percent and most of this is based on idiosyncracies of the present data.

For the population as a whole, and for the subgroup of men with college experience, the trends which contribute to the 12 percent explanatory power are reasonably clear. Men who tended to be more resentful and suspicious of other people were likely to score higher than average on Violence for Social Change. So also were those who were less trusting of others.

Table 17

Percentage of Variance in Violence for Social Change
Explained by Perceptions of Other People

	All Respondents (N=1,374)	Blacks (N=303)	Men With Some College Education (N=374)
Peer Consensus Index	2%	3%	6%
Trust Index	5	1	3
Resentment-Suspicion Index	9	3	5
All 3 jointly (R^2)	12%	6%	12%
Multiple correlations (Multiple R)	.35	.24	.35

These findings raise interesting issues about the causal dynamics involved. Do people see violence as necessary to bring about social changes because their suspiciousness and lack of trust prevents them from considering other approaches? This implies that personality predispositions determine the range of coping mechanisms. Or have these people experienced inordinate amounts of ill treatment, developed a verified suspicion and lack of trust, and thus come to the conclusion that violence is the surest way to create social change? The Trust Index (Blumenthal and Andrews 1971) and the Resentment-Suspicion Index (Blumenthal and Andrews 1971) both are related to social class—individuals in the lower classes being increasingly resentful, suspicious and distrustful. (See Appendix C for details of index construction.) This implies that past experience may be important in determining such attitudes. Irrespective of how suspicion and distrust are generated, it would be helpful to know the extent such beliefs can be modified by new and positive experiences. Our data cannot answer these questions but they are accessible to research.

The Peer Consensus Index is a variable which summarizes the extent to which the respondent believes that his friends are likely to share his beliefs in respect to violence. (See Appendix C for details of index construction.) The effect of the Peer Consensus variable is weaker and difficult to interpret. Respondents who scored above average on Violence for Social Change were more likely to feel that their friends did not agree with them. This might be regarded as an indication of alienation: perhaps people who are alienated from their social surroundings are more inclined to think of violence. Alternatively, however, it may simply be an accurate perception on the part of those who believed violence necessary to bring about social changes. This is an atypical viewpoint, and holders of this viewpoint may perceive the atypicality of their position. Regardless of the dynamics, it is interesting and perhaps heartening to discover that those who believe violence necessary for social change tended to see themselves as deviant from their friends.

Psychological Characteristics Jointly. Now that the separate sets of psychological variables have been examined, we can ask: How do the sets act when considered in various combinations? Table 18 provides the answers.

Of the five sets of psychological characteristics considered, the identification items have the most explanatory power. The respondent's views about the definition and meaning of "violence" also play an important role in the total population and both subgroups. Values are important explanatory variables for blacks and for college-educated men.

When values and group identifications are considered jointly, the values make a substantial additional contribution to the explanatory power of the identification set only among blacks. Among the population as a whole and among men with some college education, knowing how a person feels about police, white student demonstrators, and black protesters provides almost as much understanding about his attitudes on the use of Violence for Social Change as knowing these factors in combination with the five values.

When the definition set is added to the values and identification sets, explanatory power rises somewhat in each of three population groups. A person's views about the nature and definition of violence make an independent contribution to understanding his attitudes about Violence for Social Change.

Once these first three sets have been considered, neither perceptions of social issues nor perceptions of other people provide much additional explanatory power, though each makes minor contributions in some population groups.

Altogether, the psychological variables studied can explain about a third of the total variation in attitudes toward Violence for Social Change for American men generally. (The population estimate is 29 percent; the multiple correlation is slightly over .5.) There are at least two factors that act against obtaining larger values—the presence of opposite (self-cancelling) trends in certain subgroups, and unreliability in the measures themselves. Separate analysis of two subgroups, blacks and men with college experience, illuminates the problem of diverging trends; in these groups the proportion of explained variation rises to slightly over one-half. (In these groups the population estimates of the variance explained are 40 percent and 45 percent; the multiple correlations are about .7.)

Table 18

Percentage of Variance in Violence for Social Change
Explained by Psychological Factors

	Single Sets		
	All Respondents	Blacks	Men With Some College Education
	(N=1,374)	(N=303)	(N=374)
Values − 5 jointly	2%	24%	14%
Identifications − 12 jointly	22	26	44
Definitions − 5 jointly	16	21	30
Social issues − 3 jointly	9	10	19
Perceptions of others − 3 jointly	12	6	12
	Combinations of Sets		
Values + Identifications	22%	36%	47%
Multiple correlations	.47	.60	.69
Values + Identifications + Definitions	28%	47%	51%
Multiple correlations	.53	.69	.71
Values + Identifications + Definitions + Social issues	29%	51%	52%
Multiple correlations	.54	.71	.72
Values + Identifications + Definitions + Social Issues + Perceptions	33%	53%	54%
Multiple correlations	.57	.73	.73

Background and Psychological Factors Jointly

Finally, Table 19 shows the results when the five sets of psychological factors are combined with the early and later background factors. The background factors add very little to the explanatory power of the psychological characteristics. (Although the percentage of variance explained in the present data rises a few points, particularly for the more educated men, the population estimates rise by only one or two percentage points.) The overlap between background and psychological factors is most readily interpreted as a causal sequence, in which one regards psychological characteristics as developing out of the circumstances measured by background variables. All variable sets together explain about a third of the variance in attitudes toward Violence for Social

Change in the general population, and about 60 percent for blacks and for men with college experience. (Population estimates of the variance ranged from 31 percent to 47 percent.)

Table 19

Percentage of Variance in Violence for Social Change
Explained by Background and Psychological Factors

	All Respondents (N=1,374)	Blacks (N=303)	Men With Some College Education (N=374)
Background factors — 2 sets jointly	18%	18%	31%
Psychological factors — 5 sets jointly	33	53	54
Background and psychological factors jointly (R^2)	36%	57%	61%
Multiple correlation (Multiple R)	.60	.75	.78

It is interesting to compare the explanatory power achieved for attitudes about using Violence for Social Change with that summarized in Table 9 for Violence for Social Control. The figures for American men together are about the same—roughly one-third of the variance in each of the two violence indices can be explained, though background factors alone are more strongly related to Violence for Social Change than to Violence for Social Control. For blacks and for men with college experience, however, the explanatory power is considerably higher for Violence for Social Change than Violence for Social Control. And for both types of violence, explanation is more complete among men with college experience.

One distinct difference between the results for Violence for Social Control and those for Violence for Social Change is that the social change data for blacks show different trends from the general population. Such racial differences rarely occur in the data on Violence for Social Control.

A Composite Picture

We can summarize the main trends in the analyses of Violence for Social Change by describing the likely characteristics of an individual who felt that damage to property or persons would be necessary in order to bring about social changes fast enough.

He was likely to feel substantial common cause and identification with white student demonstrators and black protesters, and to be somewhat more suspicious than the average American man in his views about the police. Police acts such as shooting looters, beating students, and frisking people were likely to be seen by him as forms of "violence"—things of which he disapproved. When "violence" was viewed from a more political-instrumental standpoint, however, he tended to see it less negatively than most men. He was more likely to consider "violence" to be "necessary," "good," and "unavoidable" than the average man.[5] He was relatively likely to ascribe the causes of violence to social problems, to feel the courts tended to be unfair to poor people and blacks, and that the police-court system had too much power. He was more likely than the average man to be resentful, suspicious, and untrusting of other people generally, and he perceived himself as holding views about violence which were somewhat different from his friends. (These descriptions about resentfulness, suspicion, lack of trust, and difference from friends did not hold for blacks, for whom trends on these variables were ambiguous.)

Any statement about the basic values of persons likely to believe violence might be necessary for social change depends on the group under discussion. Among American men with some college education, most of whom were white, relatively high scores on the Index of Violence for Social Change tended to be characteristic of people who scored below average on Retributive Justice and Self-Defense, and above average on the Humanism values. In contrast, among blacks exactly opposite tendencies were observed for Retributive Justice and Self-Defense; endorsers of these values tended to score *above* average on Violence for Social Change. Also, among blacks, both Kindness and Property/Person Priority do make a difference: blacks who scored above average on Violence for Social Change tended to score lower on kindness but showed relatively greater concern for persons over property than their fellows.

Most notable among relationships involving background factors is the finding that people high on the Index of Violence for Social Change showed an over-representation of blacks and urban residents. Among blacks, those who scored above average on Violence for Social Change also tended to be above average in education and income, trends exactly opposite to those observed for the population generally.

---

[5] A report by our colleague Dean Runyan (1971) details the analyses which lead to the belief that "violence" may be viewed in both an evaluative and a political-instrumental context by the same people.

Summary

How one identifies with contending groups, what acts one considers violence, whether violence itself is perceived as necessary, what values one holds and what one believes about social issues—these appear to be the social psychological factors that underlie the justification or condemnation of violence. But these factors are not independent in their ability to explain the justification of violence; there is much overlap among them. If one allows oneself to imagine what these data might mean in combination, a picture emerges which seems sensible and coherent, and which can be readily related to the events of our day.

Violence, the data seem to say, is a tool used to attain some goal. An individual can justify violence more easily when it is used by people who share his goals and is used against those who hold antithetical goals. The individual who identifies with the police (and shares their goals, or assumes the police share his) recommends more violence as a means of social control. Such a person is likely to justify even higher levels of police force if he also regards the goals of students and blacks as inimical to his interests.

Violence is likely to be used in the service of self-defense or retribution, and both these values are related to patterns of identification. One is more likely to feel retributive toward people who hold conflicting goals than toward those who hold goals similar to one's own. And one is more inclined to feel the necessity of defending oneself against individuals whom one regards as threatening his goals and their attainment. The complementary propositions seem equally plausible. Groups or persons with whom one identifies are less likely to provide the provocation which arouses the need for self-defense or retribution than groups that hold conflicting ideals. In short, one would expect a person's values to be related to the kinds of people with whom he identifies.

While retributiveness and self-defense are action-oriented values which give rise to statements about how the individual should behave under certain circumstances, the Humanism Index is a statement of which goals seem most desirable: freedom, equality, and human dignity as contrasted to respect for law, property, and financial security. One might suppose that student and black protesters would be thought of as proponents of the first three at the expense of the second and police as proponents of the second at the expense of the first. These propositions, taken together, would lead one to suspect that there should be substantial overlap in the ability of values and identification to predict violence as, indeed, the data show there is.

Attitudes about social issues fall easily into this schema. These attitudes can be seen as a reflection of the goals to which the individual adheres. If he believes the courts are unfair, one can imagine that he would prefer a situation where justice, as he defines it, is truly to be found in the judicial system. If he believes that violence springs from social problems, one might think that he would like to see such problems solved. Students and black protesters stand for such goals; hence, one would expect attitudes about social issues would be related to identification with these groups. In addition, if the individual believes that the police need more power to function properly, and that the courts are making it more difficult to convict criminals, it is likely he will identify with the police more than individuals who do not share such beliefs. Indeed, we have shown earlier that this is the case. So, one might expect substantial overlap between beliefs on social issues and the identifications the individual makes. Attitudes about social issues are also closely related to values, particularly those which emphasize freedom, human dignity, and equality prior to respect for law and property and financial security.

The role that language plays in the justification of violence fits the picture we have been sketching. Most American men are inclined to view violence as bad. Only a few rationalize the necessity for using it by claiming violence is good. For those who cannot regard violence as good and who still wish to justify using it as a means of reaching certain goals, a problem remains. If the use of violence is recommended, and if the violent act is recognized as being violent, the user must grapple with the fact that he has done something bad, or at least supported others in evil acts. No one likes to think about himself as "bad." Such a perception is likely to lead to guilt, self doubt and pain. It is easier simply not to recognize actions as immoral, and in the present case recognition can be avoided simply by not classifying acts of violence as "violence." So, the individual who supports high levels of police force believes that it is not violent to beat students or shoot looters. Classifying such acts as "not violence" makes it possible to avoid the moral struggle which must arise when a human being becomes aware of condoning evil. So, it seems reasonable that people who identify strongly with the police would not wish to label part of the police repertoire of behavior as violence (namely bad). Similarly, it seems natural that those who regard students or black protesters as inimical groups would be more inclined to label as "violence" behaviors which are part of the repertoire of dissenters. One would expect therefore that what acts a person calls violence will be related to the kinds of identifications he holds. The substantial overlap indicated between semantics and identifications in our data is in keeping with this interpretation.

Thus the interrelationships and commonalities of the concepts of identification, values, beliefs, and semantic usage can all be seen as integral to the justification of violence.

Chapter 9

CONCLUSION

What does it all mean? What questions follow from these research results, and what answers can we provide? How can these findings be related to life in the United States as it now exists, and what implications for change do they suggest?

This study indicates that violence is widely regarded as instrumental by American men. On the face of it, this is not surprising; after all, the core interview questions inquired about violence as a tool to maintain social control and to produce social change. One might argue that the context of the interview predetermined the outcome.

Unhappily, the conclusion cannot be so easily explained. Americans justify a large amount of violence in the service of particular goals. We hardly expected that half to two-thirds of American men would justify shooting in the situations described as requiring social control. Neither did we expect that 20 to 30 percent would advise the police to shoot to kill under the circumstances described. These numbers do not imply reluctance on the part of American men to use violence for instrumental reasons.

The fact that almost 50 percent of American men felt that shooting was a good way of handling campus disturbances "almost always" or at least "sometimes" is particularly disturbing. Most campus disturbances have not involved violence to persons or major damage to property (Report of the President's Commission on Campus Unrest 1970, p. 20; Keniston and Lerner 1970, p. 28). That 20 percent of American men considered it appropriate for the police to kill in these circumstances indicates the ease with which many people will accept violence to maintain order even when force so used is entirely out of proportion to the precipitating incidents. The data imply that willingness to reach for a gun is easily evoked.

The notion that violence is looked on as instrumental by American men is augmented by another finding of this study, that attitudes toward the

243

use of violence for social control are greatly influenced by the individual's values, particularly his beliefs in retributiveness and self-defense. We may infer from the data that for some Americans, consciously or unconsciously, police force is thought of as a means of providing retribution for wicked deeds.

It has been pointed out by many authorities that violence is not necessarily related to anger, hostility or rage,[1] and that violence can consist of acts carried out without ostensible emotion. However, there is a general tendency among laymen and professionals to think of violence as the result of such emotions. Bettelheim (as quoted by Speigel 1969), for example, has described the violent acts of students as the expression of paranoid characters who, deprived of parental warmth and affection, are looking for objects on which to project and vent their rage. Such statements tend to emphasize the affective component of violence and to overlook its instrumental nature. We believe the facts to be more complex, and to include both affective and instrumental considerations. For example, in the actual process of executing an order to perform a violent action, affect may play a considerable role. At the 1968 Democratic Convention in Chicago, some policemen apparently lost control of their emotions while attempting to control the crowd. The affective component of the police behaviors appeared so prominent that the incident was described as a "police riot" by the staff of the President's Commission on the Causes and Prevention of Violence (Walker 1968, p. xxii). However, we think it likely that the official orders which gave rise to that action were based primarily on instrumental rather than affective considerations. The orders may have been made in light of a negative perspective about the character, intent and patriotism of the protesters, but they were given with the object of maintaining social control rather than expressing angry feelings.

In this study, resentment and suspicion, which may be regarded as measures of the tendency to feel paranoid and hostile, failed to account for a significant part of the variation in attitudes about how much violence should be used to maintain social control. Another index, designed to measure empathy, failed to show any association whatsoever with

---

[1] For example, Wertham (1969, pp. 150 ff) asserts that during the Second World War, about 275,000 of the mentally ill and handicapped of all ages were quietly exterminated within the confines of mental hospitals throughout Germany and Austria by physicians who never received any orders to execute such acts, merely the power to use their own discretion. While one might postulate all sorts of unconscious hostilities to explain these actions, it is still true that the episodes apparently involved no overt anger, only the intellectual decision that the patient was "worthless."

attitudes toward violence. The skeptic may argue that few measures of hostility and other such traits were included in this study, that the measurement of these characteristics was not adequate. Against this is the fact that a very substantial part of the variation in attitudes toward violence can be explained in terms of the non-affective variables studied, and the probability that much of the unexplained variation is measurement error. It seems unlikely to us that major variations in attitudes toward violence will be explained by further measures of hostility or anger.

So far in this chapter, the discussion has revolved largely around the instrumental use of violence to maintain social control, more specifically violence used by the police for the purpose of maintaining order. The justification of such uses of violence is clearly and graphically documented by the data. But there are other forms of violence for social control. Some wars and many lesser military actions could be so defined. Such extensions of our data require thought and study rather than quick conclusions; there has been too much over-simplification of complex issues, particularly in foreign affairs. In that area as in others, we must ask to what extent the use of force is necessary and unavoidable and to what extent it is a function of that readiness to respond by violent means which is apparent in our data. The question is relevant both at the level of policy decisions and, as the killing of civilians in Vietnam reminds us, at the level of individual choice and behavior.

If we accept as fact the endorsement of American men of the instrumental use of violence, the question then arises: violence instrumental in the service of what goals?

Like social control, social change is a goal for which violence against persons or property may be an instrument. Whether it becomes so depends first of all on the sentiment for change itself. In some respects that sentiment is considerable. More than 90 percent of American men agreed that changes of the kind demanded by students and blacks might be needed. Substantial percentages of American men spontaneously voiced concern over such social problems as poverty, unequal opportunity, and discrimination. More than three out of four agreed that such issues are among the causes of violence. In short, there is overwhelming agreement that social change is desirable and appropriate.

Among American men as a whole, there is equal agreement that the needed social changes can come about fast enough without the use of violence. Fewer than 10 percent felt that protest involving deaths and extensive property damage is required to produce such changes, and only about one-fifth felt that protest involving some property damage and personal injury is required to produce such change. Nevertheless, the minority must be taken seriously. Even 10 percent of American men is a very large number of individuals, and it does not take a large number of persons to commit or instigate violence. Assassinations, even of presidents, have been brought about by single individuals. Bombing and other property damage is often the work of small groups. Consensus, rather than mere majority, is required to insure domestic tranquillity.

In considering the opposition of violence for social control to violence for social change, it is easy to forget that the difference is *only* in respect to the goal desired. Both types of violence are primarily instrumental rather than emotional or expressive (see Janowitz 1969, p. 327). The ends differ, the means remain the same; both imply a readiness for force. This readiness of human beings to see violence as a path to their goals has not been satisfactorily explained. Some recent and well-publicized books have proposed explanations that emphasize the instinctive and biological origins of violence (Lorenz 1966; Ardrey 1966). But whatever the biological heritage, human beings are not equally prone to violence under all circumstances. One can imagine a society and a normative structure in which violence would be seen as taboo or counter-productive. That it is actually seen as instrumental for social control by a majority of American men and as instrumental for social change by a significant minority raises an additional question: What are the social factors that evoke belief in force as a method of coping with problems?

One such factor appears to be a lack of faith in alternative means of control or change. This doubt is expressed most clearly by black men, half of whom believe change will not come about without some violence, and a quarter of whom believe change will not come about without violence leading to the death of at least some people. Such beliefs would be sobering as historical interpretation; as prediction, they are doubly depressing.

The fact of such beliefs raises in turn the question of their origin. We would expect them to spring largely from a perceived or real lack of access to power and resources. Either there are indeed no means of access, or the means exist but the potential users are unaware of the route and perhaps unqualified to traverse it. Both conditions may exist. For example, blacks have often been told that their economic disadvantages come not from racial barriers to success but from lack of proper qualifications—education or occupational training. This is a partial truth; training opportunities have been restricted but even well-educated blacks have been seriously and persistently disadvantaged.

Another reason why some people think that property damage and injury will be necessary in order to bring about social change may be their response, or over-response, to a fundamental fact of social life—the tendency of any social system to resist change. If an organization, or a community, or a society changed in response to every effort or proposal for change, it would have no recognizable form and continuity over time. Social organizations operate on the basis of mutual expectations and their fulfillment. Anything less tends to become chaotic and generates demands for order and predictability at almost any cost. Some resistance to change is therefore a necessary aspect of social order. The eternal dilemma of human organization is to determine in theory and practice the appropriate degree and form of resistance, and the criteria for acceptance of proposed changes. When these criteria for acceptance of change are set at difficult or unattainable levels, violence in the form of property damage and injury are likely to be among the costs of change.

Some Americans believe that our country has reached such a state, and speak in terms of violence for social change. A much larger segment of the population is willing to use high levels of violence to control the violence of those desiring change. Together these states of mind have profound implications for the future of our country.

It seems clear that violence feeds on violence; a violent act tends to evoke a violent response. The goals of the two types of violence considered in this research, violence for social control and violence for social change, stand in marked contrast to each other, yet the means by which these goals are to be accomplished are identical. It is unlikely that the use of force for social control will eliminate the desire for social change, although it may indeed suppress the expression of that desire. It is also unlikely that the use of violence for social control can be expected to teach the lesson that the use of violence as a means to an end is unacceptable. Violence for social control exemplifies the opposite lesson, and by example teaches it. Aggressive behavior can be learned by watching aggression (Berkowitz 1970), and aggressive behavior is likely to increase among those who watch. It does not seem a far step to suppose that one of the covert messages conveyed in the use of violence to maintain social control, even by official agencies, is that *it is socially acceptable to use violence for instrumental reasons.*

That message is transmitted in other ways, with the untiring redundancy of television. The tendency of that medium to concentrate on the visually "exciting" and often gory details of confrontations has made the use of violence for social control public, concrete, and explicit. If the use of violence can be taught by watching it, millions have learned that instrumental violence is indeed an appropriate means of achieving an end; it is the choice of heroes, the method that never fails. *However, the specific reason for which instrumental violence is used becomes the user's choice.* If instrumental violence is indeed learned from watching it, both social facts and social fictions act to escalate the level of such violence.

This study has emphasized the opposition of violence for social control and social change. One might ask whether or not there is some intrinsic incompatability between change and social control. Clearly there is not; the concept of social order does not imply an absence of change, but rather implies agreed-upon forms and mechanisms for change. Order and social change are compatible to the extent that procedures for change are workable, accessible, common and shared.

The problem of providing institutional means for producing orderly change is magnified in the United States because of the heterogeneity of the population. In recent years, much turmoil has been generated around demands for change by blacks and young people, and the responses of government and industry to those demands. But even if their needs and wishes were to be fulfilled, there would remain a large number of other groups of varied ethnic and social backgrounds with needs and demands of their own.

Moreover, the rule of the majority, while infinitely more democratic than most forms of decision-making, is not an instrument that does well for minorities. They can of course aspire to become part of the majority, but the prospect may be dim, distant or unattainable. Meanwhile, they may find government conspicuously and even explicitly unresponsive.

Such experiences serve to increase the frustration and sense of futility of minority groups. They may respond by leaving the scene, by becoming more extreme in their protest, or by drifting into apathy. Examples of all three are frequent and conspicuous in the contemporary United States.

To increase the likelihood that minorities will be heard, respected, and their goals served implies substantial changes in the social attitudes Americans appear to hold toward dissent and dissenters. Certainly the widespread suspicion of student demonstrators and black protesters, as evidenced in data of this survey, implies a profound distrust of these groups. Whether it extends to dissenters generally in the United States deserves study; for all change, even that which proves to be most socially useful, must come from those who object in some degree and fashion to the status quo. In some areas, proposals for change are readily accepted— for example, in technology, in styling, or in consumer goods. In other sectors of life, proposals for change are suspect and resistance to change is powerful and persistent.

Resistance to change takes many forms. The fact that so many Americans define acts of dissent as "violence" *in and of themselves* speaks to the disrespect and antipathy American men have developed toward the process of change and toward its advocates. Change in a society, even that which *is* of great benefit to that society comes about in part as a response to the activities of people who desire particular changes, believe in their importance, and give expression to those beliefs. Such expression can never begin as majority sentiments, but must always initially depend on the willingness of an articulate few to state the unpopular beliefs to which they subscribe. Freedom of speech and the right to dissent have been strongly supported by the commissions investigating problems of violence. The President's Commission on Campus Unrest asserted that student protest *per se* is not a problem, and that vigorous debate on current issues should be an integral function of the university. The Commission clearly and repeatedly distinguished among protest, or organized expression of dissent, disruption, defined as physical interference with the activities of others, and violence, defined as willful property damage and injury to persons.

But large numbers of Americans do not make such distinctions. As our data so clearly shows, many are convinced that protest is violence *in and of itself.* Moreover, this is not merely a semantic issue. When an action is labeled "violence," the level of police force recommended to control that activity escalates.

"Inflammatory rhetoric" is a cliche that contains a considerable amount of truth. Rhetoric does inflame. When an action is called "violent," irrespective of its intrinsic harmfulness or lack of harmfulness, the public becomes more willing to control that action with measures which are literally violent, i.e., police acts that will lead to substantial injury or death. One can argue from these data that the time has come for us to lower our voices, and that it is irresponsible, especially for people in public life, to label behaviors "violent" which are not destructive of property or persons. Such rhetoric escalates the level of violence which is justified as retaliation.

In addition to the direct effect of increasing the level of police violence seen as justifiable, the tendency to call acts of dissent "violence" may have other and far more serious consequences. If the expression of dissent is a first step in producing social change, then the practice of confusing protest with violence and the ensuing repressive response to protest interfere with the process of producing changes, even those which the nation may most require. Moreover, interference with the right of dissent, when it does not repress the dissenters, is likely to radicalize them. If peaceful means of working for changes are treated as violent, the distinction between violence and nonviolence may be relinquished by the dissenters as well as by their critics.

The relationship between values and attitudes toward violence as depicted by this study raises additional and disturbing questions. Retributiveness and the right to self-defense at the expense of another's life account for a substantial part of the variation in attitudes toward violence, particularly Violence for Social Control among whites and Violence for Social Change among blacks. Such values are often utilized to justify violent action at all levels, from foreign wars to domestic battles. The use of such values in defense of violence is well illustrated by our data but it is also encountered in accounts of murder as described in the press. For example, in a description of the killing of two policemen in the Mother Cabrini-Green housing development in Chicago in July of 1970, the New York Times reported that:

> . . . a teenage black youth in the project strolled by a slightly older black, and, with a grin, said: "An eye for an eye, a tooth for a tooth, a life for a life, a head for a head—and two for Fred."

—the referent being Fred Hampton, the Illinois chairman of the Black Panther party who was killed in a pre-dawn raid by the police (New York Times Aug. 9, 1970). It is apparently as easy for some blacks to use the value of retribution to justify the death of policemen as it is for some whites to so justify the death of Black Panthers. The principle of retribution is primitive but egalitarian.

The agreement of American men to the values of retribution and self-defense raises issues of origin as well as effect. Where do Americans learn such values? Are we teaching such values in the early school years when we urge our boys to "hit back?" Do we teach such values in the typical courses in American history, with their uncritical justification of the slaughter of the Indians, the fight for independence, the frontier wars and all the other domestic and international conflict in which this country has engaged? Or is the endless violent retribution served daily by television and the movies as damaging as some critics allege?

We do not know the answers to these questions, but the widespread endorsement of retribution and homicidal self-defense urges that the search for answers be encouraged.

Along with the explanation of the violence-justifying values and their strength, we must explain the violence-opposing values and their weakness. For example, the value of kindness does not have much of an effect on attitudes toward violence. How is it that a positive value, which seems to imply so much for our relations with others, has so little influence on attitudes toward violence? And why, for the average American, is there so little apparent integration within his value system and between his values and his beliefs about violence? Are there ways in which more integrated attitudes can be taught and the consequences of beliefs and actions considered more carefully?

Although such questions are not answered by the present research, some suggestions are evoked by the relationships of education to the phenomena under study. Among men with at least some college education, there is a great deal more consistency among beliefs than there is for Americans in general. For the educated, attitudes toward violence are more closely related to individual values, identifications, and beliefs about social issues. Moreover, there is more consistency among these characteristics. For example, if an educated man has strong humanistic values, we know that he will be more likely to identify with protesters, and less likely to call protest violence. The same predictions would be much less certain for persons with the same humanistic values but with less education. We do not know, of course, whether the tendency to achieve cognitive consistency is something that is taught in the process of higher education, or whether people who are inclined to seek such consistency choose or are chosen for higher education. Probably both an educational and a selection effect are present to some extent.

Neither do we know that cognitive consistency operates to reduce the tendency to justify violence. Nevertheless, it seems plausible that the individual who integrates his view of the world and recognizes the consequences of his ideas might be less willing to justify violence. If cognitive consistency does act to reduce the level of violence tolerated and if the need and process of achieving cognitive consistency is somehow being taught in college, then it should be possible to teach it also at lower levels of education.

What conclusions might we draw from the relationship between identification and attitudes toward violence? On the one hand, we have seen that the more the individual identifies with white student demonstrators and black protesters, the less likely he is to advocate force as a means of maintaining social control. The more he identifies with the police, the less likely he is to consider violence necessary for social change. Identification with the group which is attacked, whether police or protesters, accounts for a larger fraction of the variation in attitudes toward violence than identification with the aggressor group, whichever it may be. Positive attitudes toward those victimized by violence tend to diminish attitudinal support for violence.

In considering the importance of identification as a process which serves to diminish the extent to which violence is justified, it is instructive to consider the role that identification played in the conduct of the war in Vietnam.

Such facts have long been part of pragmatic knowledge. In every war there is a process of dehumanizing the enemy and making him improbable or impossible as an object of identification. Among others, Taylor (1970) has described the tendency of American combat troops to think of the

Vietnamese as "gooks" or "dinks," and not to regard them as human beings. He asserts that this makes killing and brutal treatment of civilians and captured prisoners more justifiable.

Nevertheless, it is a dangerous psychological device. To the extent that any category of human beings can be excluded from considerations due all persons on the basis of their humanity, it becomes possible to so exclude others for reasons convenient at other times. Fortune sets a fickle course, and today's friend becomes tomorrow's foe. World War II characterizations of the Japanese people read strangely today.

The speed with which nations reverse their beliefs about a whole people, and the frequency with which nations do so, imply commitments made more on the basis of imaginary categorical traits than on the basis of the characteristics of a real and different people, accurately perceived. Certainly the mass media have propagated such simplistic caricatures of racial, class, and national groups. Can the individual citizen be expected to behave differently? Why should he refrain from categorical judgments about classes of people distant or different from himself? Where should he learn to regard people different from himself in the full range of their complexity?

The public schools are perhaps a potential answer to these questions, but their deficiencies in these matters are conspicuous. Large numbers of texts in current usage tend to overlook the positive attributes of minorities. Much of American history is taught in terms of the justifiable violence of virtuous men against enemies of completely undesirable characteristics. The confiscation of the land of the Indians is a case in point. Moreover, we are distressingly slow to change such teaching and texts. Recently, a Michigan State Commission complained that although a report three years earlier had found the overwhelming majority of the history and civics texts used in the state schools to be inaccurate in their treatment of minority groups, almost no change in the type of text book used had been made three years later.

If we teach the justification of violence on the basis of negative attitudes toward certain groups in our public school system, how can we expect the citizen to behave otherwise on graduation? On what basis are we to expect that the principles learned in school as a justification of our past history will not be applied in those actions which will become history tomorrow?

It appears to be an almost universal wish that our domestic affairs be controlled with a minimal use of force. That fact is clear in our own data, and other evidence for it is cited in the very strong statements made by the Kerner Commission and the President's Commission on Campus Unrest. To contribute to the minimization of force in domestic affairs, it would seem wise to foster the development of positive attitudes toward minority groups. Such a policy could be judiciously pursued in the school system, where, if more consideration were given to the virtues of dissident minority groups, some appreciation and positive identifications with such groups might be generated and in turn might lead to a decline in the level of force viewed as justifiable by the American public. Change in the level of violence viewed as justifiable would lead, one hopes, to a subsequent decline in the actual levels of force employed. The chain of causality is long and the links uncertain, but they can be tested, and the reasons for doing so are compelling.

We have also seen that persons who identify negatively with the police, and who identify positively with student demonstrators and black protesters, are more apt to agree that violence is necessary to produce needed social change fast enough. One might argue that attitudes supporting this kind of violence could be reduced by increasing the antipathy toward dissident minorities (in this case student demonstrators and black protesters). However, such a policy, even if effective, will probably lead to an increase in the amount of violence used to maintain order, an undesirable consequence.

An alternative to such a policy is to reduce still further the perception that violence may be necessary to produce social change. This can be approached by two means, and both will be required. The first is for the government to demonstrate the feasibility of bringing about requisite change through legitimate channels, and the second is to reduce the general tendency of American men to reach for violence as a solution to social problems. The feasibility of change without violence is relevant not only to those small groups of people who are actually prepared to commit violence to gain some end, but to that large population that develops and defines the social climate in which violence becomes more or less possible. For example, we must inquire as to what will convince those people who identify with students and blacks that indeed changes are occurring at a sufficiently rapid rate so that there is neither need nor justification for property damage and personal injury. The answer lies partly in communication, but more in objective and visible improvement in opportunity structure and rewards.

Reducing the general tendency to violence is more difficult. Violence has been widespread in our history, traditions, and everyday life, and such things do not change easily. One could, of course, piously take to teaching in our school systems and in the mass media that violence won't work. Unfortunately, the truth is that violence does indeed work, at least sometimes and for some periods. The President's Violence Commission sadly concluded that in many instances violence has produced results desired by those who perpetrated it. All three of the Presidential Commissions which since 1967 have addressed themselves to problems of violence have concluded that a massive expenditure of funds will be required to still domestic disorder. Such expenditures require a gross reorganization of priorities at the national level, and these the Commissions called for. No such rearrangement of priorities has occurred. The suggestions of the Commissions reflect the needs and goals of minorities. If elite Commissions of governors, university presidents and the like have so little impact on national policy, one wonders how the voices of the unprestigious poor are to be heard.

Our data suggest that there is substantial attitudinal support for the instrumental use of violence in the United States. The questions used to measure such attitudes do not imply that the holder of such opinions will himself resort to violence, but the answers do imply that the level of cynicism about alternative ways of changing the American social system is so high in some groups that those who do use violence to produce social change will be met with considerable sympathy. Indeed, the President's Commission on Campus Unrest points out that students, regardless of their personal political predilections are extremely reluctant to provide information on those few students who are in fact planning serious violence such as bombing and arson. Our data show that half of all black men in the United States believe that social change will not occur without some violence. Such facts are consistent with the warnings that we are on the brink of a racial war, and perhaps also on the brink of a war against our own young.

The meaning of this research, however, is not fully comprehended in terms of dangers and warnings, real and necessary as these may be. If we were to summarize the implications of our work as a message to the majority of Americans, we would do so in terms of two propositions and an inference:

1. The vast majority of American men are willing to consider the need for social change, including some of the changes proposed by students and blacks, and they are convinced that such changes can be made fast enough without violence.

2. A small minority of all American men and a much larger minority of blacks are skeptical that such changes will be made, are angry at their delay, and are ready to justify the violence of property damage and personal injury for their attainment.

3. Therefore, it can be argued that the majority must persuade the minority, not by rhetoric but by good

works. They must convince the minority that they acknowledge the existence of social problems and accept the requirement of their solution.

A complementary message might be offered to the minority that considers social change unlikely without the violence of property damage and personal injury:

1. Most people in the United States are not pessimistic about the likelihood of social change, nor do they believe that violence is necessary to achieve it.

2. Moreover, the vast majority of American men endorse the use of violence by the police to put down minority protest that involves property damage or injury, and they are quick to read threats of such violence into protest actions. Any minority that uses violence in an attempt to produce social change is likely to face a majority response of counter-violence, and at an escalated level of destructiveness.

3. Therefore, it can be argued that minorities must find non-violent ways to appeal to the conscience of the majority so that change may be produced.

A conclusion more general than any of these is that all Americans must learn to give up the use of violence as a means of solving problems. The use of violence to achieve social control seems to generate the use of violence to achieve social change; and no less the use of violence for social change leads to the retributive violence of social control. Such cycles end only when the destruction reaches levels that one party or another cannot sustain. The logical outcome of such continuing cycles of violence is revolution or repression. The mode of life engendered by either one of these extracts a heavy toll from all.

Such messages are over-simplifications, of course. Social reality is more complex and less consistent, full of simultaneous beliefs in kindness and revenge, professed willingness for social change and distrust of those who advocate it, condemnation of violence and endorsement of violence by police. Such reality is difficult to accept, but acceptance of it is necessary. It is necessary and difficult also to give up visions of certainty and instead to think in terms of uncertain and alternative futures, determined by our acts or failures to act.

If one thinks in such terms, social information and understanding acquire tremendous importance. If our actions determine the future, we cannot afford the luxury of self-delusion, either individually or nationally.

We need to learn who and what we are, and what factors make us so. To act wisely in respect to a wanted future requires knowledge of the present, understanding of the factors that determine present states, and measurement of progress toward future goals.

The acceptance of the present as imperfect and the future as uncertain and socially determined implies a high valuation of dissent as well as information. Dissent reflects present dissatisfaction and often includes statements of preferred alternative conditions. Both knowledge and dissent are important to the continuous process of assessment, the setting of goals, and the search for appropriate means. It is difficult to imagine that sequence coming to life without competing visions, argument, protest and deep division of opinion. Social research does not replace that process, but can contribute to making it constructive.

The present study of violence is an attempt to make such a contribution. It seeks to provide descriptive facts about a crucial aspect of American life, the justification of violence. It seeks also to explain this justification, to show some of its apparent causes and explore its consequences. It remains for future work to improve the quality of the description and to deepen the understanding of causes and effects. We hope that future studies of violence for social change and social control will find those concepts increasingly alien to American life.

APPENDIX A

METHODOLOGICAL ASPECTS OF THE STUDY

Sample Design
Weighting Procedures
Response Rates
Expansion to the National Population
Comparisons with Census Data
Coding Reliabilities
Respondent Cooperativeness and Understanding

Sample Design

Universe Sampled

The universe covered in this study consists of males aged 16-64 living in dwelling units[1] in the coterminous United States during the summer of 1969.

Two Samples

Sampling procedures were designed to yield approximately 1,400 completed interviews, of which approximately 300 would be blacks. Since blacks account for only about 10 percent of the population in the United States, some over-sampling of blacks was required if there were to be

---

[1] A "dwelling unit" is defined as: a group of two or more rooms which are lived in, or which are intended to be lived in, and which have separate cooking equipment or a separate entrance; or a single room which is lived in, or intended to be lived in, which has separate cooking equipment, or is the only living quarters in the structure, or which is a one-room apartment house. (Dwelling units on military reservations are excluded.)

sufficient cases for separate analysis by race within a total sample of just 1,400. Two procedures were adopted to increase the number of blacks interviewed: one was to supplement the national cross-section sample with an additional sample of black dwelling units (as described in the following paragraph); the other was to attempt interviews with more people in black dwelling units than in other dwelling units.

The "primary sample" consisted of dwelling units selected with equal probability (1/25,850) in the approximately 620 segments (small compact geographic areas) of the Survey Research Center's national sample of dwellings. The "supplementary sample" was selected as follows: for each primary segment a nearby secondary segment was identified. If it seemed likely that this secondary segment would contain some black households, and if the necessary maps and listings were available in the sampling office (as they were in nearly all cases) a probability sample of households was selected in these secondary segments at the same rate (1/25,850) as in the primary segments.

(A minor problem occurred for those few primary segments which were discovered to contain one or more black households and for which there was no associated secondary segment. This occurred either (1) because of an inaccurate estimate of the likelihood of finding blacks in the area, or (2) because the cost of developing needed materials for the secondary segment seemed too high. In such cases the black households in the primary segment were weighted to compensate for the lack of an associated secondary segment.)

Six Categories of Respondents

Eligible respondents were defined as males aged 16-64. In nonblack households in cross-section (i.e., "primary") segments, one person was randomly designated as the principal eligible respondent and an interview attempted. In black households in both the primary and secondary segments, interviews were attempted with *all* eligible respondents. (Subsequently, one of the eligible respondents in black households from primary segments was designated as the principal. While the same could be done in black households from secondary segments, there seemed no need to do this.) No interviews were conducted in nonblack households located in secondary segments.

As a result of the above design, six categories of respondents are distinguished in Table 1.

Weighting Procedures

Since respondents in different categories were selected with different

Table 1

Six Categories of Respondents

1. Principal respondents from nonblack households in primary segments (N=1,070).

2. Principal respondents from black households in primary segments for which there was an associated secondary segment (N=79).

3. Principal respondents from black households in primary segments for which there was no associated secondary segment (N=24).

4. Extra (i.e., nonprincipal) respondents from black households in primary segments for which there was an associated secondary segment (N=21).

5. Extra respondents from black households in primary segments for which there was no associated secondary segment (N=8).

6. Respondents from black households in secondary segments (N=172).

sampling probabilities, it was necessary to weight them differentially during analysis. The weights appear in Table 2.

Table 2

Sampling Weights by Respondent Category

Respondent Categories (from Table 1)	Weight
1	Number of eligible R's in the dwelling unit.
2,4,6	0.5
3,5	1.0

Response Rates

The obtained response rates are shown in Table 3.

It is clear that the representation of whites and blacks is very similar, but that large cities and the Eastern states are slightly under-represented relative to other places. (Most of the large cities were in the Eastern states.)

The response rates shown in the table were based on an "unweighted" approach which compared the number of people actually interviewed with the number of people who *might* have been interviewed. A "weighted" response rate (which compared the people *represented* by the

Table 3

Response Rates for Designated Groups

All sampled persons	80%
Race:	
White	80
Black	78
Size of place:	
Large cities	75
Other places	82
Region:	
Eastern states	75
Southern states	81
Middle states	81
Western states	82

obtained respondents with those who might have been represented) was also calculated for whites. This weighted rate was 81 percent—virtually identical with the 80 percent obtained via the unweighted approach. Since there was no reason to expect that discrepancies between weighted and unweighted rates would be larger in other groups, the considerable additional effort of actually carrying out the calculations was not undertaken.

Having discovered the slight under-representation of people from large cities and the Eastern states in the data, we considered introducing an additional set of weights which would compensate for this. It turned out, however, that the effect of incorporating such a compensation would be negligible. Percentages based on compensated data would have differed from uncompensated figures by less than one point in all but the most extreme situations. Accordingly, no such compensation was made.

Expansions to the National Population

For some purposes it is desirable to use sample data to estimate the actual number of people having a certain characteristic in the universe from which the sample was drawn. Given a sampling rate of 1/25,850 in each of the samples, an obtained response rate of 80 percent, an estimated coverage rate of 94 percent, and the weights described above, the appropriate expansion factor is 34,548. This is the number by which an obtained weighted number of respondents would be multiplied to estimate the corresponding number of people in our universe.

When the total weighted number of respondents (1,472) is multiplied by the expansion factor, one obtains an estimate of approximately

51,000,000 males aged 16-64 living in dwelling units. From the *Statistical Abstract of the United States 1969*[2] it is possible to develop an estimate of approximately 58,000,000 as the number of all males 16-64 in the coterminous United States. Part of the discrepancy between the sample estimate of 51,000,000 males and the 58,000,000 estimated from the Census arises from a difference in who is included in the two universes. Our sample, which consisted of dwelling units, excludes people living in quarters such as barracks, dormitories, fraternities, hospitals, rooming houses, hotels, prisons, etc.[3] It seems safe to conclude, however, that use of this expansion factor produces estimates correct at least to within 10 percent. The actual error may be substantially less than that.

Comparisons with Census Data

The race and age distributions of the respondents compared satisfactorily with similar distributions obtained from the Bureau of the Census. This helped confirm the representativeness of our sample. Tables 4 and 5 present the comparisons.

Table 4

Estimates of Racial Distribution from
Project Data and Census Bureau Data

	Project Data	Census Bureau Data[a]
Whites	87	89
Blacks	11	10
Other	2	1
Total	100%	100%

[a] This estimate based on all males aged 16-64 as of July 1, 1967. Source: Current Population Reports, Series P-25, No. 385, Table 1.

With respect to Tables 4 and 5, it should be noted that Census Bureau Data were estimates for *all* males in the relevant age ranges— including members of the armed forces overseas, residents of Alaska and Hawaii, and people living in all types of quarters. The project data, on the other hand, referred only to males living in dwelling units within the 48 states.

2 See Tables 8, 24, and 26 of the Statistical Abstract.
3 See the first footnote in this appendix for the definition of a dwelling unit.

Table 5

Estimates of Age Distribution from
Project Data and Census Bureau Data

Age	Project Data	Census Bureau Data[a]
16-19	13	13
20-29	20	24
30-39	19	19
40-49	22	20
50-59	17	17
60-64	9	7
Total	100%	100%

[a] This estimate based on all males aged 16-64 on July 1, 1967.
Source: Current Population Reports, Series P-25, No. 385, Table 1.

Coding Reliabilities

Coding is the process of assigning numeric categories to the information appearing on an interview schedule and writing those numbers on a special form (from which the information is subsequently punched onto cards which can be read by a computer). This process is one in which measurement error may be introduced, hence effort was taken to estimate how much error occurred and to minimize it.

To assess the measurement error associated with coding, a predetermined proportion of interviews were independently recoded by a person more centrally involved with the management of the study than the original coder. It is convenient to report the degree of their agreement (i.e., the coding reliability) in "percentage agreement" terms. If the coding reliability were, say, 99 percent, this would mean that the original coder and the check coder assigned the same category number to 99 out of every 100 responses. The proportion of interviews check-coded in the present study ranged from 6 to 28 percent, depending on the type of question.

The likelihood of measurement error occurring during coding of information from closed questions is small. In these cases, the respondent or interviewer had marked one of a limited number of possible answers in the interview schedule, and the coder had only to select the correct category number for this answer and write that number on the form. In the present study, coding reliabilities for closed questions were consistently above 99 percent. Most of the analysis reported in this book is based on answers to closed questions.

Also included in the interview, however, were some open questions, which required the interviewer to transcribe the respondent's answer in his own words. Coding this information was considerably more difficult since the coder had to make a judgment as to the appropriate category number to assign to the answer. For some open questions this required selecting an appropriate category from among several hundred possibilities. The coding reliability averaged 90 percent agreement for open questions used in the analyses described in this book.

Respondent Cooperativeness and Understanding

After the interview was completed, interviewers were asked to rate the cooperativeness of the respondent and his understanding of the questions. Tables 6 and 7 present the results:

Table 6

Cooperativeness of Respondents

Very cooperative	83
Somewhat cooperative	15
Not cooperative	1
Not ascertained	1
Total	100%

Table 7

Respondent's Understanding of the Questions

Good understanding	62
Fair understanding	29
Poor understanding	8
Not ascertained	1
Total	100%

Note: Unlike most presentations in this book, Table 6 and 7 are based on *unweighted* data. Hence they refer explicitly to the 1,374 respondents who participated in the study rather than estimating what would be true for American men as a whole.

It can be seen that virtually all of the respondents from whom an interview was obtained were judged to be at least somewhat cooperative, and most of these were judged "very" cooperative.

Ninety-one percent of the respondents were judged to have understood the questions at least moderately well (62 percent were said to have a "good" understanding). Further analysis showed that respondents having a "poor" understanding tended to include disproportionately high numbers of blacks, of people with little education, and of people living in rural areas and/or the South.

APPENDIX B

INTERVIEW SCHEDULE

The questionnaire used in the survey on attitudes toward violence conducted in the summer of 1969 is reproduced here.

INTRODUCTION

INTRODUCTION

In this study we are interested in finding out something about how people in the United States feel about problems in society nowadays. There has been a lot of talk lately about how life in this country is changing, and we are interested in finding out how you feel about some of the things that have been going on.

SECTION A:

A1. In this study we are interested in people's views about many different things.
     What things going on in the United States these days worry or concern you?

_____

_____

_____

     A1a. Anything else? _____

           _____

           _____

A2. Could you mention some (other) things you've heard about in the last few years
     that involve violence?

_____

_____

_____

A3. What violent events in the United States are of the most concern to you?

_____

_____

_____

A4. Here are some words that have been used to describe violence. (HAND R RING CARD A) The first words are strong and weak. Do you think violence belongs at the <u>strong end</u> or at the <u>weak end</u> or <u>in between</u>? Please point to where you think it belongs. (INTERVIEWER: CIRCLE NUMBER NEAREST R'S POSITION. REPEAT INSTRUCTION FOR SECOND ITEM AND OTHERS IF NEEDED)

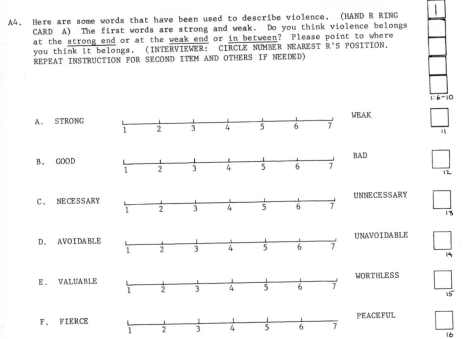

A. STRONG   1 2 3 4 5 6 7   WEAK

B. GOOD   1 2 3 4 5 6 7   BAD

C. NECESSARY 1 2 3 4 5 6 7   UNNECESSARY

D. AVOIDABLE 1 2 3 4 5 6 7   UNAVOIDABLE

E. VALUABLE   1 2 3 4 5 6 7   WORTHLESS

F. FIERCE   1 2 3 4 5 6 7   PEACEFUL

A5a. Here is a list of nine things that have been in the news. Tell me if you think about these as violence. I don't mean if they lead to violence, but if you think about them <u>as violence in themselves</u>.

Do you think of <u>student protest</u> as violence?

| 1. YES | 3. NO | 2. BOTH |

A5b. Do you think of <u>police beating students</u> as violence?

| 1. YES | 3. NO | 2. BOTH |

A5c. Do you think of <u>police shooting looters</u> as violence?

| 1. YES | 3. NO | 2. BOTH |

A5d. Do you think of <u>burglary</u> as violence?

| 1. YES | 3. NO | 2. BOTH |

A5e. Do you think of <u>sit-ins</u> as violence?

| 1. YES | 3. NO | 2. BOTH |

A5f. Do you think of <u>draft card burning</u> as violence?

| 1. YES | 3. NO | 2. BOTH |

A5g. Do you think of <u>looting</u> as violence?

| 1. YES | 3. NO | 2. BOTH |

A5h. Is it violence <u>not to let people have their civil rights</u>?

| 1. YES | 3. NO | 2. BOTH |

A5i. Do you think of <u>police stopping to frisk people</u> as violence?

| 1. YES | 3. NO | 2. BOTH |

A6. People, nowadays, have many ideas about what causes violence. Thinking about the problem generally, what do <u>you</u> think causes violence?

_____

_____

_____

A7. Do you think that one cause of violence is that the average person feels he can't live up to what is expected of him?

    | 1. YES | | 3. NO |

1:26

A8. Do you think that poverty helps cause violence?

    | 1. YES | | 3. NO |

27

A9. Would there be less violence if more people had good jobs?

    | 1. YES | | 3. NO |

28

A10. Do you think a poor education helps cause violence?

    | 1. YES | | 3. NO |

29

A11. In your opinion, does discrimination help cause violence?

| 1. YES | | 3. NO |

1:30

A12. When people get the feeling that changes are happening so fast they can't keep up with them, are they more likely to cause violence?

| 1. YES | | 3. NO |

31

A13. Do you ever feel changes are happening too fast for you?

| YES | | 3. NO | (GO TO Q. A14)

32

A13a. Do you feel this way a lot of the time or just occasionally?

| 1. LOT OF THE TIME | | 2. OCCASIONALLY |

A14. Some people have told us that it's harder and harder for a person to feel important nowadays. Do you think that helps cause violence?

| 1. YES | | 3. NO |

33

A15. Do you think it is harder for a person to feel important nowadays?

| 1. YES | | 3. NO |

34

A16. How safe do you feel it is for people to go out alone at night in your neighborhood?

| 4. Completely Safe | 3. Usually Safe | 2. Not Too Safe | 1. Not Safe At All |

35

P A S T E   C A R D   # 1   H E R E

A17. There have been times when gangs of hoodlums have gone into a town, terrified people, and caused a lot of property damage. How do you think the police should handle this situation? (HAND R PASTE CARD #1. INSTRUCT R TO FILL OUT CARD BY CHECKING ONE ANSWER IN EACH ROW)

	ALMOST ALWAYS	SOMETIMES	HARDLY EVER	NEVER	
A. The police should let it go, not do anything.	4	3	2	1	1:36
B. Police should make arrests without using clubs or guns.	4	3	2	1	37
C. Police should use clubs, but not guns.	4	3	2	1	38
D. The police should shoot, but not to kill.	4	3	2	1	39
E. The police should shoot to kill.	4	3	2	1	40

A18. How many of your friends do you think would agree with your answers?

| 3. Most | 2. Some | 1. A few or none |

41

SECTION B:

B1. There have been a lot of disturbances by white students at colleges around the country. What do you think about these?

_____

_____

_____

B2. On the whole, would you say that <u>most</u> white student demonstrators are <u>trying to be helpful</u>, or that they are <u>looking for trouble</u>, or they aren't one way or the other?

| 3. TRYING TO BE HELPFUL | 1. LOOKING FOR TROUBLE | 2. NOT ONE WAY OR THE OTHER |

1:42

B3. Think of how white student demonstrators think of people like yourself. Do you think that <u>none</u> dislike people like yourself, only <u>a few</u>, <u>many</u>, or <u>almost all</u> dislike people like yourself?

| 4. NONE | 3. A FEW | 2. MANY | 1. ALMOST ALL |

43

B4. Would you say that most white student demonstrators <u>can be trusted</u>, or that you <u>can't be too careful in dealing with them</u>?

| 3. CAN BE TRUSTED | 1. CAN'T BE TOO CAREFUL IN DEALING WITH THEM | 2. D.K. |

44

PASTE   CARD   # 2   HERE

B5. As you know, many white students feel changes are needed in society. Do you agree with the students that some changes are <u>might</u> be needed?

1. YES, CHANGE IS NEEDED	8. D.K.	3. NO CHANGE IS NEEDED

(PASTE IN BLANK CARD; TURN TO PAGE 10, Q. B8)

1:45

B6. In trying to bring about change, students sometimes demonstrate in such a way that property is damaged and the police have to be called. We would like to know how much you agree with each of these opinions about how much violence is necessary for the students to bring about change. (HAND R PASTE CARD #2. INSTRUCT R TO FILL OUT CARD)

	AGREE A GREAT DEAL	AGREE SOMEWHAT	DISAGREE SOMEWHAT	DISAGREE A GREAT DEAL	
A. Changes can be made fast enough without action involving property damage or injury.	4	3	2	1	46
B. Protest in which some people are hurt is necessary for changes to come fast enough.	4	3	2	1	47
C. Protest in which there is <u>some</u> property damage is necessary for changes to be brought about fast enough.	4	3	2	1	48
D. Protest in which there is <u>much</u> property damage is necessary before changes can be brought about fast enough.	4	3	2	1	49
E. Protest in which some people are killed is necessary before changes will take place fast enough.	4	3	2	1	50

B7. How many of your friends do you think would agree with your answers?

3. Most	2. Some	1. A few or none

51

B8. When you think about student disturbances on campuses and elsewhere, which involve a lot of property damage, how do you think police should handle the situation? (HAND R PASTE CARD #3. INSTRUCT R TO FILL OUT CARD SAYING:) "This card is like the one you filled out before, but now we want to know how you feel about <u>student disturbances</u>."

		ALMOST ALWAYS	SOMETIMES	HARDLY EVER	NEVER
A.	The police should let it go, not do anything.	4	3	2	1
B.	Police should make arrests without using clubs or guns.	4	3	2	1
C.	Police should use clubs, but not guns.	4	3	2	1
D.	The police should shoot, but not to kill.	4	3	2	1
E.	The police should shoot to kill.	4	3	2	1

1:52

53

54

55

56

B9. How many of your friends do you think would agree with your answers?

| 3. Most | | 2. Some | | 1. A few or none |

57

B10. If white student demonstrators get the things they want, do you think <u>your</u> life will change?

WILL CHANGE	2. WON'T CHANGE	8. D.K.
	(GO TO Q. C1)	(GO TO Q. C1)

1:58

B10a. IF "WILL CHANGE": Do you think <u>your</u> life will change for <u>better</u> or <u>worse</u>?

3. BETTER	1. WORSE	7. D.K.

SECTION C:

C1. Do you think <u>student demonstrators</u> are more likely to <u>cause</u> violence, or more likely to be <u>victims</u> of violence, or are they likely not to be involved?

1. CAUSE	3. VICTIMS	4. NOT INVOLVED	2. BOTH CAUSE AND VICTIMS

59

C2. Do you think <u>Negroes</u> (black people/colored people) are more likely to <u>cause</u> violence, or more likely to be <u>victims</u> of violence, or are they likely not to be involved?

1. CAUSE	3. VICTIMS	4. NOT INVOLVED	2. BOTH CAUSE AND VICTIMS

60

C3. Do you think <u>police</u> are more likely to <u>cause</u> violence, or more likely to be <u>victims</u> of violence, or are they likely not to be involved?

1. CAUSE	3. VICTIMS	4. NOT INVOLVED	2. BOTH CAUSE AND VICTIMS

61

C4. Do you think <u>businessmen</u> are more likely to <u>cause</u> violence, or more likely to be <u>victims</u> of violence, or are they likely not to be involved?

1. CAUSE	3. VICTIMS	4. NOT INVOLVED	2. BOTH CAUSE AND VICTIMS

62

SECTION D:

D1. How people think problems should be handled depends on how they imagine the
other fellow's situation. In this study, we are interested in finding out
how people go about putting themselves in someone else's shoes. So, I will
describe several real-life situations -- things that really happen to people --
and then ask how those situations look to you.

STORY 1; PART A: *After a lot of pleading, a boy finally persuades his father
to let him use the new car. When he comes back to the car after seeing a
movie, he finds one fender crumpled.*

How do you think the boy was <u>feeling</u> in this situation? (INTERVIEWER: TRY TO
GET R TO STATE A <u>FEELING</u>.)

_____

_____

D2. STORY 1; PART B: *When the father asks the boy about the fender, his son tells
him that the car was all right when he brought it home and that some other
family member must have crumpled it.*

How do you think the boy was <u>feeling</u> when he lied like that? (INTERVIEWER:
TRY TO GET R TO STATE A <u>FEELING</u>.)

_____

_____

D3. How likely is it that anyone among your friends <u>could</u> feel like
this boy if a similar thing happened to them? (HAND R RING CARD B)

4. Very likely	3. Somewhat likely	2. Not too likely	1. Not likely at all

D4. How likely is it that you <u>could</u> feel like this boy if a similar
thing happened to you?

4. Very likely	3. Somewhat likely	2. Not too likely	1. Not likely at all

SECTION E:

E1. STORY 2; PART A: *The young mother of two children has a difficult birth with the third child. The infant does not do well, and when the child is three years old the mother learns from the doctor that the child will probably never be able to learn as well as his brother and sister, and cannot be expected to get past the third or fourth grade in school.*

How do you think the mother was <u>feeling</u> in this situation? (INTERVIEWER: TRY TO GET R TO STATE A <u>FEELING</u>.)

_____

_____

E2. STORY 2; PART B: *Actually, in this case, the mother becomes very impatient with the retarded child, and is often cross with him about the things he cannot do.*

How do you think this mother was <u>feeling</u> when she treated her child like that? (INTERVIEWER: TRY TO GET R TO STATE A <u>FEELING</u>.)

_____

_____

E3. How likely is it that anyone among your friends <u>could</u> feel like this mother if a similar thing happened to them? (HAND R RING CARD B)

4. Very likely	3. Somewhat likely	2. Not too likely	1. Not likely at all	

1:65

E4. How likely is it that you <u>could</u> feel like this mother if a similar thing happened to you?

4. Very likely	3. Somewhat likely	2. Not too likely	1. Not likely at all	

66

SECTION F:

F1. Over the last few years there have been a lot of big city riots (ghetto disturbances/inner city disturbances). What do you think about those?

_____

_____

_____

F2. On the whole, would you say that <u>most</u> Negro (black/colored) protesters are <u>trying to be helpful</u>, or that they are <u>looking for trouble</u>, or they aren't one way or the other?

3. TRYING TO BE HELPFUL	1. LOOKING FOR TROUBLE	2. NOT ONE WAY OR THE OTHER

F3. Think of how Negro (black/colored) protesters think of people like yourself. Do you think that <u>none</u> dislike people like yourself, only <u>a few</u>, <u>many</u>, or <u>almost all</u> dislike people like yourself?

4. NONE	3. A FEW	2. MANY	1. ALMOST ALL

F4. Would you say that most Negro (black/colored) protesters <u>can be trusted</u> or that you <u>can't be too careful in dealing with them</u>?

3. CAN BE TRUSTED	1. CAN'T BE TOO CAREFUL IN DEALING WITH THEM	2. D.K.

2

2:6-10

11

12

13

PASTE   CARD   #4   HERE

F5. Many Negroes (black people/colored people) feel changes are needed in our society. Do you agree that some changes <u>might</u> be needed in the United States to make life better for Negroes (black people/colored people)?

1. YES, CHANGE IS NEEDED	8. D.K.	3. NO CHANGE IS NEEDED

2:14

(PASTE IN BLANK CARD; TURN TO PAGE 16, Q. F8)

F6. In trying to bring about changes, some Negroes (black people/colored people) have protested sometimes in such a way that the police had to be called. We would like to know how much you agree with each of these opinions about how much violence is necessary for the Negro (black people / colored people) to bring about changes. (HAND R PASTE CARD #4. INTERVIEWER: INSTRUCT R TO FILL OUT CARD)

	AGREE A GREAT DEAL	AGREE SOMEWHAT	DISAGREE SOMEWHAT	DISAGREE A GREAT DEAL
A. Changes can be made fast enough without action involving property damage or injury.	4	3	2	1
B. Protest in which some people are hurt is necessary for changes to come fast enough.	4	3	2	1
C. Protest in which there is <u>some</u> property damage is necessary for changes to be brought about fast enough.	4	3	2	1
D. Protest in which there is <u>much</u> property damage is necessary before changes can be brought about fast enough.	4	3	2	1
E. Protest in which some people are killed is necessary before changes will take place fast enough.	4	3	2	1

15
16
17
18
19

F7. How many of your friends do you think would agree with your answers?

3. Most	2. Some	1. A few or none

20

PASTE   CARD   # 5   HERE

F8. When you think about big city riots (ghetto disturbances/inner city disturbances) involving Negroes (black people/colored people) and police, how do
you think the police should handle the situation? (HAND R PASTE CARD #5.
INSTRUCT R TO FILL OUT CARD)

	ALMOST ALWAYS	SOMETIMES	HARDLY EVER	NEVER
A. The police should let it go, not do anything.	4	3	2	1
B. Police should make arrests without using clubs or guns.	4	3	2	1
C. Police should use clubs, but not guns.	4	3	2	1
D. The police should shoot, but not to kill.	4	3	2	1
E. The police should shoot to kill.	4	3	2	1

F9. How many of your friends do you think would agree with your answers?

| 3. Most | | 2. Some | | 1. A few or none |

F10. If Negro (black/colored) protesters get the things they want, do you think your life will change?

WILL CHANGE	2. WON'T CHANGE	8. D.K.
	(GO TO Q. F11)	(GO TO Q. F11)

F10a. IF "WILL CHANGE": Do you think your life will change for better or worse?

2:27

3. BETTER	1. WORSE	7. D.K.	(GO TO Q. F11)

F10b. In what way? _____

_____

_____

F11. What do you think should be done to prevent big city riots (ghetto disturbances/inner city disturbances)?

_____

_____

_____

SECTION G:

G1. Some people say that stealing or damaging property is as bad as hurting
     people. Others say that damaging property is not as bad as hurting people.
     What do you think?

1. STEALING OR DAMAGING PROPERTY IS AS BAD AS HURTING PEOPLE	2. DAMAGING PROPERTY IS NOT AS BAD AS HURTING PEOPLE

2:28

G2. Do you think it would be worse to become a permanent cripple, or to lose an
     uninsured home through fire, or are they equally bad?

BECOMING A CRIPPLE IS WORSE	LOSING HOME IS WORSE	3. THEY ARE EQUALLY BAD

(GO TO Q. G3)

G2a. Would you say it was a
      lot worse, or just
      somewhat worse?

5. A LOT WORSE	4. SOMEWHAT WORSE

G2b. Would you say it was a
      lot worse, or just
      somewhat worse?

1. A LOT WORSE	2. SOMEWHAT WORSE

29

G3. How do you think that robbery and stealing can be reduced?

_____

_____

_____

G3a. (IF R MENTIONS ONLY ONE WAY, PROBE FOR ADDITIONAL MATERIAL) Any other ways?

_____

_____

_____

G3b. Which of these do you favor? (INTERVIEWER: CIRCLE WHICHEVER ALTERNATIVE
      IN G3 OR G3a IS FAVORED)

G4. Some people have told us the courts nowadays treat some people better or worse than others. Do you think that <u>rich</u> people and <u>poor</u> people are likely to be <u>treated the same</u> by the courts or <u>not</u>?

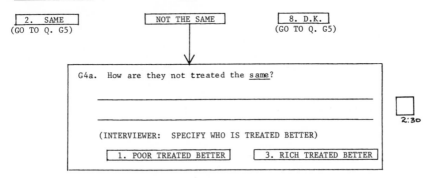

| 2. SAME |
| NOT THE SAME |
| 8. D.K. |
(GO TO Q. G5)   (GO TO Q. G5)

G4a. How are they not treated the <u>same</u>?

_____

_____

(INTERVIEWER: SPECIFY WHO IS TREATED BETTER)

| 1. POOR TREATED BETTER | | 3. RICH TREATED BETTER |

2:30

G5. Do you think that white people and Negroes (black people/colored people) are likely to be <u>treated the same</u> by the courts or <u>not</u>?

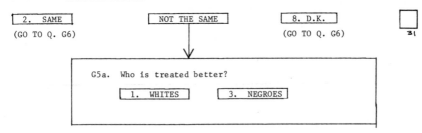

| 2. SAME |
| NOT THE SAME |
| 8. D.K. |
(GO TO Q. G6)   (GO TO Q. G6)

31

G5a. Who is treated better?

| 1. WHITES | | 3. NEGROES |

G6. Do you think the courts treat people like yourself <u>better</u> or <u>worse</u> than others, or <u>about the same</u>?

| 3. BETTER | | 1. WORSE | | 2. SAME |

32

G7. On the whole, would you say that most policemen are <u>trying to be helpful</u>, or that they are <u>looking for trouble</u>, or they aren't one way or the other?

| 3. TRYING TO BE HELPFUL | | 1. LOOKING FOR TROUBLE | | 2. NOT ONE WAY OR THE OTHER |

33

G8. Think of how policemen think of people like yourself. Do you think that <u>none</u> dislike people like yourself, only <u>a few</u>, <u>many</u>, or <u>almost all</u> dislike people like yourself?

| 4. NONE | | 3. A FEW | | 2. MANY | | 1. ALMOST ALL |

34

G9.   Would you say that most policemen can be trusted or that you can't be too careful in dealing with them?

| 3. CAN BE TRUSTED | 1. CAN'T BE TOO CAREFUL IN DEALING WITH THEM | 2. D.K. |

G10. If the police get the things they want, do you think your life will change?

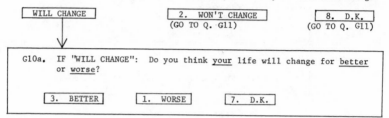

| WILL CHANGE | 2. WON'T CHANGE (GO TO Q. G11) | 8. D.K. (GO TO Q. G11) |

G10a. IF "WILL CHANGE": Do you think your life will change for better or worse?

| 3. BETTER | 1. WORSE | 7. D.K. |

G11. Think of people who run things like the government, big business and such. Is the way they are trying to run things generally favorable for you, bad for you, or somewhere in between?

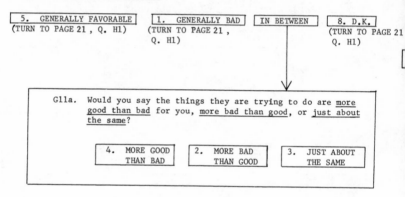

| 5. GENERALLY FAVORABLE (TURN TO PAGE 21 , Q. H1) | 1. GENERALLY BAD (TURN TO PAGE 21 , Q. H1) | IN BETWEEN | 8. D.K. (TURN TO PAGE 21 Q. H1) |

G11a. Would you say the things they are trying to do are more good than bad for you, more bad than good, or just about the same?

| 4. MORE GOOD THAN BAD | 2. MORE BAD THAN GOOD | 3. JUST ABOUT THE SAME |

SECTION H:

H1. (HAND R RING CARD C) We would like you to list these in the order you feel is
most important for the kind of world you want to live in. Please tell
me which you think is <u>most</u> important. Now which do you think is the next most
important? (INTERVIEWER: CONTINUE ASKING UNTIL R HAS ORDERED ALL ITEMS. MARK
THE NUMBER <u>1</u> IN FRONT OF THE ITEM WHICH IS <u>MOST</u> IMPORTANT, <u>2</u> IN FRONT OF THE
ITEM WHICH <u>IS</u> NEXT MOST IMPORTANT AND SO ON UNTIL ALL ITEMS HAVE BEEN ASSIGNED
A NUMBER FROM ONE TO SIX)

A. ( ) EQUALITY

B. ( ) HUMAN DIGNITY

C. ( ) RESPECT FOR PROPERTY

D. ( ) RESPECT FOR LAW

E. ( ) FREEDOM

F. ( ) FINANCIAL SECURITY FOR SELF AND LOVED ONES

H2. Here are some things people have told us. We would like to know whether you
<u>agree a great deal</u>, <u>agree somewhat</u>, <u>disagree somewhat</u>, or <u>disagree a great</u>
<u>deal</u>. (HAND R RING CARD D. READ STATEMENTS TO R)

	AGREE A GREAT DEAL	AGREE SOMEWHAT	DISAGREE SOMEWHAT	DISAGREE A GREAT DEAL	
People who commit murder deserve capital punishment.	4	3	2	1	☐ 2:38
H3. Violence deserves violence.	4	3	2	1	☐ 39
H4. It's important to be kind to people even if they do things you don't believe in.	4	3	2	1	☐ 40
H5. "An eye for an eye and a tooth for a tooth" is a good rule for living.	4	3	2	1	☐ 41
H6. It is often necessary to use violence to prevent violence.	4	3	2	1	☐ 42
H7. When a person harms you, you should turn the other cheek and forgive him.	4	3	2	1	☐ 43

		AGREE A GREAT DEAL	AGREE SOMEWHAT	DISAGREE SOMEWHAT	DISAGREE A GREAT DEAL
H8.	When someone does wrong, he should be paid back for it.	4	3	2	1
H9.	Many people only learn through violence.	4	3	2	1
H10.	Even if you don't like a person, you should still try to help him.	4	3	2	1
H11.	A man has a right to kill another man in a case of self defense.	4	3	2	1
H12.	A man has the right to kill a person to defend his family.	4	3	2	1
H13.	A man has the right to kill a person to defend his house.	4	3	2	1
H14.	Even if it means giving up something, you should help others get what they want.	4	3	2	1
H15.	People who make speeches stirring people up should be put in prison before they cause serious trouble.	4	3	2	1
H16.	Police are getting so much power the average citizen has to worry.	4	3	2	1
H17.	Courts nowadays are much too easy on criminals.	4	3	2	1
H18.	Recent Supreme Court decisions have made it more difficult to punish criminals.	4	3	2	1
H19.	Police nowadays should have more power (authority) to enforce the law adequately.	4	3	2	1

2:44
45
46
47
48
49
50
51
52
53
54
55

P A S T E   C A R D   # 6   H E R E

SECTION J:

J1. Some people feel that important changes can only be brought about through
     violence; others say violence is not necessary. What do you think?
     (HAND R PASTE CARD #6. INSTRUCT R TO FILL OUT CARD)

		AGREE A GREAT DEAL	AGREE SOMEWHAT	DISAGREE SOMEWHAT	DISAGREE A GREAT DEAL	
A.	Changes can be made fast enough without action involving property damage or injury.	4	3	2	1	☐ 2:56
B.	Protest in which some people are hurt is necessary for changes to come fast enough.	4	3	2	1	☐ 57
C.	Protest in which there is some property damage is necessary for changes to be brought about fast enough.	4	3	2	1	☐ 58
D.	Protest in which there is much property damage is necessary before changes can be brought about fast enough.	4	3	2	1	☐ 59
E.	Protest in which some people are killed is necessary before changes will take place fast enough.	4	3	2	1	☐ 60

J2. How many of your friends do you think would agree with your answers?

| 3. Most | 2. Some | 1. A few or none | ☐ 61 |

P A S T E   C A R D   # 7   H E R E

SECTION K:

K1. Here is a list of statements about the way some people may feel. Please
     read each statement and check the way you feel. (HAND R PASTE CARD #7.
     INSTRUCT R TO FILL OUT CARD)

     TRUE   FALSE

     [1]   [2]   A. I don't seem to get what's coming to me.

     [1]   [2]   B. Although I don't show it, I am sometimes eaten up
                             with jealousy.

     [1]   [2]   C. At times I feel I get a raw deal out of life.

     [1]   [2]   D. I tend to be on my guard with people who are
                             somewhat more friendly than I expected.

     [1]   [2]   E. I commonly wonder what hidden reason another person
                             may have for doing something nice for me.

     [1]   [2]   F. I used to think most people told the truth but now
                             I know otherwise.

K2. Generally speaking, would you say that <u>most people can be trusted</u> or that you <u>can't be too careful in dealing with people</u>?

| 3. MOST PEOPLE CAN BE TRUSTED | 2. D.K. | 1. CAN'T BE TOO CAREFUL IN DEALING WITH PEOPLE |

☐
2:68

K3. Would you say that most of the time people <u>try to be helpful</u> or that they are mostly just <u>looking out for themselves</u>, or they aren't one way or the other?

| 3. TRY TO BE HELPFUL | 1. LOOKING OUT FOR THEMSELVES | 2. NOT ONE WAY OR THE OTHER |

☐
69

K4. Do you think most people would <u>try to take advantage</u> of you if they got a chance or would they <u>try to be fair</u>?

| 1. TRY TO TAKE ADVANTAGE | 3. TRY TO BE FAIR | 2. D.K. |

☐
70

SECTION M:

M1. Here are two more stories about real-life situations like the ones we talked about before.

STORY 3; PART A: *A policeman is giving a ticket to a man for reckless driving. The driver takes the ticket, begins to swear, and calls the policeman a pig.*

How do you think the policeman was <u>feeling</u> in this situation? (INTERVIEWER: TRY TO GET R TO STATE A <u>FEELING</u>.)

_____

_____

M2. STORY 3; PART B: *Actually, the policeman hauls off and punches the driver in the nose and knocks him down.*

Considering how the policeman acted, how do you think he was <u>feeling</u>? (INTERVIEWER: TRY TO GET R TO STATE A <u>FEELING</u>.)

_____

_____

M3. How likely is it that anyone among your friends <u>could</u> feel like that policeman if a similar thing happened to them? (HAND R RING CARD B)

4. Very likely	3. Somewhat likely	2. Not too likely	1. Not likely at all	

2:71

M4. How likely is it that you <u>could</u> feel like that policeman if a similar thing happened to you?

4. Very likely	3. Somewhat likely	2. Not too likely	1. Not likely at all	

72

SECTION N:

N1. STORY 4; PART A: *A middle-aged woman with six children who has lived on relief most of her life is offered an opportunity to train for a good job.*

How do you think this woman was <u>feeling</u> in this situation? (INTERVIEWER: TRY TO GET R TO STATE A <u>FEELING</u>.)

_____

_____

N2. STORY 4; PART B: *Actually, when this woman is told about the program she says that she can't see much point to it, and, anyway, she's too old to learn.*

How do you think this woman was <u>feeling</u> when she turned down that job like that? (INTERVIEWER: TRY TO GET R TO STATE A <u>FEELING</u>.)

_____

_____

N3. How likely is it that anyone among your friends <u>could</u> feel like that woman if a similar thing happened to them? (HAND R RING CARD B)

4. Very likely	3. Somewhat likely	2. Not too likely	1. Not likely at all	

2:73

N4. How likely is it that you <u>could</u> feel like that woman if a similar thing happened to you?

4. Very likely	3. Somewhat likely	2. Not too likely	1. Not likely at all	

74

SECTION P:

P1. Here is a list of clubs and organizations that some people belong to. Please
     look at this list and tell me which of these organizations you belong to, if any.
     (SHOW R RING CARD E)
     (CHECK APPROPRIATE BOX FOR EACH ORGANIZATION R GIVES. AFTER GOING THROUGH LIST
     THEN ASK Q. P1a FOR EACH ORGANIZATION BETWEEN 1 and 7)

P1a. What is the name of that ____ ?

1. ☐ Labor Unions ——————→ _____ _____

2. ☐ Veteran's Organizations ——→ _____ _____

3. ☐ Organizations of People of
        the Same Nationality ——→ _____ _____

4. ☐ Youth Groups ——————→ _____ _____

5. ☐ Political Clubs or
        Organizations ——————→ _____ _____

6. ☐ Neighborhood Associations ——→ _____ _____

7. ☐ Fraternal Organizations
        or Lodges ——————→ _____ _____

8. ☐ Church Connected Groups

9. ☐ Business or Civic Groups

10. ☐ Parent Teachers Associations

11. ☐ Community Centers

12. ☐ Sport Teams

13. ☐ Country Clubs

14. ☐ Professional Groups

15. ☐ Charity or Welfare Organizations

16. ☐ Other (SPECIFY) _____

17. ☐ None (GO TO NEXT PAGE, Q. P2)

P2. Now in this last section, I'd like to ask some questions about yourself.
     Are you married, widowed, separated, divorced, or single?

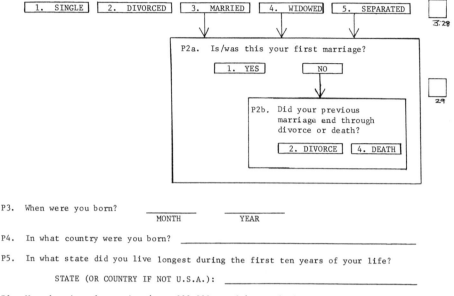

| 1. SINGLE | 2. DIVORCED | 3. MARRIED | 4. WIDOWED | 5. SEPARATED |

3:28

P2a. Is/was this your first marriage?

| 1. YES | | NO |

29

P2b. Did your previous
marriage end through
divorce or death?

| 2. DIVORCE | 4. DEATH |

P3. When were you born?   _____   _____
                             MONTH   YEAR

P4. In what country were you born?   _____

P5. In what state did you live longest during the first ten years of your life?

     STATE (OR COUNTRY IF NOT U.S.A.):   _____

P6. Was that in a large city (over 100,000 people), a suburb, a small city, a small
     town, or on a farm?

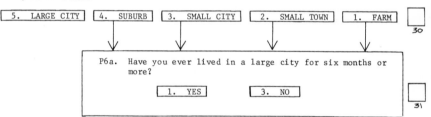

| 5. LARGE CITY | 4. SUBURB | 3. SMALL CITY | 2. SMALL TOWN | 1. FARM |

30

P6a. Have you ever lived in a large city for six months or
more?

| 1. YES | | 3. NO |

31

P7. (IF NON-SOUTHERN STATE IN P5 [LONGEST RESIDENCE BEFORE AGE 10]): Have you ever
     lived for six months or more in the South?

| 1. YES | | 3. NO |

32

(SOUTHERN STATES: ALA., ARK., FLA., GA., KY., LA., MD., MISS., N.C., OKLA., S.C.,
TENN., TEX., VA., WASH. D.C.)

P8. Was your father born in the United States?

| 1. YES | | 3. NO |

☐ 3:33

P8a. What country did he come from?

_____

P9. Was your mother born in the United States?

| 1. YES | | 3. NO |

☐ 3†

P9a. What country did she come from?

_____

P10. Are you working now, laid off, a student, unemployed, retired, or what?

| 1. WORKING OR LAID OFF | 2. RETIRED | 3. UNEMPLOYED | 4. STUDENT |
(GO TO Q. P11)   (ASK Q. P11 IN   (TURN TO PAGE 31
                    PAST TENSE)   Q. P15)

☐ 35

P10a. Did you ever work regularly at all?

| 1. YES | 3. NO |
(ASK Q. P11   (TURN TO
IN PAST   PAGE 31 ,
TENSE)   Q. P15)

☐ 36

P11. What is/was your main job? _____

P12. Specifically, what do/did you do on your job? _____

_____

P13. What kind of business is/was that in? _____

P14. Do/did you work for yourself, or for someone else?

| SELF | | 0. SOMEONE ELSE | (GO TO Q. P15)

P14a. About how much would it cost to buy a business (farm/ranch) such as
yours, nowadays? Just tell me the letter on the card. (HAND R
RING CARD   F)

3:37

   A. | 1. LESS THAN $3000 | E. | 5. $20,000 - $34,999 |

   B. | 2. $3000 - $5999 | F. | 6. $35,000 - $99,999 |

   C. | 3. $6000 - $9999 | G. | 7. MORE THAN $100,000 |

   D. | 4. $10,000 - $19,999 | H. | 8. BUSINESS IS RENTED |

(ASK EVERYBODY)

P15. (INTERVIEWER: IF R DOES NOT KNOW FATHER, OR KNOW OF FATHER, ASK ABOUT MALE
HEAD OF HOUSEHOLD WHEN R WAS GROWING UP, OR MOTHER)

What is/was your father's main job? _____

P16. Specifically, can you tell me what your father does/did?

_____

P17. What kind of a business is/was that in? _____

P18. Does/did he work for himself, or for someone else?

| SELF | | 0. SOMEONE ELSE |
                    (TURN TO PAGE 32 , Q. P19)

P18a. About how much would it cost to buy a business (farm/ranch) such
as your father's, nowadays? Just tell me the letter on the card.
(HAND R RING CARD   F)

38

   A. | 1. LESS THAN $3000 | E. | 5. $20,000 - $34,999 |

   B. | 2. $3000 - $5999 | F. | 6. $35,000 - $99,999 |

   C. | 3. $6000 - $9999 | G. | 7. MORE THAN $100,000 |

   D. | 4. $10,000 - $19,999 | H. | 8. BUSINESS IS RENTED |

(GO TO Q. P15) ... (TURN TO PAGE 32 , Q. P19)

(ASK ALL RESPONDENTS)

P19. What is the highest grade of school or year of college you have finished?

_____ Grade of School   or _____ Year of College

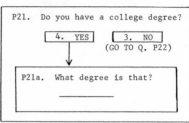

(IF 11th OR 12th GRADE, ASK
Q. P20; OTHERS SKIP TO Q. P22)   (IF COLLEGE)

P20. Did you get a high school   P21. Do you have a college degree?
      graduation diploma?
                                               ☐ 4. YES ☐   ☐ 3. NO ☐
      ☐ 2. YES ☐   ☐ 1. NO ☐   (GO TO Q. P22)

                                               P21a. What degree is that?

                                               _____

P22. (IF R IS A STUDENT ASK; OTHERS GO TO Q. P23) Are you attending school at the
      present time?
            ☐ 1. YES ☐   ☐ 3. NO ☐
                                      (GO TO Q. P23)

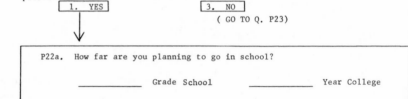

      P22a. How far are you planning to go in school?

             _____ Grade School   _____ Year College

P23. Have you had any other schooling?
            ☐ 1. YES ☐   ☐ 3. NO ☐ (TURN TO PAGE 33 , Q. P24)

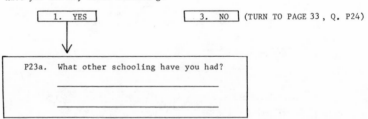

      P23a. What other schooling have you had?

             _____

             _____

P24. <u>(IF R IS MARRIED AND OVER 30 YEARS OF AGE ASK)</u>   Do you have any children in college?

| 1. YES | | 3. NO |

P25. What was the highest grade of school your father (OR PERSON SPECIFIED IN Q. P15) completed? (CIRCLE NUMBER)

Grade School   0   1   2   3   4   5   6   7   8

High School   1   2   3   4

College   1   2   3   4   5/

| D.K. |

P25a. Would you guess that he had <u>less than seven years</u> of school, <u>between seven and twelve years</u> of school, <u>finished high school</u>, or had <u>some schooling past high school</u>?

| 1. LESS THAN SEVEN YEARS | 2. BETWEEN SEVEN AND TWELVE YEARS |
| 3. FINISHED HIGH SCHOOL | 4. SOME SCHOOLING PAST HIGH SCHOOL |

43

P26. What was the highest grade of school your mother completed? (CIRCLE NUMBER)

Grade School   0   1   2   3   4   5   6   7   8

High School   1   2   3   4

College   1   2   3   4   5/

| D.K. |

P26a. Would you guess that she had <u>less than seven years</u> of school, <u>between seven and twelve years</u> of school, <u>finished high school</u>, or had <u>some schooling past high school</u>?

| 1. LESS THAN SEVEN YEARS | 2. BETWEEN SEVEN AND TWELVE YEARS |
| 3. FINISHED HIGH SCHOOL | 4. SOME SCHOOLING PAST HIGH SCHOOL |

44

P27. Are you Protestant, Catholic, Jewish, or what?

1. PROTESTANT	2. CATHOLIC	3. JEWISH	4. OTHER
	(GO TO Q. P29)	(GO TO Q. P29)	

3:45

(SPECIFY)

P28. What denomination?

_____

P27a.

_____

P29. How often do you attend religious services?

7. SEVERAL TIMES A WEEK	6. ONCE A WEEK	5. TWO OR THREE TIMES A MONTH
4. ONCE A MONTH	3. A FEW TIMES A YEAR	2. ONCE A YEAR OR LESS

46

1. NEVER

P30. In general, how religious minded would you say you are -- very religious minded, more than average, less than average, or not at all religious minded?

5. VERY	4. MORE THAN AVERAGE	3. AVERAGE	2. LESS THAN AVERAGE	1. NOT AT ALL

47

P31. Now about your life when you were growing up. Did you attend Sunday School or religious instruction classes regularly, most of the time, some of the time, or never?

4. REGULARLY OR PAROCHIAL SCHOOL	3. MOST OF THE TIME	2. SOME OF THE TIME	1. NEVER

48

P32. Would you tell me how much income you and your family will get during 1969, January through December? I mean before taxes. Just tell me the letter on the card. (HAND R RING CARD G)

A. | 1. UNDER $2000 | E. | 5. $8000-9999 |

B. | 2. $2000-3999 | F. | 6. $10,000-11,999 |

C. | 3. $4000-5999 | G. | 7. $12,000-15,999 |

D. | 4. $6000-7999 | H. | 8. $16,000-AND OVER |

3:49

P33. Does that include the income of everyone in the family?

| 1. YES | | 3. NO |
(GO TO Q. P34)

P33a. How much is your income altogether? (CHECK CORRECT BOX IN Q. P32 TO INCLUDE TOTAL FAMILY INCOME)

P34. How many people depend on this income for their support? (CIRCLE NUMBER)

1   2   3   4   5   6   7   8+

50

P35. Were you ever in any of the armed services, including the national guard?

| YES | | 4. NO | (GO TO PAGE 36 , Q. P36)

P35a. When you were in the service, did you ever have combat duty?

| YES | | 3. NO | (GO TO PAGE 36, Q. P36)

P35b. Were you ever involved in any active combat during a war?

| 1. YES | | 2. NO |

51

P36. Have you thought about making any change in your life as a result of the violent events going on in the United States nowadays?

| YES | | NO |

P36a. IF "YES": What have you planned? _____

FOR INTERVIEWER ONLY

SECTION Z:

Z1. This interview was taken in a:

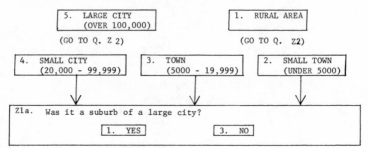

| 5. LARGE CITY (OVER 100,000) | | 1. RURAL AREA |

(GO TO Q. Z 2)   (GO TO Q. Z2)

| 4. SMALL CITY (20,000 - 99,999) | 3. TOWN (5000 - 19,999) | 2. SMALL TOWN (UNDER 5000) |

Z1a. Was it a suburb of a large city?

1. YES   3. NO

Z2. Race of Respondent:

1. WHITE   2. NEGRO   3. OTHER   (SPECIFY) _____

Z3. Cooperation of respondent:

3. VERY COOPERATIVE   2. SOMEWHAT COOPERATIVE   1. NOT COOPERATIVE

Z4. Respondent's understanding of questions:

3. GOOD UNDERSTANDING   2. FAIR UNDERSTANDING   1. POOR UNDERSTANDING

Z5. THUMBNAIL SKETCH

APPENDIX C

DERIVED MEASURES

Introduction

The general rules governing the construction of indices were as follows:

(a) Constituent items must be statistically related.

(b) Structural relationships between items must be stable across heterogeneous subgroups of the population.

(c) The final result of combining several items was to be a three to seven category scale with an approximately rectangular distribution.

(d) For respondents for whom not all the data were available, the index value was estimated based on the available data, if more than half of the data were available.

(e) In general, a high score on the index implies a high amount of the characteristic being measured.

In the brief descriptions of each of the indices referred to in the text, the following sequence will be adhered to: wording of constituent items and response categories; item interrelationships; test of the stability of these relationships; item combination and recoding scheme; and a note on questionnaire items considered for inclusion in the index but rejected due to failure to meet rules (a) or (b) above.

The population subgroups on which the stability of inter-item relationships were examined were defined as follows:

1) Education:

    a) Low education (those with an eighth grade education or less)

      b) High education (those with one year of college or more)

2) Income:

      a) Low income (those making less than $4,000 per year)

      b) High income (those making $16,000 a year or more)

3) Region of the country in which the interview was taken:

      a) Solid South or Border states (Alabama, Arkansas, Georgia, Louisiana, Mississippi, North Carolina, South Carolina, Texas, Virginia, Kentucky, Maryland, Oklahoma, Tennessee, Washington, D.C.)

      b) Pacific states (California, Oregon, Washington)

4) Age:

      a) Youth (those born in 1944 or later)

      b) Older (those born in 1929 or before)

5) Race:

      a) Blacks

      b) Whites

Are Police Acts Violence? Index

Table 1 shows the original questions whose responses were summed to form the Are Police Acts Violence? Index. To each item, the respondent could answer "yes," coded 1, "both," coded 2, or "no," coded 3.

Table 1

Are Police Acts Violence? Index Items

V11 Do you think of police beating students as violence?
V12 Do you think of police shooting looters as violence?
V18 Do you think of police stopping to frisk people as violence?

The relationships among these three items for the total population is shown in Table 2.

Table 2

Relationships Between Are Police Acts Violence?
Index Items for All Respondents

(gammas)

	V12 Shooting Looters	V18 Frisking
V11 Beating students	.6	.3
V12 Shooting looters		.4

To test the stability of the relationships among the three constituent items, the gammas were examined in a variety of subgroups (Table 3).

Table 3

Relationships Between Are Police Acts Violence? Index Items
for Designated Demographic Subgroups

(gammas)

	V11 Beating Students vs. V12 Shooting Looters	V11 Beating Students vs. V18 Frisking	V12 Shooting Looters vs. V18 Frisking
Low education	.6	.4	.6
High education	.7	.3	.4
Low income	.7	.6	.4
High income	.6	.2	.3
South and Border	.6	.3	.3
Pacific	.8	.5	.5
Age: 25 and under	.6	.3	.4
Age: 40 and older	.6	.4	.4
Blacks	.3	.4	.3
Whites	.6	.3	.4

Table 3 shows a reasonable degree of consistency in the relationships between definitions of police action as violence by the different population subgroups. The one exception to this general statement is that the relation between definitions of beating students and police frisking people was small for the high income group. Nevertheless, responses to the items referring to police beating students, police shooting looters, and police frisking people were summed to form the Are Police Acts Violence? Index (Table 4).

Table 4

Construction of the Are Police Acts Violence? Index

Are Police Actions Violence?	No			Yes	Total
Original score	9	7-8	5-6	3-4	
Recoded score	1	2	3	4	
Percent	22	35	31	12	100%
(0.1% missing data)					

Court Fairness Index

The Court Fairness Index was constructed by cumulating "fair" replies (scored "1") to the three questions reproduced below (Table 5).

Table 5

Court Fairness Index Items

V80	Some people have told us the courts nowadays treat some people better or worse than others. Do you think that rich people and poor people are likely to be treated the same by the courts or not?

	(unfair)	(fair)	(unfair)
	Poor treated better	Poor and rich treated same	Rich treated better

V81	Do you think that white people and black people are likely to be treated the same by the courts or not? ... Who is treated better?

	(unfair)	(fair)	(unfair)	(unfair)
	Whites treated better	Same treatment whites, blacks	Blacks treated better	Depends on region

V82	Do you think the courts treat people like yourself better or worse than others, or about the same?

	(unfair)	(fair)	(unfair)
	Worse	Same	Better

The relationships among the Court Fairness Index items for the total population are shown below (Table 6).

Table 6

Relationships Between Court Fairness Index Items
for All Respondents

(gammas)

	V81 White/Black	V82 Self/Others
V80 Rich/poor	.7	.7
V81 White/black		.8

To see whether or not we could combine these three items into a Court Fairness Index, respondents' answers to each item were reclassified as "fair" (scored "1") or "unfair" (i.e., all other valid responses scored "0"), and the gammas were calculated for each possible pair of items. This was done for the entire sample and also for the various demographic subgroups that we used routinely to test inter-item consistency. The gammas turned out to be high and reasonably consistent, all but two of them over .6 (Table 7).

Table 7

Relationships Between Court Fairness Index Items for
Designated Demographic Subgroups

(gammas)

	V80 Rich/Poor vs. V81 White/ Black	V80 Rich/Poor vs. V82 Self/ Others	V81 White/ Black vs. V82 Self/ Others
Low education	.9	.6	.8
High education	.7	.8	.7
Low income	.3	(1.00)[a]	.9
High income	.8	.9	.8
South and Border	.6	.8	.8
Pacific	.5	.6	.9
Age: 25 and under	.7	.8	.9
Age: 40 and older	.6	.8	.9
Blacks	.9	.8	.9
Whites	.6	.7	.7

[a] Artifact of the gamma formula: one cell has zero frequency.

Scores on the index based on cumulated "fair" responses to the three items ranged from "3," indicating "fair" responses to all three questions, to "0," indicating "unfair" responses to all questions (Table 8).

Table 8
Construction of the Court Fairness Index

Court Fairness:	Unfair			Fair	Total
Score	0	1	2	3	
Percent	19	33	33	15	100%
(2.4% missing data)					

Evaluative Index

Table 9 reproduces the semantic differential card shown to respondents from which items B, C and E were drawn to form the Evaluative Index. The card was introduced to each respondent in the following manner:

> Here are some words that have been used to describe violence. The first words are strong and weak. Do you think violence belongs at the *strong end* or at the *weak end* or *in between?* Please point to where you think it belongs.

Table 9
Item Pool for Evaluative Index

A. Strong							Weak
	1	2	3	4	5	6	7
B. Good							Bad
	1	2	3	4	5	6	7
C. Necessary							Unnecessary
	1	2	3	4	5	6	7
D. Avoidable							Unavoidable
	1	2	3	4	5	6	7
E. Valuable							Worthless
	1	2	3	4	5	6	7
F. Fierce							Peaceful
	1	2	3	4	5	6	7

Items B, C and E were found to form a cluster of interrelationships, which is shown for the total population in Table 10.

Table 10

Relationships Between Evaluative Index Items
for All Respondents

(gammas)

	V6 Necessary-Unnecessary	V8 Valuable-Worthless
V5 Good-bad	.6	.5
V6 Necessary-unnecessary		.6

To test the stability of the relationships among the three constituent items, the gammas were examined in a variety of subgroups (Table 11).

Table 11

Relationships Between Evaluative Index Items
for Designated Demographic Subgroups

(gammas)

	V5 Good-Bad vs. V6 Necessary-Unnecessary	V5 Good-Bad vs. V8 Valuable-Worthless	V6 Necessary-Unnecessary vs. V8 Valuable-Worthless
Low education	.7	.6	.7
High education	.6	.5	.6
Low income	.7	.6	.7
High income	.6	.4	.7
South and Border	.7	.6	.7
Pacific	.5	.6	.6
Age: 25 and under	.6	.4	.6
Age: 40 and older	.6	.5	.7
Blacks	.6	.6	.7
Whites	.6	.5	.6

Table 11 shows a reasonable degree of consistency in the relationships among the several evaluative semantic differential items for the different population subgroups. Accordingly, the original seven-point items were summed to form the Evaluative Index as is shown in Table 12. A high score indicates a relatively negative evaluation of violence.

Table 12

Construction of the Evaluative Index

Evaluation (of violence):	Good				Bad	Total
Original score	3-13	14-16	17-18	19-20	21	
Recoded score	1	2	3	4	5	
Percent	15	18	19	16	32	100%
(1% missing data)						

Humanism Index

Due to the rank-order basis for this index, the usual rules for construction of indices did not apply. For a description of the index, see Chapter 5, Values and Violence.

Identification

The four basic identification stem questions are shown in Table 13.

The relationships among the four identification items for each contender group are shown in Table 14.

On the basis of these relationships, it might be assumed that three indices could have been built from the items, considerably simplifying the analysis. However, Tables 15 and 16 show that the strength of the relationships was not consistent among different subgroups of our population. The relationships were especially affected by level of income. Accordingly, no indices were built from the identification items.

Table 13

Identification Items

On the whole, would you say that *most* (white student demonstrators) (black protesters) (police) are *trying to be helpful*, or that they are *looking for trouble*, or that they aren't one way or the other?

| Looking for
trouble | Not one way
or the other | Trying to
be helpful |

Think of how (white student demonstrators) (black protesters) (police) think of people like yourself. Do you think that *none* dislike people like yourself, only *a few, many* or *almost all* dislike people like yourself?

| Almost all | Many | A few | None |

Would you say that most (white student demonstrators) (black protesters) (police) *can be trusted,* or that you *can't be too careful in dealing with them?*

| Can't be too
careful in dealing
with them | Don't know | Can be trusted |

If (white student demonstrators) (black protesters) (police) get the things they want, do you think *your* life will change? (IF "WILL CHANGE"): Do you think *your* life will change for *better* or *worse?*

| Worse | Won't change | Better |

Table 14

Relationships Between Identification Items
For All Respondents
(gammas)

White student demonstrators	V36	V37	V51
V35 Helpful	.3	.6	.4
V36 None dislike respondent		.3	.3
V37 Trustworthy			.5
V51 Better life			

Black protesters	V62	V63	V77
V61 Helpful	.4	.7	.5
V62 None dislike respondent		.4	.3
V63 Trustworthy			.6
V77 Better life			

Police	V84	V85	V86
V83 Helpful	.6	.8	.5
V84 None dislike respondent		.6	.2
V85 Trustworthy			.6
V86 Better life			

Table 15

Relationships Between Identification Items
Among Designated Demographic Subgroups
(gammas)

	V84 vs. V86	V84 vs. V83	V62 vs. V77	V62 vs. V61	V36 vs. V51	V36 vs. V35
Low education	.3	.7	.4	.5	.2	.3
High education	.3	.4	.4	.3	.4	.3
Low income	.4	.8	.6	.6	.5	.5
High income	.0	.2	.2	.3	.4	.3
South and Border	.1	.6	.4	.4	.2	.3
Age: 25 and under	.3	.7	.4	.5	.4	.4
Blacks	.6	.7	.4	.3	.1	.4
Whites	.2	.5	.3	.3	.3	.3

V35 White student demonstrators helpful
V36 No white student demonstrators dislike respondent
V37 White student demonstrators trustworthy
V51 White student demonstrators better life

V61 Black protesters helpful
V62 No black protesters dislike respondent
V63 Black protesters trustworthy
V77 Black protesters better life

V83 Police helpful
V84 No police dislike respondent
V85 Police trustworthy
V86 Police better life

Is Burglary-Looting Violence? Index

Table 17 shows the original questions whose responses were summed to form the Is Burglary-Looting Violence? Index. To both items, the respondent could answer "yes," coded 1, "both," coded 2, or "no," coded 3.

The gamma between these two items for all respondents was .8. To test the stability of the relationship between the two constituent items, the association was examined in a variety of population subgroups.

Table 18 shows that whether respondents defined looting and burglary as violence or not violence was consistently and highly related in all population subgroups, justifying the combination of these two items.

Table 16
Relationships Between Identification Items for Designated Income Groups
(gammas)

	V36 No Students Dislike R			V37 Students Trustworthy			V51 Students Better Life		
	$0-3,999	$8,000-9,999	$16,000 & Over	$0-3,999	$8,000-9,999	$16,000 & Over	$0-3,999	$8,000-9,999	$16,000 & Over
V35 Students helpful	.3	.2	.5	.5	.5	.6	.6	.5	.4
V36 No students dislike R				.3	.4	.3	.5	.4	.4
V37 Students trustworthy							.5	.5	.6
V51 Students better life									

	V84 No Police Dislike R			V85 Police Trustworthy			V86 Police Better Life		
	$0-3,999	$8,000-9,999	$16,000 & Over	$0-3,999	$8,000-9,999	$16,000 & Over	$0-3,999	$8,000-9,999	$16,000 & Over
V83 Police helpful	.8	.6	.2	.9	.7	.1	.6	.2	.0
V84 No police dislike R				.7	.4	.4	.4	.2	.0
V85 Police trustworthy							.7	.6	.5
V86 Police better life									

	V62 No Blacks Dislike R			V63 Blacks Trustworthy			V77 Blacks Better Life		
	$0-3,999	$8,000-9,999	$16,000 & Over	$0-3,999	$8,000-9,999	$16,000 & Over	$0-3,999	$8,000-9,999	$16,000 & Over
V61 Blacks helpful	.6	.3	.3	.7	.7	.6	.7	.6	.4
V62 No blacks dislike R				.6	.5	.3	.6	.3	.2
V63 Blacks trustworthy							.8	.5	.5
V77 Blacks better life									

Table 17

Is Burglary-Looting Violence? Index Items

V13 Do you think of burglary as violence?
V16 Do you think of looting as violence?

Table 18

Relationships Between Burglary-Looting Definition Items For Designated Demographic Subgroups
(gammas)

	V16 Looting vs. V13 Burglary
Low education	.6
High education	.8
Low income	.8
High income	.8
South and Border	.8
Pacific	.8
Age: 25 and under	.9
Age: 40 and older	.7
Blacks	.7
Whites	.8

Details of index construction are shown in Table 19.

Table 19

Construction of the Is Burglary-Looting Violence? Index

Is Burglary-Looting Violence?	No		Yes	Total
Original score	5-6	3-4	2	
Recoded score	1	2	3	
Percent	11	27	62	100%
(0.4% missing data)				

Is Protest Violence? Index

Table 20 shows the original questions whose combined responses constitute the Is Protest Violence? Index. To each item, the respondent could answer "yes," coded 1, "both," coded 2, or "no," coded 3.

Table 20

Is Protest Violence? Index Items

V10 Do you think of student protest as violence?
V14 Do you think of sit-ins as violence?
V15 Do you think of draft card burning as violence?

The relationships among these three items for the total population is shown in Table 21.

Table 21

Relationships Between Is Protest Violence?
Index Items for All Respondents

(gammas)

	V14 Sit-ins	V15 Draft Card Burning
V10 Student protest	.6	.5
V14 Sit-ins		.8

To test the stability of the relationships among the three constituent items, the gammas were examined in a variety of subgroups (Table 22).

Table 22 shows the respondents' definitions of student protest, sit-ins and draft card burning were reasonably consistent. These items were combined into one index, the Is Protest Violence? Index.

Details of index construction are presented in Table 23. The higher a score on the index, the more a respondent called the actions in the index violence.

Table 22

Relationships Between Is Protest Violence? Index Items
for Designated Demographic Subgroups
(gammas)

	V10 Student Protest vs. V14 Sit-ins	V10 Student Protest vs. V15 Draft Card	V14 Sit-ins vs. V15 Draft Card
Low education	.6	.5	.7
High education	.6	.3	.7
Low income	.7	.7	.9
High income	.5	.2	.7
South and Border	.6	.4	.8
Pacific	.7	.5	.7
Age: 25 and under	.6	.5	.8
Age: 40 and older	.6	.4	.8
Blacks	.7	.6	.6
Whites	.6	.5	.8

Table 23

Construction of the Is Protest Violence? Index

Is Protest Violence?	No			Yes	Total
Original score	9	7-8	5-6	3-4	
Recoded score	1	2	3	4	
Percent	23	30	27	20	100%
(0.3% missing data)					

A fourth item, concerned with denial of civil rights, did not relate to the other items in a consistent fashion. This item was worded as follows:

V18   Do you think of not letting people have their
civil rights as violence?

Kindness Index

Table 24 shows the original questions whose responses were combined to form the Kindness Index.

The possible response choices and their corresponding values for each of the constituent items are as follows: "agree strongly" coded 4; "agree somewhat" coded 3; "disagree somewhat" coded 2; "disagree a great deal" coded 1.

Table 24

Kindness Index Items

V90 It's important to be kind to people even if they do things you don't believe in.

V93 When a person harms you, you should turn the other cheek and forgive him.

V96 Even if you don't like a person, you should still try to help him.

Note: These items were based on those of Scott (Scott, W. *Values and Organizations.* Chicago: Rand McNally, 1965).

Table 25 shows the relationships among the constituent items of the Kindness Index.

Table 25

Relationships Between Kindness Index Items
for All Respondents
(gammas)

	V93 Turn the Other Cheek	V96 A Person Should Try to Help
V90 Kindness is important	.4	.6
V93 Turn the other cheek		.4

Table 26 indicates the stability of the inter-item relationships across a variety of demographic subgroups, for a representative pair of items.

Table 27 shows how the constituent items were combined to form the Kindness Index. The values for each item were summed and the sum was recoded to provide index scores convenient for analysis. A high score indicates a strong belief in kindness values.

Table 26

Relationships Between a Representative Pair of Kindness Index Items for Designated Demographic Subgroups

(gammas)

	V93 Turn Other Cheek vs V96 Try to Help
Low education	.4
High education	.4
Low income	.5
High income	.4
South and Border	.5
Age: 25 and under	.5
Blacks	.4
Whites	.4

Table 27

Construction of the Kindness Index

Kindness Values:	Low				High	Total
Original score	3-7	8	9	10	11-12	
Recoded score	1	2	3	4	5	
Percent (0.4% missing data)	16	21	24	17	22	100%

Peer Consensus Index

Each of the six sets of "attitudes toward violence" items from which the criterion variables were developed was followed by this question:

> *How many of your friends do you think would agree with your answers?*

The relationships among these six variables for the total population is shown in Table 28.

Table 28

Relationships Between Peer Consensus Index Items for All Respondents

(gammas)

Perceived Peer Consensus		V44	V50	V70	V76	V111
V34	On violence for hoodlum gang control	.7	.8	.7	.7	.7
V44	On violence for student change		.8	.8	.7	.8
V50	On violence for student control			.8	.8	.8
V70	On violence for black change				.9	.9
V76	On violence for black control					.9
V111	On violence for social change in general					

Table 29

Relationships Between Three Representative Pairs of Peer Consensus Index Items for Designated Demographic Subgroups

(gammas)

	V34 vs V44	V34 vs V50	V70 vs V111
Low education	.8	.8	.9
High education	.6	.8	.9
Low income	.7	.8	.9
High income	.6	.7	.9
South and Border	.8	.8	.9
Pacific	.6	.8	.9
Age: 25 and under	.4	.7	.8
Age: 40 and older	.8	.8	.9
Blacks	.7	.7	.9
Whites	.7	.8	.9

V34   On violence for hoodlum gang control
V44   On violence for student change
V50   On violence for student control
V70   On violence for black change
V111 On violence for social change in general

To test the stability of the inter-item relationships, gammas between three representative item pairs were examined in a variety of subgroups (Table 29).

As can be seen, the relationship between the items of the three pairs remained reasonably stable across a number of population subgroups. Accordingly, a single index was created by summing the six items and collapsing the resulting raw scores as shown in Table 30. A high score indicates high belief in peer consensus.

Table 30

Construction of the Peer Consensus Index

Peer Consensus:	Low			High	Total
Original score	6-12	13-15	16-17	18	
Recoded score	1	2	3	4	
Percent	17	17	21	45	100%
(1% missing data)					

Police/Court Power Index

The Police/Court Power Index was based on responses to three attitudinal statements with Likert-type, four-point response choices. For each of the three statements reproduced below in Table 31, the respondent could answer "disagree a great deal," coded 1, "disagree somewhat," coded 2, "agree somewhat," coded 3, or "agree a great deal," coded 4.

Table 31

Police/Court Power Index Items

V103 Courts nowadays are much too easy on criminals.

V104 Recent Supreme Court decisions have made it more difficult to punish criminals.

V105 Police nowadays should have more power to enforce the law adequately.

The relationships among these three items for all respondents are shown in Table 32.

Table 32

Relationships Between Police/Court Power Index Items
for All Respondents

(gammas)

	V104 Supreme Court Decisions	V105 Police Need More Power
V103 Courts easy on criminals	.7	.5
V104 Supreme Court decisions		.5

To test the stability of the relationships among three constituent items, the gammas were examined in a variety of subgroups (Table 33).

Table 33

Relationships Between Police/Court Power Index Items
for Designated Demographic Subgroups

(gammas)

	V103 Courts Easy vs. V104 Supreme Court	V103 Courts Easy vs. V105 More Power	V104 Supreme Court vs. V105 More Power
Low education	.6	.5	.5
High education	.8	.5	.7
Low income	.6	.4	.6
High income	.8	.4	.5
South and Border	.7	.5	.6
Blacks	.5	.4	.4
Whites	.7	.5	.5

A respondent's score on the Police/Court Power Index was arrived at by adding his scores on Variables 103, 104 and 105 and then recoding his total score according to the scheme in Table 34. Police/Court Power Index scores of 5 or 6 indicate a strong endorsement of police/court power.

Table 34

Construction of the Police/Court Power Index

Police/Court Power:	Low					High	Total
Original score	0-6	7-8	9	10	11	12	
Recoded score	1	2	3	4	5	6	
Percent	10	17	18	14	16	25	100%
(0.8% missing data)							

Two other items covering the area of police power were found to be inconsistently related to the three Police/Court Power Index items either among all respondents or among blacks. These items, which had the same response format as the index items, are as follows:

V101   People who make speeches stirring people up should be put in prison before they cause serious trouble.

V102   Police are getting so much power the average citizen has to worry.

Property/Person Priority Index

Table 35 shows the original questions whose responses were combined to form the Property/Person Priority Index.

Table 35

Property/Person Priority Index Items

V78   Some people say that stealing or damaging property is as bad as hurting people. Others say that damaging property is not as bad as hurting people. What do you think?

Stealing as bad   Hurting worse

V79   Do you think it would be worse to become a permanent cripple, or to lose an uninsured home through fire, or are they equally bad?

Home loss lot worse	Home loss somewhat worse	Both equally bad	Crippled somewhat worse	Crippled lot worse

The relationship between these two variables for the total population and for various population subgroups is shown in Table 36.

Table 36

Relationships Between Property Items for
Designated Demographic Subgroups
(gammas)

	V78 Stealing/Hurting vs. V79 Home/Cripple
All respondents	.4
Low education	.4
High education	.5
Low income	.6
High income	.6
South and Border	.6
Pacific	.3
Age: 25 and under	.5
Age: 40 and older	.5
Blacks	.4
Whites	.5

As can be seen, the relationship between the two constituent variables of the Property/Person Priority Index remained reasonably stable across a number of population subgroups. Under the assumption that the hypothesized value dimension could more usefully be analyzed by a single index than by two separate variables, we collapsed the bivariate distribution into a single index according to the following scheme (Table 37).

Table 37

Combination of the Property Variables and
Index Values Assigned

	Variable 79				
Variable 78	Losing Home a Lot Worse	Losing Home Somewhat Worse	Equally Bad	Crippled Somewhat Worse	Crippled a Lot Worse
Property damage as bad as hurting people	1	1	1	2	3
Property damage not as bad as hurting people			2	3	4

Note: Empty cells were treated as missing data. See text for explanation.

Table 38 shows the distribution of the Property/Person Priority Index. A higher score indicates a relative valuation of person over property.

Table 38

Distribution of the Property/Person Priority Index

Property/Person Priority:	Property			Person	Total
Original score	1	2	3	4	
Percent	16	10	31	43	100%
(3.4% missing data)					

Excluded from this distribution as well as the 1.7 percent missing data are respondents whose replies on the two items were judged to be extremely inconsistent. This latter group came to 1.6 percent of the population, resulting in a total of 3.4 percent excluded from the analysis.

Resentment-Suspicion Index

The Resentment-Suspicion Index was based on responses to five "true-false" statements, reproduced below (Table 39). "True" was assigned a value of 1, and "false" a value of 2.

Table 39

Resentment-Suspicion Index Items

V112 I don't seem to get what's coming to me.

V114 At times I feel I get a raw deal out of life.

V115 I tend to be on my guard with people who are somewhat more friendly than I expected.

V116 I commonly wonder what hidden reason another person may have for doing something nice for me.

V117 I used to think most people told the truth but now I know otherwise.

Since blacks and whites answered individual constituent items at very different frequencies, matrices of relationships (gammas) between items were calculated for the white and black populations separately, as well as for the population as a whole (Tables 40, 41 and 42).

Table 40

Relationships Between Resentment-Suspicion Index Items for All Respondents

(gammas)

	V114	V115	V116	V117
V112 Don't get what's coming	.8	.4	.5	.6
V114 Get raw deal		.3	.4	.4
V115 Guard with friendly people			.8	.5
V116 Why people nice				.5
V117 Know people lie				

Table 41

Relationships Between Resentment-Suspicion Index Items for White Respondents

(gammas)

	V114	V115	V116	V117
V112 Don't get what's coming	.7	.3	.5	.6
V114 Get raw deal		.2	.4	.4
V115 Guard with friendly people			.8	.5
V116 Why people nice				.5

Table 42

Relationships Between Resentment-Suspicion Index Items for Black Respondents

(gammas)

	V114	V115	V116	V117
V112 Don't get what's coming	.8	.3	.3	.5
V114 Get raw deal		.2	.3	.3
V115 Guard with friendly people			.8	.5
V116 Why people nice				.2

Inspection of these tables shows that the gammas between items are almost identical for whites and the population as a whole. Cluster diagrams based on these gammas show a similar, though somewhat looser, relationship for blacks and the total population (Figure 1).

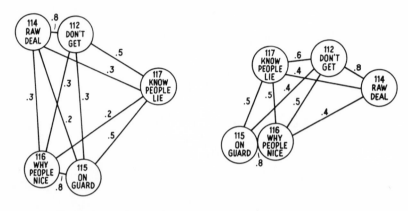

BLACK RESPONDENTS (N = 303)   ALL RESPONDENTS (N = 1,374)

Figure 1. Interrelationships among resentment-suspicion items for all respondents and black respondents (gammas).

An additional test of stability was performed on the relationship between V117 and the other items for high and low income groups (Table 43).

Table 43

Relationships Between V117 (Know People Lie)
and Other Resentment-Suspicion Index
Items for High and Low Income Groups

(gammas)

V117 (Know People Lie) versus	High Income	Low Income
V112 I don't get what's coming	.6	.6
V114 I get a raw deal	.4	.4
V115 On guard with friendly people	.5	.6
V116 Why people are nice	.4	.6

It can be seen that the structure of the relationships as measured by gammas is not markedly affected by income. So, a single index was created, combining Variables 112, 114, 115, 116 and 117. All items were summed, and the cumulated scores collapsed as shown in Table 44.

Table 44

Construction of the Resentment-Suspicion Index

Resentment-Suspicion:	Low				High	Total
Original score	10	9	8	7	5-6	
Recoded score	1	2	3	4	5	
Percent	23	21	23	18	15	100%
(0.5% missing data)						

The scoring system implies that high scores on the index indicate more resentful or suspicious answers.

One other item covering the area of resentment-suspicion was found to be inconsistently related to the other items and was excluded from the index. The excluded item, which also had a "true-false" response choice, is as follows:

V113 Although I don't show it, I am sometimes eaten up with jealousy.

Retributive Justice Index

The Retributive Justice Index was based on responses to five attitudinal items with Likert-type, four-point response choices. For each of the statements shown in Table 45, the respondent could answer "disagree a great deal," coded 1, "disagree somewhat," coded 2, "agree somewhat," coded 3, or "agree a great deal," coded 4.

Table 45

Retributive Justice Index Items

V88 People who commit murder deserve capital punishment.

V89 Violence deserves violence.

V91 "An eye for an eye and a tooth for a tooth" is a good rule for living.

V92 It is often necessary to use violence to prevent violence.

V94 When someone does wrong, he should be paid back for it.

Table 46 shows the relationship among the constituent items of the Retributive Justice Index. Table 47 indicates the stability of these inter-item relationships over a variety of demographic subgroups, for a representative pair of items. The relationships were considered stable enough to permit construction of the index.

Table 46

Relationships Between Retributive Justice Index Items for All Respondents

(gammas)

	V89 Violence Deserves Violence	V91 Eye for an Eye	V92 Violence Prevents Violence	V94 Wrong Should Be Paid Back
V88 Murder – capital punishment	.4	.3	.2	.2
V89 Violence deserves violence		.4	.4	.3
V91 Eye for an eye			.3	.3
V92 Violence prevents violence				.2

Table 47

Relationships Between a Representative Pair of Retributive Justice Index Items for Designated Demographic Subgroups

(gammas)

	V89 Violence Deserves Violence vs. V91 Eye for an Eye
Low education	.3
High education	.5
Low income	.6
High income	.4
South and Border	.5
Age: 25 and under	.5
Blacks	.5
Whites	.4

The values for each item were summed and the sum was recoded to provide index scores convenient for analysis. The recoding scheme is shown in Table 48. A high score indicates a strong belief in retributive justice.

Table 48

Construction of the Retributive Justice Index

Retributive Justice:	Low					High	Total
Original score	5-8	9-10	11-12	13-14	15-16	17-20	
Recoded score	1	2	3	4	5	6	
Percent	10	16	23	24	15	12	100%
(0.3% missing data)							

Self-Defense Index

The Self-Defense Index was based on responses to three attitudinal items with Likert-type, four-point response choices. For each of the statements shown in Table 49, the respondent could answer "disagree a great deal," coded 1, "disagree somewhat," coded 2, "agree somewhat," coded 3, or "agree a great deal," coded 4.

Table 49

Self-Defense Index Items

> V97 A man has a right to kill another man in a case of self-defense.
>
> V98 A man has the right to kill a person to defend his family.
>
> V99 A man has the right to kill a person to defend his house.

Table 50 shows the relationships among the constituent items of the Self-Defense Index. Table 51 indicates the stability of the inter-item relationships across demographic subgroups, for two representative pairs of items.

Table 50

Relationships Between Self-Defense Index Items
for All Respondents

(gammas)

	V98 Kill to Defend your Family	V99 Kill to Defend your House
V97 Kill in self-defense	.9	.4
V98 Kill to defend your family		.5

Table 51

Relationships Between Representative Self-Defense
Index Items for Designated Demographic Subgroups

(gammas)

	V97 Self-Defense vs. V99 Defend House	V98 Defend Family vs. V99 Defend House
Low education	.5	.5
High education	.5	.6
Low income	.7	.7
High income	.3	.4
South and Border	.5	.6
Age: 25 and under	.4	.5
Blacks	.6	.7
Whites	.4	.5

The relationships were considered stable enough to permit construction of the index. Accordingly, the values for each item were summed and the sum was recoded to provide index scores convenient for analysis. The recoding scheme is shown in Table 52. A high score indicates a strong belief in self-defense values.

Table 52
Construction of the Self-Defense Index

Self-Defense:	Low				High	Total
Original score	3-8	9	10	11	12	
Recoded score	1	2	3	4	5	
Percent	22	19	19	20	20	100%
(0.8% missing data)						

Social Causes Index

The Social Causes Index was based on the cumulated total of positive responses to five questions suggesting different social causes of violence. The wording of the four items, each of which offered a response choice of "yes," coded 1, or "no," coded 3, is in Table 53.

Table 53
Social Causes Index Items

V20 Do you think that poverty helps cause violence?

V21 Would there be less violence if more people had good jobs?

V22 Do you think a poor education helps cause violence?

V23 In your opinion, does discrimination help cause violence?

As can be seen in Tables 54 and 55, the relationships among the four items were quite high for all respondents and remained high across a variety of subgroups in our population. Inspection of the bivariate distribution of the one apparent exception, the gamma of .01 between Variables 23 and 20 for high-income respondents, revealed virtually no variance in responses on which a correlation could be based.

Table 54

Relationships Between Social Causes Index Items
for All Respondents

(gammas)

	V21 Jobs	V22 Education	V23 Discrimination
V20 Poverty	.7	.7	.8
V21 Jobs		.5	.6
V22 Education			.6

Table 55

Relationships Between Social Causes Index Items
for Designated Demographic Subgroups

(gammas)

	V21 vs. V20	V22 vs. V20	V23 vs. V20	V21 vs. V22	V21 vs. V23	V22 vs. V23
Low education	.8	.6	.7	.7	.7	.5
High education	.8	.7	.7	.5	.7	.5
Low income	.8	.7	.8	.6	.5	.4
High income	.7	.7	.0	.3	.4	.3
South and Border	.8	.7	.8	.5	.6	.7
Pacific	.6	.7	.8	.5	.6	.6
Age: 25 and under	.5	.7	.7	.2	.5	.8
Age: 40 and older	.8	.6	.8	.5	.7	.5
Blacks	.7	.7	.8	.4	.4	.6
Whites	.7	.7	.8	.5	.6	.6

V20 Poverty
V21 Jobs
V22 Education
V23 Discrimination

Table 56 presents the details of constructing the Social Causes Index, together with the percent distribution. The index was constructed by collapsing the summed response codes for Variables 20 through 23.

Table 56

Construction of the Social Causes Index

Social Causes of Violence:	No				Yes	Total
Original score	12	9-10	7-8	6	4	
Recoded score	1	2	3	4	5	
Percent	4	8	14	23	51	100%
(0% missing data)						

The higher the score on the Social Causes Index, the more agreement that social problems cause violence.

Trust Index

The Trust Index was based on responses to three questions shown in Table 57.

Table 57

Trust Index Items

V118 Generally speaking, would you say that most people can be trusted or that you can't be too careful in dealing with people?

Can't be too careful in dealing with people	Don't know	Most people can be trusted

V119 Would you say that most of the time people try to be helpful or that they are mostly just looking out for themselves, *or* they aren't one way or the other?

Looking out for themselves	Not one way or the other	Try to be helpful

V120 Do you think most people would try to take advantage of you if they got a chance or would they try to be fair?

Try to take advantage	Don't know	Try to be fair

The relationships between the three items of the Trust Index are Shown in Table 58.

Table 58

Relationships Between Trust Index Items
for All Respondents

(gammas)

	V119 People Try to Help	V120 Try to be Fair
V118 Can trust people	.7	.7
V119 People try to help		.7

The consistency of these relationships was checked by obtaining gammas between Variables 118 and 119 for different population subgroups. As can be seen in Table 59, all the gammas obtained were .7 with the exceptions of the high-income group, where the gamma was .8, and for those under 25, where the gamma was .6. On the basis of this information, relationships seemed sufficiently stable to justify combining these items into a single index.

Table 59

Relationships Between a Representative Pair of Trust
Items for Designated Demographic Subgroups

(gammas)

	V118 Can Trust People vs. V119 People Try to Help
Low education	.7
High education	.7
Low income	.7
High income	.8
South and Border	.7
Age: 25 and under	.6
Blacks	.7
Whites	.7

The variables were combined by assigning one point for each low-trust answer, three points for each high-trust answer, and two points for each intermediate answer. The resulting scores were then grouped as shown in Table 60 to provide a four-point variable with a convenient distribution for analysis.

Table 60

Construction of the Trust Index

Trust:	Low			High	Total
Original score	3	4-6	7-8	9	
Recoded score	1	2	3	4	
Percent	13	21	25	41	100%
(0.3% missing data)					

A higher score indicates a higher sense of trust.

Violent Behaviors Index

The Violent Behaviors Index, whose distribution is shown in Table 61, is composed of the sum of the scores on four variables coded from the prisoners' personal records. The following four variables were dichotomized on the basis of mention or no mention of a violent act: violence of present offense, violent offenses on past juvenile or adult prison records, violent misconduct on misconduct reports, and mention of violent actions in personal history.

Table 61

Distribution of Violent Behaviors among Prisoners[a]

Violent Behaviors:	None	One	Two	Three	Four	Total
Percent	33	33	20	14	0	100%

[a] A random sample of prisoners in Federal Correctional Institution, Milan, Michigan.

APPENDIX D

MEASURING ATTITUDES TOWARD
THE USE OF VIOLENCE

Good measures of attitudes about the use of violence were deemed crucial to the present study. Furthermore, we expected that good measures of such attitudes might find utilization by other investigators, and as social indicators. Therefore, considerable information was collected about people's attitudes in this area and much analytic effort was devoted to measure construction. This appendix describes how people's willingness to justify violence for certain specified purposes was measured, and—in the light of our subsequent experience—considers how those measures might be further improved or made more efficient.

For reasons described elsewhere in the book, two types of purposes for which violence might be used were distinguished: achieving social control and achieving social change.

Measuring Attitudes Toward the Use of Violence
for Achieving Social Control

Data Sources

Since the police are the principal group charged with maintaining social control, three sets of questions were included in the interview which assessed attitudes about personal injury as a form of violence which might be used by police. As noted in Chapter 2 (where exact question wording is given), one set of questions inquired about violence by police when confronting hoodlum gangs; in the second set the contending parties were police and white student demonstrators; and in the third set the contenders were police and black protesters. Each set consisted of five questions asking how frequently a specified police action seemed appropriate:

A. The police should let it go, not do anything
B. Police should make arrests without using clubs or guns
C. Police should use clubs, but not guns
D. Police should shoot, but not to kill
E. Police should shoot to kill

In answer to each question, the respondent indicated whether he thought the action was appropriate "almost always," "sometimes," "hardly ever," or "never."

Searching for a Violence Dimension

One question which needed to be answered was whether respondents had treated the set of items A-B-C-D-E as a single dimension ranging from least violence to most violence. This was examined in two ways. The first involved an examination of the interrelationships among the items to see whether their relative similarities were such as to suggest a unidimensional structure.[1] The second consisted of an examination of the patterns of responses to determine the frequency with which patterns inconsistent with an assumption of order had occurred.

Interrelationships. Interrelationships among the five items, for each of the three data sets, are shown in Table 1.[2] One thing immediately apparent is that the overall pattern of the gammas was very similar for the three data sets. A plot—based on a Smaller Space Analysis—makes clear the relationship between these items. The plot for Hoodlum Gangs is shown in Figure 1. (Plots for the other two situations were very similar.) Note that the "A" item lay to one side of the line defined by the other four items, and that the order among these items—as expected—was B-C-D-E. Since the "A" item asked *whether* the police should do anything, rather than *what* they should do (as the remaining items asked), this was not surprising. These findings suggested the "A" item be omitted from the scaling effort and that a scale be developed using items B-C-D-E.

---

[1] The notion of dimensionality is similar to that used in Smallest Space Analysis (Lingoes, J.C. and Guttman, L. Non-metric factor analysis: a rank reducing alternative to linear factor analysis. *Multivariate Behavioral Research,* 1967, 485-505 and Guttman, L. A general non-metric technique for finding the smallest Euclidean space for a configuration of points. *Psychometrika,* 1968, *33*, 469-506).

[2] Many of the interrelationships reported in this Appendix were computed without use of the sampling weights described in Appendix A. Such relationships are descriptive of our respondents but not of the population sampled. The tables and figures indicate whether sampling weights were used. As a practical matter, use of the weights would rarely produce a sufficient change to affect the sizes of the gammas.

Table 1

Relationships Among the Social Control Items
for the Three Interview Situations
(gammas, unweighted data)

	Hoodlum Gangs					White Student Demonstrators					Black Protesters			
	B	C	D	E		B	C	D	E		B	C	D	E
A	.1	-.0	-.1	-.2	A	.1	-.2	-.3	-.3	A	.1	-.2	-.2	-.3
B		.2	-.1	-.2	B		.1	-.2	-.4	B		.3	-.1	-.3
C			.3	.1	C			.4	.1	C			.4	.1
D				.3	D				.5	D				.4

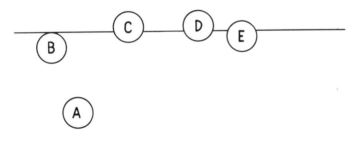

Figure 1. Relative distances among five items dealing with hoodlum gang disturbances (based on gammas in Table 1).

Response Consistency. It was also possible to examine the "rationality" or "consistency" of individual responses. It seemed likely that some responses might be inconsistent with the assumed order owing to the respondent's using a different order or through his misunderstanding the question.

By examining the individual answer patterns of each respondent, it was possible to determine the proportion of people who seemed to be treating the items B-C-D-E in the same order as the general population and to examine separately those respondents who did not. It turned out, as described below, that over 90 percent of respondents gave answers which were reasonably consistent with the B-C-D-E order. Furthermore, no population subgroup could be identified which regularly gave answers inconsistent with this order. In short, the inconsistencies seemed to arise from random response perturbations rather than the perception of some alternative order among these items.

The consistency analysis began with a set of rules defining response patterns that violated the assumption of B-C-D-E order in some manner, or seemed otherwise inconsistent with the nature of the reduced item set. These were as follows:

1. Response values must be monotonically decreasing on each side of the action picked by the respondent as being most frequently appropriate. That is, the indicated frequencies must be either the same or less in each adjacent item.

2. If the response to item "E" is "almost always," the response to item "B" must be either "hardly ever" or "never."

3. Four responses at the "never" level are inconsistent.

4. Multiple responses at the "almost always" level are inconsistent.

A wide variety of response patterns would be considered inconsistent under this set of specifications, some of these being very nearly consistent and some wildly inconsistent. Since some of the mildly inconsistent responses were certainly acceptable, certain rule "relaxations" were considered. The following is a list of the rule relaxations allowed, ordered from the least serious infringement of response consistency to most serious.

a. Nonmonotonic increment between "hardly ever" and "never responses."

b. Two adjacent "almost always" responses.

c. Disregard rule number 2.

d. Nonmonotonic increment between "sometimes" and "hardly ever" responses.

e. Three adjacent "almost always" responses.

All other infringements were treated as patterns inconsistent with the B-C-D-E order.

When these rule relaxations were applied to the data, in the order given above, the percentages shown in Table 2 resulted.

Table 2

Percentage of Respondents Giving Answers Consistent
with the B-C-D-E Order and Intent of the Item Set

(unweighted data)

	Item Set		
Consistency Rules Met	Hoodlum Gangs	White Student Demonstrators	Black Protesters
All	72%	75%	79%
All, if relaxation *a* allowed	74	77	81
All, if relaxations *a,b* allowed	81	84	86
All, if relaxations *a,b,c* allowed	81	84	86
All, if relaxations *a,b,c,d* allowed	87	87	90
All, if relaxations *a,b,c,d,e* allowed	90	91	93

Note that from 72 to 79 percent of respondents (depending on which item set was examined) gave answers fully satisfying all the original specifications for a response pattern consistent with the B-C-D-E order. After introducing five relatively minor relaxations of these specifications, the percentage of respondents giving answers consistent with this order ranged from 90 to 93 percent.[3]

The implication from these analyses is that in three different contexts the items denoted as B,C,D, and E were consistently treated by nearly all respondents as indicating a range of behaviors varying from least to most violent. Furthermore, the sequence was shown to be B-C-D-E.

Deriving Scores for Justification of Violence for Social Control

Having demonstrated that the items B,C,D,E, in that order, were treated by nearly all respondents as a reasonably unidimensional set, it

[3] The reader may be interested to note that the percentage of respondents giving answers consistent with the B-C-D-E order increased with each successive item set. (The set asking about actions appropriate for hoodlum gangs appeared first; black protesters appeared last.) We attribute this to some people learning how to respond to this item format during the course of the interview.

was necessary to find a way to combine answers to these four items into a single score.

After considerable exploration of alternative techniques, a simple two-factor scoring system was settled upon.[4] The system was derived to give scores which agreed closely in rank order to the average of the ranks independently assigned by three judges to a heterogeneous group of 27 possible answer patterns.[5] Subsequently, a cross validation showed a rank order agreement of $\rho = .99$ with scores assigned by the model and the average rank assigned by the same judges on 23 additional answer patterns. For the eight answer patterns that occurred most frequently in the data, agreement between the average for three judges and the model was also $\rho = .99$. A later test using 14 answer patterns produced a rank order agreement of .97 between the average of scores assigned independently by six *other* judges and the scoring system. In short, for the tests made, the scoring system worked well.

The two-factor scoring system is expressed mathematically as follows:

$$\text{Raw Score} = \Sigma A_i / \Sigma B_i$$

The numbers which sum to form the numerator are selected from Matrix A according to the answers given by the respondent to each of the four items, and similarly from Matrix B for the denominator.[6]

		Matrix A				Matrix B			
		Almost Always	Some- times	Hardly Ever	Never	Almost Always	Some- times	Hardly Ever	Never
Item	B	-3	0	1	3	4	3	1	0
	C	5	2	1	1	4	3	1	0
	D	35	8	2	-2	4	3	1	0
	E	100	61	4	-4	4	3	1	0

[4] Further documentation of the exploratory steps appears in Technical Memorandum #4, "Measuring the Acceptability of Violence Used for Social Control," available as publication #3234 from the Publications Division, Institute for Social Research, University of Michigan.

[5] Average inter-judge agreement (Spearman rho) was .97 on a set of 50 response patterns which included the 27 used to develop the scoring system. Stability reliability (over a period of several days) was $\rho = .96$.

[6] In the event the denominator was zero (possible only if the respondent gave a highly inconsistent set of answers), a -2.00 was arbitrarily assigned as the value of the raw score. This had the effect of grouping these responses in the lowest category of the 10-point scale described later.

Example. Assume a respondent felt that police, when faced with a hoodlum gang damaging property, should almost always make arrests without using clubs or guns, might sometimes use clubs, but should never use their guns. The raw score for this person would be: $\Sigma A_i / \Sigma B_i = [(-3) + 1 + (-2) + (-4)] \ / \ [4 + 1 + 0 + 0] = -8 \ / \ 5 = -1.6$.

A person more in favor of violence by the police might feel they should sometimes shoot (but hardly ever to kill), might sometimes use clubs, and might sometimes make arrests without using clubs or guns. The raw score for this person would be: $\Sigma A_i / \Sigma B_i = [0 + 2 + 8 + 4] \ / \ [3 + 3 + + 3 + 1] = 14 \ / \ 10 = +1.4$.

Transformation to 10-point scores. The magnitude of the raw scores is entirely arbitrary, and for ease of subsequent analysis they were transformed to a more convenient 10-point form using the equivalences shown in Table 3. The 10-point scores, *when averaged across the three item sets,* provided an approximate deciling of the respondents. (This deciling is a convenient baseline—dated 1969—against which changes in attitudes about using Violence for Social Control can be measured in the future.)

Table 3

Transformation of Raw Scores to 10-Point Scale

Range of Raw Scores	10-point Scale
-6.00 to - 0.83	0
-0.84 to - 0.17	1
-0.18 to + 0.49	2
+0.50 to + 0.83	3
+0.84 to + 1.16	4
+1.17 to + 2.49	5
+2.50 to + 3.49	6
+3.50 to + 5.83	7
+5.84 to + 6.83	8
+6.84 to +25.50	9

Some specific answer patterns. After the various manipulations involved in converting answer patterns to a 10-point scale, it becomes rather difficult to see intuitively the meaning of a particular scale score in other than purely relative terms. Table 4 is included for readers who wish to make the "translation" from scale category back to original answers. For each category of the 10-point violence scale, the table shows the most common pattern of answers to the set of questions inquiring about how police should handle black protesters. Of course, many different patterns can result in the same final scale value, and to show all would not be feasible. The table does, however, provide an indication of the different attitudes of respondents classified at various positions along the violence continuum. The top row, for example, shows that a common set of answers from respondents in the lowest violence category was that police should almost always make arrests using neither clubs nor guns and that they should never use clubs, never shoot to maim, and never shoot to kill.

Table 4

Most Common Answer Pattern Among Respondents Classified
in Designated Categories of the 10-Point
Violence for Social Control Scale

	How Police Should Handle Big City Riots Involving Blacks:			
10-point scale category	Make arrests without using clubs or guns	Use clubs but not guns	Shoot but not to kill	Shoot to kill
0	almost always	never	never	never
1	almost always	sometimes	hardly ever	never
2	sometimes	sometimes	hardly ever	never
3	sometimes	sometimes	sometimes	never
4	sometimes	sometimes	hardly ever	hardly ever
5	sometimes	sometimes	sometimes	hardly ever
6	almost always	almost always	almost always	never
7	almost always	sometimes	sometimes	sometimes
8	sometimes	sometimes	sometimes	sometimes
9	hardly ever	sometimes	sometimes	sometimes

Rationale for the scoring system. The primary justification for the scoring technique is empirical—its results proved to be almost perfectly correlated with rankings of answer patterns assigned by a variety of different judges. (Many of the judges were initially skeptical that a mathematical technique could match their own judgmental process!) Nevertheless, the highly satisfactory results from the technique suggest that it may be a reasonably close representation in mathematical form of the decision processes used by the judges.

In effect, the final judgment about the relative amount of violence implied by a certain set of answers seemed to be based on the frequency of particular actions (represented by the numerator), compensated to place all respondents in the same frame of reference with respect to total frequency (by the denominator). Conceptually, the scoring operation is somewhat analogous to computing percentages or probabilities, which have the effect of reducing numbers to a common base or frame of reference for greater ease of comparison. For comparing the levels of violence advocated by different respondents, our scoring technique puts all respondents on a common basis with respect to the *overall frequency* of score-relevant acts. The values shown in Matrix A might be regarded as the "violence weights" assigned to engaging in various actions at the specified frequencies; Matrix B contains the "frequency weights."

The actual derivation of the "weights" was by trial-and-error, continued until satisfactory results were obtained.

Combining Scores to Provide a Summary Measure

By applying the scoring and transformation procedures to each of the three answer sets, three contender-specific violence scores were derived. On the whole, people who advocated that police use relatively high levels of violence against one group (e.g., hoodlum gangs) also tended to advocate high levels of violence against other groups. The positive relationships among the several scales yielded gammas of .5 to .6 (see Table 5). Consequently it seemed reasonable to combine the contender-specific scores into a more general summary measure. This was done by averaging the three 10-point scales.[7]

Table 5

Relationships Among Contender-Specific Violence for
Social Control Scores and the Summary Measure
(gammas, unweighted data)

	White Student Demonstrators	Black Protesters	Summary Measure
Hoodlum gangs	.5	.5	.8
White student demonstrators		.6	.8
Black protesters			.8

[7] In a few cases respondents had provided incomplete information. Our general approach to handling these situations was to provide estimates of the missing data, if more than half of the required information was available. Where half or less was present, the respondent would be removed from analyses involving this variable. It turned out, however, that no respondents had to- be removed. Technical Memorandum #4, referenced in footnote 4, provides further details about assignment procedures.

Distribution of the Scores

Figure 2 shows the distributions of the several 10-point scores on Violence for Social Control. As noted previously, the score categories were set so as to divide the respondents into ten approximately equal categories on the summary measure. As is obvious from the figure, however, the 10-point scores do *not* represent a deciling of respondents on the situation-specific scales. On the whole respondents were more willing that police inflict injury on hoodlum gangs than on student demonstrators (with black protesters falling in between), and the 10-point scores reflect this.

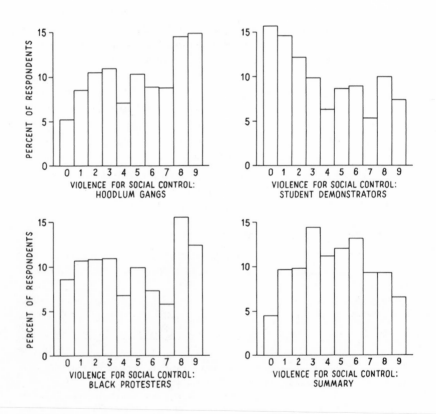

Figure 2. Percentage distributions for Violence for Social Control (weighted data).

Consistency Scores

As noted previously, the answers of each respondent to each of the three question sets were examined for the degree to which they met certain "consistency" specifications. A code was developed which grouped respondents according to whether the pattern of their answers met all of the original consistency specifications, met them after making certain "relaxations," or failed to meet even the relaxed specifications. In addition to using the consistency scores to explore the unidimensionality of the items, they proved useful as a filter for identifying respondents who had responded to the item sets in ways inappropriate for our scoring system. (While the inappropriateness might have resulted from the respondent perceiving the world in unusual ways, we subsequently concluded that many of the inconsistencies arose from the respondent misunderstanding the questions and/or how to indicate his answers. This was based on the finding that the respondents judged by the interviewers to have had a better understanding of the questions and/or to have been more coopera-tive were somewhat more likely to have given answers meeting the consis-tency specifications.)[8]

On the whole, people who gave answers which met the consistency specifications for one set of items also tended to answer other item sets in ways which met the specifications—i.e., relationships among the consis-tency scores were substantially positive (gammas were all .6).

No classificatory variable was found which related strongly to the consistency scores, but blacks and those who were older and/or less educated were slightly more likely to give answers failing to meet the specifications than other groups (gammas were about .1).

Explorations also showed that relationships between the summary measure of Violence for Social Control and numerous other variables tended to be somewhat stronger (by 10-20 percent) when analyses were restricted to the 56 percent of respondents who gave answer patterns which met *all* the original consistency specifications in *each* of the three question sets. This finding is in line with the idea that the inconsistent answer patterns included large amounts of measurement or response error: removing respondents who gave such responses resulted in a clearer picture for those who remained. While useful for exploratory analysis and model testing, filtering out inconsistent answer patterns resulted in a redefinition of the sample, and such data no longer represented all American men. For

---

[8] Gammas between consistency of response and understanding, and consistency and cooperativeness, each equalled .2.

this reason, most analyses reported in this book do *not* incorporate such a filtering.[9]

Measuring Attitudes Toward the Use of Violence
for Achieving Social Change

Data Sources

As detailed in Chapter 2, three sets of questions were devoted to assessing respondents' attitudes about the appropriateness of using violence to achieve social *change*. In two sets, the actors were specified—white student demonstrators and black protesters; the third set talked about violence to bring about "important changes" without identifying a specific group. Each set consisted of these five items:

A. Changes can be made fast enough without action involving property damage or injury.

B. Protest in which some people are hurt is necessary for changes to come fast enough.

C. Protest in which there is *some* property damage is necessary for changes to be brought about fast enough.

D. Protest in which there is *much* property damage is necessary before changes can be brought about fast enough.

E. Protest in which some people are killed is necessary before changes will take place fast enough.

In response to each question, the respondent indicated how strongly he agreed with the statement, checking one of the following: "agree a great deal," "agree somewhat," "disagree somewhat," or "disagree a great deal." Chapter 2 noted that the great majority of respondents (82-87 percent, depending on the specific situation) agreed with the statement that changes could be brought about fast enough "without action involving property damage or injury." Similarly, they tended to disagree with

---

[9] Some of the analyses reported in the chapters on Values and Identifications are the exception. Where indicated in these chapters, only respondents who gave answers meeting *all* the original specifications for consistency in *each* of the three question sets are included.

statements saying property damage or injury would be necessary. As a consequence, the derivation of even a reasonably symmetric violence-for-social-change scale proved to be impossible. Nevertheless, respondents did vary some in their attitudes, and hence some discrimination among them was possible.

Two Subdimensions: Damage to Persons and Damage to Property

The relationships among the items of each set, shown in Table 6, indicate that the four items which described actions to bring about change (items B-C-D-E) were all very highly interrelated in each of the three sets (gammas of .8 or .9) and that item A was consistently less strongly related to these four (negative gammas of .4 to .6). Under these circumstances it seemed reasonable to concentrate on the more homogeneous set B-C-D-E. Within this subset, items B and E described two levels of damage to people ("hurt" versus "kill"), and items C and D distinguished two levels of property damage. Initially it seemed wise to keep injury separate from property damage, and subscales were constructed for each. (Given the high relationships between the subscales—gammas of .8—the distinction was not useful, and the two subscales were later combined.) That American men did not make a sharp distinction between damage to persons and damage to property is an interesting finding in itself.

Table 6

Relationships Among the Social Change Items
for the Three Interview Situations
(gammas, unweighted data)

	White Student Demonstrators					Black Protesters					Change in Genral			
	B	C	D	E		B	C	D	E		B	C	D	E
A	-.4	-.5	-.5	-.4	A	-.5	-.6	-.6	-.5	A	-.5	-.6	-.6	-.5
B		.8	.8	.8	B		.8	.8	.8	B		.9	.8	.8
C			.9	.8	C			.9	.8	C			.9	.8
D				.9	D				.9	D				.9

Since the format of the two personal injury items and the property damage pair was similar, and since the elements of each pair were about equally intercorrelated (see Table 6), the same 7-point scoring technique was used for each pair. Table 7 shows the values assigned.[10] Reading from Table 7, one sees that a respondent who indicated that he "disagreed a great deal" with the idea that it was necessary for some people to be killed, would be assigned a score of "1" on the personal injury subscale of violence for social change.

Table 7

Various Combinations of Injury or Property Damage
Items and Subscale Values Assigned

| | | Item D: Much Property Damage or Item E: Some People Killed | | | |
		Disagree a great deal	Disagree somewhat	Agree somewhat	Agree a great deal
Item B: Some people hurt	Disagree a great deal	1	3	— —	— —
	Disagree somewhat	2	4	5	— —
or					
Item C: Some property damage	Agree somewhat	3	5	6	7
	Agree a great deal	4	5	7	7

Note: Empty cells were treated as missing data. See text for explanation.

The empty cells in Table 7 represent special situations. These scores, because they emphasize killing without some injury or *much* property damage without *some* property damage, seemed somewhat less logical than the other. Consequently, they required different treatment. It is possible that such responses were thoroughly rational—an assassin, for example, might want either to leave people alone or kill them. However, in our data, inconsistent responses were more likely to be due to misunderstanding the items or incorrectly marking the response card. Hence respondents whose answer placed them in an empty cell were removed from the analysis. The number of people who gave such responses was very small.

---

[10] Technical Memorandum #7, "Attitudes Toward the Use of Violence for Producing Social Change," (available as publication #3235 from the Publications Division, Institute for Social Research, University of Michigan) details several intermediate steps in this assignment procedure.

One manner of response to the original five items is not represented in the above scoring scheme. The first two item-sets were preceded by a screening question which filtered out respondents who felt social changes were not needed.[11] For them, questions about protest by students or blacks to produce change were simply irrelevant. These people (6 percent on the student situation, 8 percent on the black situation) were simply removed from analyses using these scales.

Combining Scores to Provide Summary Measures

The procedures detailed above yielded six basic subscales which could be combined in various ways. Table 8 shows the subscales (within the cells of the table), and the various combinations which were constructed. (Table 9 presents the interrelationships among the subscales.) In each case, the combined scale was derived by averaging the relevant subscales, resulting in a new 7-point scale.

Table 8

Violence for Social Change Subscales and Their Combinations

	Student Demonstrators	Black Protesters	Change In General	
Personal Injury	Personal Injury by Student Demonstrators	Personal Injury by Black Protesters	Personal Injury in General	Violence for Social Change Involving Personal Injury
Property Damage	Property Damage by Student Demonstrators	Property Damage by Black Protesters	Property Damage in General	Violence for Social Change Involving Property Damage
	Violence for Social Change by Student Demonstrators	Violence for Social Change by Black Protesters	Violence for Social Change in General	

---

[11] These two items read as follows:

As you know, many white students feel changes are needed in society. Do you agree with the students that some changes *might* be needed?

Many Negroes (black people/colored people) feel changes are needed in our society. Do you agree that some changes *might* be needed in the United States to make life better for Negroes (black people/colored people)?

Table 9

Interrelationships Among Six Subscales of
Violence for Social Change
(gammas, unweighted data)

	Personal Injury by Black Protesters	Personal Injury in General	Property Damage by White Student Demonstrators	Property Damage by Black Protesters	Property Damage in General
Personal injury by white student demonstrators	.7	.7	.8	.7	.7
Personal injury by black protesters		.8	.7	.8	.7
Personal injury in general			.7	.7	.9
Property damage by white student demonstrators				.8	.8
Property damage by black protesters					.8

An examination of the interrelationships among the various combined scales, shown in Table 10, demonstrated that each was highly related to the other (gammas = .8 to .9) and suggested it would be appropriate to compute an overall summary measure. This was achieved by averaging the three situation-specific scales, again yielding a 1-7 range.

In all combining operations the general rule for handling respondents who had some missing data was as follows: if half or more of the data were missing, the summary scale was also coded as missing data; in other cases, an assignment based on the available data was made.

Score Distributions

Figure 3 shows the percentage distributions on the five combined scales and the summary measure of Violence for Social Change. Most notable is the marked skew, a feature inconvenient for analysis, but unavoidable if a scale of more than two points was to be obtained from the present data. As with the decile distribution of the summary measure of Violence for Social Control, mentioned previously, the data in Figure 3 provide a set of benchmarks showing the distribution of attitudes toward violence for social change among American men in 1969.

Table 10

Interrelationships Among Five Scales of
Violence for Social Change

(gammas, unweighted data)

	Violence for Social Change by Black Protesters	Violence for Social Change in General	Violence for Social Change Involving Personal Injury	Violence for Social Change Involving Property Damage
Violence for social change by white student demonstrators	.8	.8	.9	.9
Violence for social change by black protesters		.8	.9	.9
Violence for social change in general			.9	.9
Violence for social change involving personal injury				.9

Comments

Violence for Social Control

On the whole we are well pleased with the scales measuring attitudes toward the use of violence for social control. The distributional characteristics of the measure are fine, they seem sensitive even to small shadings of opinion, and the data collection is easy and interesting for most respondents. We learned that the "A" item in each of the question sets proved not to be needed for actual measurement, and we suspect the B-C-D-E items would be little affected by omitting item "A." If this proves to be the case, some gain in efficiency could be achieved by leaving it out of a subsequent measurement effort.

Still further gains in efficiency might be possible by asking fewer than three sets of questions. While this remains a possibility worth investigating, we are not prepared to recommend it at this time since the interrelationships among the three situation-specific scales were only moderate (shown in Table 5).

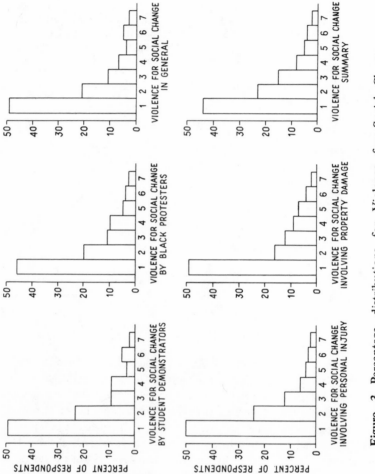

Figure 3. Percentage distributions for Violence for Social Change (weighted data).

Violence for Social Change

The Violence for Social Change scales, while satisfactory for our purposes, represent a substantially less-than-ideal set of measuring instruments. While they do differentiate well among people who feel some violence is necessary to produce social change (and they distinguish these people from other people), almost half of the respondents fell together as a single group in the lowest category of our scale. For some analytic purposes, it would be desirable to have more sensitive indications of the attitudes of this latter group.

If different shades of feelings on the part of the low-violence group could be distinguished, it might well be that the distinctions between damage to persons and damage to property would prove more useful than in the present study. Although we attempted to measure these two forms of violence separately, they proved so highly related, given our scales (Table 10), we chose not to analyze them separately.

A further problem lies in the 7-9 percent of respondents who were not asked the sets of questions on personal injury and property damage by student demonstrators and black protesters because they were opposed to the changes these groups were seeking. A special analysis showed that such people were not necessarily opposed to using violence for changes *they* thought were needed. While one "change in general" set of questions was included in our interview, it would be desirable to develop other such questions to reduce the problem of having certain items irrelevant for even a small portion of the respondents. Since the set of questions asking about "change in general" correlated highly with other question sets and was applicable to everyone, we consider this the best of our three sets.

As with the Violence for Social Control items, some saving in interviewing time could be achieved by omitting the "A" item from the Violence for Social Change sets if further investigation shows it is not needed to set the general context.

BIBLIOGRAPHY

Act of mercy. *The Nation,* 1971, *211,* 772-773.

Andrews, F. M., Morgan J. N., and Sonquist, J. A. *Multiple Classification Analysis.* Ann Arbor, Mich.: Survey Research Center, Institute for Social Research, The University of Michigan, 1967.

Ardrey, R. *The Territorial Imperative: A Personal Inquiry into Animal Origins of Property and Nations.* New York: Atheneum, 1966.

Berkowitz, L. Experimental investigations of hostility catharsis. *Journal of Consulting and Clinical Psychology,* 1970, *35,* 1-7.

Blum, S. The police. In S. Endleman (Ed.), *Violence in the Streets.* Chicago: Quadrangle Books, 1968.

Blumenthal, M. D. and Andrews, F. M. Resentment and suspicion. Unpublished manuscript, 1971. Ann Arbor, Mich.: Publications Division, Institute for Social Research, The University of Michigan (ISR code no. 3316).

Blumenthal, M. D. and Andrews, F. M. The trust index. Unpublished manuscript, 1971. Ann Arbor, Mich.: Publications Division, Institute for Social Research, The University of Michigan (ISR code no. 3317).

Burnstein, R. When the Panther came to Yale. *New York Times Magazine,* June 21, 1970, 7 ff.

Caplan, N. Identity in transition: A theory of black militancy. In R. Aya and N. Miller (Eds.), *Revolution Reconsidered.* New York: Free Press, 1970.

Clark, R. *Crime in America: Observations on Its Nature, Causes, Prevention and Control.* New York: Simon and Schuster, 1970.

Cleaver, E. *Post-prison Writings and Speeches.* New York: Vintage Books, 1969.

Clemens, S. L. *Adventures of Huckleberry Finn.* H. N. Smith (Ed.), Boston: Houghton-Mifflin, 1958.

Daniels, D. N., Gilula, M. F., and Ochberg, F. M. (Eds.), *Violence and the Struggle for Existence.* Boston: Little, Brown & Co., 1970.

Deloria, V. *Custer Died for Your Sins.* New York: Avon, 1970.

Dynes, R., and Quarantelli, E. L. What looting in civil disturbances really means. *Transaction,* 1968, *5*(6), 9-14.

Epstein, E. J. The Panthers and the police: A pattern of genocide? *The New Yorker,* 1970, *46*(39), 45 ff.

Erikson, E. H. *Identity, Youth and Crisis.* New York: W. W. Norton, 1968.

Erskine, H. The polls: Freedom of speech. *Public Opinion Quarterly,* 1970, *34,* 483-496.

Fogelson, R. M. Violence and grievances: Reflections on the 1960's riots. *Journal of Social Issues,* 1970, *26*(1), 141-163.

Freeman, L. C. *Elementary Applied Statistics.* New York: Wiley, 1965.

Gamson, W. A. *Power and Discontent.* Homewood, Ill.: Dorsey Press, 1968.

Gardner, V. W. *The Recovery of Confidence.* New York: W. W. Norton, 1970.

Garver, N. What violence is. In T. Rose (Ed.), *Violence in America.* New York: Random House, 1969.

Gillen, J. C., and Ochberg, F. M. Firearms control and violence. In D. N. Daniels, M. F. Gilula, and F. M. Ochberg (Eds.), *Violence and the Struggle for Existence.* Boston: Little, Brown & Co., 1970.

Graham, F. T. A contemporary history of American crime. In H. D. Graham, and T. R. Gurr (Eds.), *Violence in America: Historical and Comparative Perspectives.* (A staff report to the National Commission on the Causes and Prevention of Violence) Washington, D.C., United States Government Printing Office, 1969.

Grimshaw, A. D. Three views of urban violence: Civil disturbance, racial revolt, class assault. *American Behavioral Scientist,* 1968, *11*(4), 2-7.

Gurr, T. R. *Why Men Rebel.* Princeton: Princeton University Press, 1970.

Hackney, S. Southern violence. In H. D. Graham, and T. R. Gurr (Eds.), *Violence in America: Historical and Comparative Perspectives.* (A staff report to the National Commission on the Causes and Prevention of Violence) Washington, D.C., United States Government Printing Office, 1969.

Hahn, H. D. Civic responses to riots: A reappraisal of Kerner Commission data. *Public Opinion Quarterly,* 1970, *34*(1), 101-107.

Heider, F. *The Psychology of Interpersonal Relations.* New York: Wiley, 1958.

Homicides on the increase. *Statistical Bulletin,* Metropolitan Life Insurance Company, March 1970.

Horn, J. L., and Knott, P. D. Activist youth of the 1960's: Summary and prognosis. *Science,* 1971, *171,* 977-985.

Janowitz, M. Patterns of collective racial violence. In H. D. Graham, and T. R. Gurr (Eds.), *Violence in America: Historical and Comparative Perspectives.* (A staff report to the National Commission on the Causes and Prevention of Violence) Washington, D.C., United States Government Printing Office, 1969.

Keniston, K., and Lerner, M. The unholy alliance against the campus. *New York Times Magazine,* November 8, 1970, 28 ff.

Kirkhan, J. F., Levy, S., and Crotty, W. J. *Assassination and Political Violence.* (A staff report to the National Commission on the Causes and Prevention of Violence) Washington, D.C., United States Government Printing Office, 1969.

Knopf, T. A. Sniping—A new pattern of violence? *Reflections,* 1970, *5*(13), 13-30.

Lane, R. E., and Lerner, M. Why the hard hats hate hairs. *Psychology Today,* 1970, *4*(6), 45-48, 104-105.

Lorenz, K. *On Aggression.* M. K. Wilson (Tr.), New York: Harcourt Brace Jovanovich, 1966.

Luby, E. D., Mendelsohn, R. A., Fishhoff, J., and Wehmer, G. The Detroit riot: Some characteristics of those on the street. *Psychiatric Opinion,* 1968, *5,* 29-35.

Manchester, W. *Arms of Krupp: 1587-1968.* New York: Bantam Books, 1970.

Morris, N., and Hawkins, G. From murder and from violence. *Midway,* 1969, *10,* 64-70.

Newcomb, T. M. *Personality and Social Change.* New York: Dryden, 1943.

Newcomb, T. M. The prediction of interpersonal attraction. *American Psychologist,* 1956, *11,* 575-586.

Orrick, W. H. *Shut It Down! A College in Crisis.* (A staff report to the National Commission on the Causes and Prevention of Violence) Washington, D.C., United States Government Printing Office, June 1969.

Osgood, C. E., Suci, F. J., and Tannenbaum, P. H. *The Measurement of Meaning.* Urbana, Ill.: University of Illinois Press, 1957.

Pettigrew, T. Social evaluation theory: Convergences and applications. In D. Levine (Ed.), *Nebraska Symposium on Motivation.* Lincoln, Nebraska: University of Nebraska Press, 1967.

Report of the National Advisory Commission on Civil Disorders. New York: Bantam Books, 1968.

Report of the President's Commission on Campus Unrest. Washington, D.C., United States Government Printing Office, September 1970.

Robinson, J. P. Public reaction to political protest, Chicago, 1969. *Public Opinion Quarterly,* 1970, *34*(1), 1-9.

Rokeach, M. *Beliefs, Attitudes, and Values.* San Francisco: Jossey-Bass, 1968.

Rosenthal, R., and Jacobson, L. F. Teacher expectations for the disadvantaged. *Scientific American,* 1968, *218*(4), 19-23.

Rossi, P. Alienation in the white community (Interview). *Social Action,* May 1970, *36*(9), 6-10.

Runyan, D. What violence means to American men. Unpublished manuscript, 1971. Ann Arbor, Mich.: Publications Division, Institute for Social Research, The University of Michigan (ISR code no. 3309).

Sanford, N. and Comstock, C. (Eds.), *Sanctions for Evil.* San Francisco: Jossey-Bass, 1971.

Schira, F. J. The war in America the American public refuses to face. In S. Endleman (Ed.), *Violence in the Streets.* Chicago: Quadrangle Books, 1968.

Schrag, P. The law-and-order issue. *Saturday Review,* 1970, *53*(47), 26, 86.

Singer, B. The Detroit riot of July 1967. A report prepared for the United States Department of Labor—Manpower Administration Research Contract No. 81-24-68-03.

Skolnick, J. *The Politics of Protest: Violent Aspects of Protest and Confrontation.* (A staff report to the National Commission on the Causes and Prevention of Violence) Washington, D. C., United States Government Printing Office, March 1969.

Smelser, N. J. *Theory of Collective Behavior.* New York: Free Press, 1963.

Spiegel, J. P. Campus conflict and professorial egos. *Transaction,* 1969, *6*(11), 41-50.

Spiegel, J. Hostility, aggression and violence. Paper presented at a Lowell Lecture Series, Tufts-New England Medical Center, Boston, March 1968.

Spitzer, S. An exploratory study of police attitudes as a factor in the process of criminalization. *Sociological Focus,* 1969 *2*(4), 45-60.

Taylor, T. *Nuremberg and Vietnam: An American Tragedy.* Chicago: Quadrangle Books, 1970.

Tilly, C. From mobilization to political conflict. Unpublished manuscript. Ann Arbor, Mich.: The University of Michigan, March 1970.

To Establish Justice, to Insure Domestic Tranquility. (Final report of the National Commission on the Causes and Prevention of Violence) Washington, D. C., United States Government Printing Office, December 1969.

Walker, D. *Rights in Conflict.* New York: New American Library, 1968.

Webster's Seventh New Collegiate Dictionary. (7th ed.) Springfield, Mass.: G. & C. Merriam, 1969.

Wertham, F. *A Sign for Cain.* New York: Paperback Library, 1969.

Wolfgang, M. E. *Patterns in Criminal Homicide.* Philadelphia: University of Pennsylvania, 1958.

Wolfgang, M. E., and Ferracuti, F. *The Subculture of Violence.* London: Tavistock Publications, 1967.

Zinn, H. Violence and social change in American history. In T. Rose (Ed.), *Violence in America.* New York: Random House, 1969.

INDEX